Gifts, Goods and Money

Comparing currency and circulation systems in past societies

edited by

Dirk Brandherm, Elon Heymans and Daniela Hofmann

ARCHAEOPRESS PUBLISHING LTD
13-14 Market Square
Bicester
Oxfordshire OX26 6AD

www.archaeopress.com

ISBN 978 1 78491 835 4
ISBN 978 1 78491 836 1 (e-Pdf)

Cover image courtesy of the Megiddo Expedition, Tel Aviv University

Contents

List of contributors

Dirk Brandherm
Queen's University Belfast
School of Natural and Built Environment
Archaeology & Palaeoecology Centre
Belfast BT7 1NN
UK
d.brandherm@qub.ac.uk

Constanze Dupont
Graduiertenkolleg "Wert und Äquivalent"
Goethe-Universität - Campus Westend
Norbert-Wollheim-Platz 1, Fach 50
60629 Frankfurt am Main
Germany
C.Dupont@em.uni-frankfurt.de

Elon D. Heymans
Amsterdam Centre for Ancient Studies and Archaeology
University of Amsterdam, The Netherlands
Department of Archaeology and Ancient Near Eastern Cultures
Tel Aviv University
Israel
elonheymans@gmail.com

Daniela Hofmann
Institut für Vor- und Frühgeschichtliche Archäologie
Universität Hamburg
Edmund-Siemers-Allee 1 (West)
20146 Hamburg
Germany
daniela.hofmann@uni-hamburg.de

Nicola Ialongo
Georg August Universität Göttingen
Seminar für Ur- und Frühgeschichte
Nikolausberger Weg 15
37073 Göttingen
Germany
nicola.ialongo@uni-goettingen.de

Lene Melheim
Universitetet i Oslo
Kulturhistorisk museum
Frederiks gate 2
0164 Oslo
Norway
a.l.melheim@khm.uio.no

Joanna Ostapkowicz
Research Associate in Caribbean Archaeology
School of Archaeology
University of Oxford
OX1 2PG
UK
joanna.ostapkowicz@arch.ox.ac.uk

Thibaud Poigt
TRACES, Université Toulouse-Jean-Jaurès
Ausonius, Université Bordeaux-Montaigne
Maison de l'Archéologie
Domaine universitaire
8, esplanade des Antilles
33607 Pessac CEDEX
France
thibaud.poigt@gmail.com

Agnese Vacca
Università di Roma 'La Sapienza'
Dipartimento di Scienze dell'Antichità
Piazzale Aldo Moro 5
00185 Rome
Italy
agnese.vacca@gmail.com

Alessandro Vanzetti
Università di Roma 'La Sapienza'
Dipartimento di Scienze dell'Antichità
Piazzale Aldo Moro 5
00185 Rome
Italy
alessandro.vanzetti@uniroma1.it

David Wigg-Wolf
Römisch-Germanische Kommission des
Deutschen Archäologischen Instituts
Palmengartenstraße 10–12
60325 Frankfurt a. Main
Germany
david.wigg-wolf@dainst.de

Introduction: comparing currency and circulation systems in past societies

Dirk Brandherm
Elon Heymans
Daniela Hofmann

Abstract

In this brief introduction, the editors summarise the main themes of the volume and place them in relation to the wider framework of exchange studies. While the volume makes important points regarding the introduction of new prestige items, the process of monetisation and the way societies reacted to periods of rapid and fundamental change in the availability of certain goods, the next step is to work towards an integrated approach combining both prestige items and bulk commodities.

Zusammenfassung

In dieser kurzen Einleitung erläutern die Herausgeber die Schwerpunkte der verschiedenen Beiträge und ordnen diese in den weiteren Rahmen der Diskussion um Austauschnetzwerke ein. Dieser Band bietet vor allem Ansätze zu Themen wie der Einführung neuartiger Prestigegüter, dem Prozess der Monetisierung und der Art und Weise, wie Gesellschaften auf schnelle und tiefgreifende Veränderungen in der Verfügbarkeit bestimmter Güter reagierten. Der nächste Schritt ist eine Integration dieser Überlegungen in weitreichendere Modelle, die sowohl Prestige- als auch Gebrauchsgüter gemeinsam berücksichtigen.

Résumé

Dans cette brève introduction, les éditeurs résument les principaux thèmes du volume et les replacent au sein d'un cadre plus large d'études sur les réseaux d'échanges. Alors que le volume aborde de nombreux aspects concernant l'introduction de nouveaux biens de prestige, le processus de monétisation et la manière dont les sociétés ont réagi aux périodes de changement rapide et fondamental dans la disponibilité de certaines marchandises, la prochaine étape est de travailler vers une approche intégrée considérant à la fois les biens de prestige et les marchandises en vrac.

The present volume brings together the proceedings from two separately held conference sessions: 'Premonetary currency systems in past societies', organised by Dirk Brandherm and Stefan Wirth as session B22 on the occasion of the XVII World Congress of the Union Internationale de Sciences Préhistoriques et Protohistoriques (Burgos, Spain, 1–7 September 2014), and 'A crystal formed of necessity – Gifts, goods and money: the role of exchange in processes of social transformation', organised by Daniela Hofmann and Nicholas Wells as session T05S011 at the 20th Annual Meeting of the European Association of Archaeologists (Istanbul, Turkey, 10–14 September 2014).

Both sessions fundamentally aimed at exploring the economic and social roles of exchange systems in past societies, but approached these issues from slightly different perspectives. The Burgos UISPP session, from which the first four papers are drawn, focused specifically on questions surrounding the identification of premonetary currencies in the archaeological record, the part played by weight measurement systems in their development, the role of premonetary currencies in the transition from staple to wealth finance systems (and vice versa), the ideological underpinnings of premonetary currencies and prestige economies and the interrelationship between socioeconomic change and premonetary currency systems. The Istanbul EAA session examined the role of exchange networks as agents of social change in a wider setting, trying to answer what happens when new objects of value are introduced into a system, or when existing objects go out of use. This resulted in a focus on the potentially changing role of objects as they shift between different spheres of exchange, for instance from commodity to prestige item. In particular, situations of change and upheaval in general, such as collapses, crises or the emergence of new polities and social constellations formed a main theme.

As a consequence, the different approaches taken by the two sessions in their attempt to attain a better understanding of the economic and social roles played by exchange systems in past societies complement each other rather well. Not all papers presented at Burgos and Istanbul found their way into the present volume, and others were added later, but the contributions assembled here nevertheless offer a broad range of perspectives. Indeed, there are also productive linkages cross-cutting the contributions that emerged from the two sessions.

One theme that unites both sets of papers is the tension between what is introduced from the outside and changes that are driven by social transformations within a given group. As an absolute contrast, this is likely overdrawn, but it remains a main focus of research for instance in the Mediterranean, where various weight systems are used concurrently. Scholars have long worked on the basis of an attenuated kind of core-periphery model, whereby the ultimate inspiration for such metrological systems is thought to lie in the proto-urban societies in the eastern part of the region. In how far the weights attested in other areas correspond to such standards is thus generally one of the first questions addressed, thereby perpetuating an inherent normative assumption. Ialongo and colleagues go furthest in critiquing this basic tenet. They show that a given weight can quite easily match units within several different systems, so that tracing exact lines of derivation is neither possible, nor perhaps terribly relevant. Instead, using a variety of historical, contemporary and prehistoric examples, they urge us to focus on the pragmatic aspects by which weight divisions could emerge in the practical context of transactions, based for instance on quantities such as 'how much a man can reasonably carry'. This would lead to the establishment of several very similar systems without any direct link of (asymmetric) influence.

Similar arguments are made in several other papers. In Poigt's Spanish Iron Age cemetery, for example, the weight sets buried with two individuals who lived about a generation apart do not match each other, so that even within the same burial community different systems were apparently in operation, either concurrently or in rapid succession. There is no indication of a central authority imposing a coherent standard here. In his contribution, Heymans also argues that the token aspect of trade in hacksilber and other fragmented metal items was present and exploited even in contexts in which no state or equivalent power had ordered it. Similarly, the Scandinavian prehistoric trading sites discussed by Melheim were places in which imported metals were recast into regionally familiar forms using crucibles of relatively standardised sizes. These common standards apparently emerged through practice, creating items of the 'right' size for potential customers. This more heterarchical emergence of weight systems is an aspect that deserves to be more fully explored in the future. On the other hand, in his discussion of metalwork assemblages from the European Bronze Age, Brandherm argues that premonetary currency systems using standardized ingot forms and those based on 'hackbronze' generally appear not to have operated side by side coevally in the same region.

Other papers, most clearly those by Ostapkowicz and Wigg-Wolf, are mainly concerned with how items of foreign origin come to be incorporated into existing value systems, so that their character as straightforwardly 'alien' objects comes to be compromised. In the case of the Caribbean Taíno, Spanish goods were incorporated into locally valued items denoting a chief's authority, for instance by being sown onto cotton belts. Similarly, the adoption of coinage in Gaul, discussed by Wigg-Wolf, initially proceeded through incorporation into existing elite strategies of interaction. In both cases, too, the consequences of such transactions, the developing dependencies between coloniser and colonised, could not have been fully foreseen by the individuals involved. Here, the pursuit of traditional power strategies eventually led to changes on a much wider scale.

The cases discussed in the respective papers challenge us to think about how cultural and geographic distance contribute to the construction of value.

While objects or ideas that are tied in with external relations are internally appropriated for new strategies of value, the distance through which they are obtained appears to form an important aspect of their value. This brings to mind the work of Mary Helms, which explores cultural understandings of geographical distance and how these are related to supernatural, mythical and political power (Helms 1988). She argues that 'not only exotic materials but also intangible knowledge of distant realms and regions can be politically valuable "goods"' (Helms 1988: 4), thereby providing a basis for their use and significance in a local context. The political power associated with the objects discussed in this volume – whether representing value themselves, such as an exotic coin, or a system of valuation, such as a weight standard – could have substituted the need for a formal authority to assert their value or enforce their use, partly explaining the heterarchical framework in which they appear.

The intimate association of currency with political status and elite activities, as for instance argued by Wigg-Wolf, thus forms a second key theme, even if measurement systems may not have necessarily been centrally imposed. The role of particular individuals as beneficiaries and brokers in transactions involving new kinds of currency are crucial here. In the case of Iron Age Gaul, the first coinages carried associations of military prowess and commanding a following, but were also considered appropriate for ritualised consumption in hoards. They were objects that had acquired biographies and were intimately connected to the achievements of their owners. As such, they fitted seamlessly with the significance and treatment of other metal items. A major change occurred only with the introduction of Roman-inspired smaller denominations, but Wigg-Wolf argues that the way of seeing money did not substantially alter, as alliance with Rome was now a major source of power and authority. Throughout, then, coinage served mainly the interests of elites. Similarly, in Poigt's example, sets of weights were found in the richest graves, suggesting that owning and using such items was restricted. Here, elites may have bolstered their renown partly by being able to undertake even relatively complex mathematical operations connected with the use of scales. Perhaps – although this is not the focus of Poigt's analysis – this even aligned with other kinds of esoteric knowledge possessed by those in power (cf. Helms 1988) and was part of the motivation why the uptake of coinage, potentially more practical in use, was delayed in Iberia.

In contrast, Dupont's paper shows that such hegemonic relations can be challenged and must be rather laboriously maintained. On Palau, glass beads imported from a variety of sources are used as key items in certain exchange transactions. While the amount of beads in circulation had long been static, relying on stock acquired from Asian and possibly European traders in historical times, the much more recent import of virtually indistinguishable beads from the Philippines has upset traditional hierarchies. Even relatively low-ranking families can now afford large pieces in desirable colours. To avoid inflation, a time-consuming system of checking and registration has been set up, although the outcome is still uncertain. There are hence situations in which elite control can be challenged and perhaps circumvented, and it would be interesting to see if parallel processes can be identified in prehistoric Europe.

The significance of the various types of objects used within elite discourse also provides an indication of their role in social strategies and dynamics, rather than representing static categories of value. Understanding such objects as serving political interests provides a credible context for their emergence, without reference to a central authority. It is worthwhile noting in that respect that several of the objects discussed can be regarded as serving to adorn the social body, whether as grave goods or as a material extension/reflection of certain activities and, as such, functioned as an expression of prestige. Interestingly, David Graeber observes that the types of objects adopted as currencies were often personal ornaments. Referring to past achievements and transactions, objects of adornment enhance the bearer's prestige, while when hidden or hoarded they reflect the owner's capacity to act in the future, described by Graeber as a characteristic of money (Graeber 1996; 2001: 91–115).

The importance of the visual or aesthetic properties of the exchanged goods themselves is a final theme that is worthwhile drawing attention to. All the papers assembled here deal with items that are hard, lustrous and easily portionable: metals, glass beads, mirrors and so on. Metal is also fundamentally malleable, which means that it could be adapted to culturally acceptable forms (as in Melheim's case), stamped with the names and symbols of authority of the powerful (as in the case of coinage), or indeed easily broken up and transformed from tradeable commodity to elite object and back again (as drawn out in Brandherm's and Heymans' studies). This is a prime example for how the physical properties of materials are crucial to the kinds of social and historical processes that can play out in the first place. As Heymans illustrates, using evidence from Iron Age Israel, rigid distinctions between the 'spheres' of commodities and gifts are inappropriate in these cases.

Material qualities are also discussed in detail by Ostapkowicz, who shows how the Caribbean Taíno very selectively focused on trade in those items which could be integrated into existing value systems. These were generally made from lustrous or reflective materials, such as specific metal alloys, jet or mirror glass. These materials were associated not only with chiefly power, but also with establishing contact with the numinous, just as metalwork hoards in prehistoric Europe and the Near East may well have been. In addition, further qualities may have been valued which are less apparent to archaeologists today. The Taíno, for example, appreciated some alloys because of their distinctive smell. On Palau, the authentication of glass beads is partly based on the special sheen 'real' money acquires when rubbed against the human skin, as well as on its perceived greater hardness and on details of manufacture. There are hence many gradations of value and desirability, and not any 'foreign' material will become equally prestigious when incorporated into a new context.

This point also draws attention to the selective nature of the objects treated here. Due partly to the initial conception of our conference sessions, most pieces deal with hard and shiny materials, and side-line soft, organic goods perhaps traded in bulk quantities. In this sense, we are only focusing on a subset of items, but we do not wish to create the impression that these are the only ones that had a substantial social impact. Narratives of elite manipulation and interests aside, it is very likely, as Poigt reminds us, that systems for the exchange of bulk quantities existed alongside and in relation to the high-precision transactions associated with metals and other exotica. These may have been less circumscribed in terms of access, and Poigt mentions cattle, salt or textiles as possibilities.

Assessing to what extent such systems of exchange of subsistence/bulk goods and portable prestige items were disparate or integrated is challenging when based on archaeological evidence alone. One question is that of the different weighing or measuring systems involved, and in how far these would have been commensurable. Yet we must avoid the conclusion that larger or bulkier items were necessarily less prestigious, or indeed excluded from functioning as currencies. For instance, cattle hold considerable prestige value in many different societies, from the Nuer of Sudan (Evans-Pritchard 1940: 16–50) to Homeric Greece (Gallant 1982: 118; Schaps 2004: 69–70; McInerney 2010), medieval Ireland (Grierson 1978: 12) and Neolithic Britain (Parker Pearson 2000). Similarly, various ethnographic studies stress the value of specific kinds of cloth in local value systems. Although not normally circulating in a market context, raffia cloth functioned akin to a coupon system among the Lele of Congo (Douglas 1982a; 1982b) and Tugudu cloth was used as a form of currency in Tiv exchange (Bohannan 1955). In the Late Bronze Age eastern Mediterranean, the weight standards for wool were commensurable with those for (precious) metals, so arguably textile had some characteristics of a currency (Alberti and Parise 2005: 383–4; Breniquet and Michel 2014; Zaccagnini 1999/2001: 48–54). Among the Baruya of Papua New Guinea, salt was considered a luxury item important for ritual occasions, but as it could be exchanged for virtually any other item, it functioned in some ways like money (Godelier 1969:

26–8). In the case of Neolithic central Europe, Weller (2002) has argued that the concentrations of rare Alpine axes near salt springs implies that salt could have been part of the realm of prestige goods exchange.

These examples challenge easy divisions between currency, prestige good and bulk commodity. In particular, they clearly show that the correlation between bulk trade and lower-prestige transactions is premature. However, it is currently still difficult to estimate the volumes of bulky organic items which were traded, and therefore to characterise the social roles they could fulfil. Using a wider set of methods, as in the isotopic studies tracing cattle movement (Knipper 2011) or even the long-distance transports of (parts of) pigs (Madgwick and Mulville 2015), it may one day be possible to gain a deeper understanding of the extent and reach of such networks of bulky and/or organic items, and to finally establish whether they partly followed a similar logic as the hard, shiny and small objects focused on here. Only then will it be possible to gain a full picture of how exchange relations as a whole contributed to change and transformation in past societies and to disentangle the complexities of these extensive economic systems.

Acknowledgements

We gratefully acknowledge the financial support received from the School of Geography, Archaeology and Palaeoecology (now School of Natural and Built Environment), Queen's University Belfast, which allowed the publication of these joint proceedings in open access. We would also like to thank our authors for their patience during the production of this volume, and last but not least Linda Boutoille for her help with the French translation of the abstracts.

Bibliography

Breniquet, C. and Michel, C. 2014. *Wool economy in the Ancient Near East and the Aegean: from the beginnings of sheep husbandry to institutional textile industry*. Oxford, Oxbow Books.

Douglas, M. 1982a [1967]. Primitive rationing. In M. Douglas (ed.), *In the active voice*: 57–81. London, Routledge.

Douglas, M. 1982b [1958]. Raffia cloth distribution in the Lele economy. In M. Douglas (ed.), *In the active voice*: 38–56. London, Routledge.

Evans-Pritchard, E.E. 1940. *The Nuer: a description of the modes of livelihood and political institutions of a Nilotic people*. Oxford, Oxford University Press.

Gallant, T.W. 1982. Agricultural systems, land tenure, and the reforms of Solon. *The Annual of the British School at Athens* 77: 111–24.

Godelier, M. 1969. La 'monnaie de sel' des Baruya de Nouvelle-Guinée. *L'Homme* 9: 5–37.

Graeber, D. 1996. Beads and money: notes toward a theory of wealth and power. *American Ethnologist* 23(1): 4–24.

Graeber, D. 2001. *Toward an anthropological theory of value : the false coin of our own dreams*. New York, Palgrave.

Grierson P. 1978. *The origins of money*. London, Athlone Press.

Helms, M.W. 1988. *Ulysses' sail: an ethnographic odyssey of power, knowledge, and geographical distance*. Princeton, Princeton University Press.

Knipper, C. 2011. *Die räumliche Organisation der linearbandkeramischen Rinderhaltung: naturwissenschaftliche und archäologische Untersuchungen*. Oxford: British Archaeological Reports.

Madgwick, R. and Mulville, J. 2015. Feasting on fore-limbs: conspicuous consumption and identity in later prehistoric Britain. *Antiquity* 89: 629–44.

McInerney, J. 2010. *The cattle of the sun: cows and culture in the world of the ancient Greeks*. Princeton, Princeton University Press.

Parker Pearson, M. 2000. Eating money. *Archaeological Dialogues* 7: 217–32.

Schaps, D.M. 2004. *The invention of coinage and the monetization of ancient Greece*. Ann Arbor, University of Michigan Press.

Weller, O. 2002. Aux origines de l'exploitation du sel en Europe. Vestiges, fonctions et enjeux archéologiques. In O. Weller (ed.), *Archéologie du sel. Techniques et sociétés*: 163–75. Rahden, Marie Leidorf.

Zaccagnini, C. 1999/2001. The Mina of Karkemiš and other Minas. *State Archives of Assyria Bulletin* 13: 39–56.

Indeterminacy and approximation in Mediterranean weight systems in the third and second millennia BC

Nicola Ialongo
Agnese Vacca
Alessandro Vanzetti

Abstract

Research on weight systems used during the Bronze Age, prior to the introduction of writing, generally assumes that the widespread use of metal as 'commodity currency' eventually resulted in the adoption of widely shared systems of measurement. Many studies aimed at the identification of recurrent weight values as multiples and/or submultiples of theoretical standard units. This approach faces two limitations: 1) the absence of written sources, or at least statistically sound samples, makes it difficult to either validate or reject any reconstruction of prehistoric systems; 2) in the literate Ancient World, different polities usually retained distinct systems. Here an alternative analytical framework is outlined, making use of elementary statistics and cross-historical comparisons, and relying positively on 'indeterminacy' and 'approximation' rather than on 'exactness'. Recurrent weight measures can correspond to 'Standard Average Quantities', rather than representing arrays of exact multiples/submultiples of given units. By departing from a 'fractional' theoretical logic, one can observe that constant exchange practice may have produced the normalisation of 'tradable quantities' and that this can happen without necessarily implying the unification of local systems.

Keywords: weight systems, Bronze Age, indeterminacy, approximation, Standard Average Quantities

Résumé

Indétermination et approximation dans les systèmes pondéraux du Méditerranée, pendant le 3ème et 2ème millénaires av. J.-C.

La recherche sur les unités de poids employées à l'Âge du Bronze présuppose qu'une utilisation courante du métal, sous forme de matière première, comme monnaie d'échange permit une généralisation d'échelles de mesures communes. Plusieurs études ont été menées afin d'identifier les valeurs de poids récurrentes représentant des multiples et/ou sous-multiples d'unités de mesure théoriques standardisées. Ces études ont deux limites : 1) l'absence de sources écrites ou au moins d'un échantillonnage statistique fiable, rendant difficile de valider ou de rejeter toute tentative de reconstruction de systèmes préhistoriques; 2) dans le monde ancien les différentes entités politiques utilisent des unités de mesures distinctes qui leur sont propres. Cet article présente une analyse alternative mettant en comparaison divers cas historiques connus avec des statistiques élémentaires, en s'appuyant sur les concepts 'd'indétermination' et 'd'approximation', et non sur la notion 'd'exactitude'. Les mesures de poids répétées peuvent davantage correspondre à des *Standard Average Quantities* (quantités moyennes standardisées) qu'à des séries exactes des multiples ou des sous-multiples des unités données. En s'écartant d'une logique 'fractionnelle' théorique, on peut observer que la pratique des échanges constants peut avoir donné lieu à une normalisation des 'quantités échangeables' sans la nécessité d'une unification des différents systèmes locaux.

Mots-clés: systèmes de poids, Âge du Bronze, indétermination, approximation, quantités moyennes standardisées

Zusammenfassung

Unbestimmtheit und Approximation in mediterranen Gewichtssystemen während des 3. und 2. Jahrtausends v. Chr.

Die Forschung zu bronzezeitlichen Gewichtssystemen geht davon aus, dass unter schriftlosen Bedingungen eine generelle Verwendung von Metall als ‚Primitivgeld' zur weiträumigen Verbreitung identischer Messskalen führte. Zahlreiche Studien haben versucht, wiederkehrende Gewichtswerte als Vielfache bzw. Teiler von theoretischen Standardeinheiten zu identifizieren. Diesem Ansatz stehen zwei Einschränkungen gegenüber: 1) das Fehlen schriftlicher Quellen oder zumindest einer statistisch belastbaren Stichprobe macht es schwierig, Rekonstruktionen prähistorischer Systeme zu bestätigen oder zu widerlegen; 2) in der antiken Welt behielten verschiedene politische Gemeinwesen in der Regel unterschiedliche Systeme bei. Der vorliegende Beitrag stellt einen alternativen Ansatz vor, beruhend auf einfachen statistischen Grundsätzen und einem Vergleich unterschiedlicher historischer Fallbeispiele. Als Grundbegriffe dienen hierbei ‚Unbestimmtheit' und ‚Näherungswert', anstelle von ‚Genauigkeit'. Wiederkehrend gemessene Gewichte können demnach *Standard Average Quantities* (standardisierten Durchschnittsmengen) entsprechen, anstatt einer Reihe von genauen Vielfachen bzw. Teilern von bestimmten Grundeinheiten. Ausgehend von einer theoretischen Bruchlogik lässt sich konstatieren, dass kontinuierlicher Warentausch zu einer Normierung ‚austauschbarer Mengen' geführt haben kann, und dass dies ohne eine Vereinheitlichung verschiedener lokaler Messsysteme möglich ist.

Schlüsselwörter: Gewichtssysteme, Bronzezeit, Unbestimmtheit, Approximation, standardisierte Durchschnittsmengen

Introduction

The extensive adoption of balances and balance weights since the third millennium BC in the Near East and in the Aegean (e.g. Ascalone and Peyronel 2006; Petruso 1978; Rahmstorf 2003), and in the second millennium BC in the rest of Europe (Pare 1999), has led archaeologists to assume that it was during these periods that widely shared conventional weight systems were first developed, serving as standards for the assessment of economic value. The same general consensus can be recognised in the argument that the circulation of metal was the crucial factor in the spread of conventional weight systems (Pare 2013; Peroni 2006; Renfrew 2008). Moreover, it has been of general interest to understand whether weight systems were shared, or at least accepted, over wide areas, and if their adoption could be explained as the outcome of a diffusion process (Alberti *et al.* 2006; Pare 1999; Peroni 1998).

A main problem of research is rooted in the imbalance of the available evidence between literate Ancient Near Eastern societies and preliterate European societies.[1] In the Ancient Near East, the availability of marked and inscribed weights and written records allows for a refined understanding of different yet interconnected standards. In Europe, while the identification of limited sets of proper weights has become generally accepted (Cardarelli *et al.* 2004; Pare 1999), research is bound to material evidence alone and weight systems are often sought for by assuming that the origin of European standards has to be found outside Europe itself. There is, in this case, a risk of circular reasoning, as the dependence on external standards is assumed as both the question and the proof. This approach has much in common with the beginnings of metrological research: the comparison of different systems of units, in the belief that they were somehow connected to each other, was popular in Ancient Near Eastern studies in the nineteenth century (the so-called 'comparative metrology'; Ascalone and Peyronel 2006: 17–40; Chambon 2011: 28–38; Powell 1979). Relations were established through the observation of apparent correspondences between different systems and equivalences intuitively defined following a fractional logic. It must be considered, however, that individual metrological systems, in the detailed form in which we currently know them, still took a long time to be identified. In the early 1900s (Viedebantt 1917; 1923; Weissbach 1907; 1916), sharp critiques of this approach were published, which came to the conclusion that 'comparative metrology could be of value only after the specialised metrologies had created a more secure basis for comparison' (Powell 1979: 76). In fact, comparative metrology runs the risk of overestimating the value of correspondences when attempting to infer relations between different 'systems' whose internal structure has not yet been independently defined (Alberti *et al.* 2006; Rahmstorf 2010).

Conversion of different systems is not only an analytical problem for the archaeologist, but was also a concern for ancient economic operators. A wealth of ancient texts from the Near East addresses the issue of conversion: the same quantity can be (and in fact is) counted and recorded according to different systems, and rounded down in order to fit 'exact' multiples (or submultiples) of any given scale. This raises the question of the indeterminacy of nominal

[1] This article focuses on fully prehistoric societies located within the territories of modern Europe. Therefore, the terms 'Europe' and 'European' are used in this article to indicate Bronze Age societies other than those located in the Aegean (following Harding 2000: 4).

weight standards that can be calculated differently according to different systems of measurement. The *mina* represents, since the Ancient Near Eastern Bronze Age, the most evident example of this practice, providing 'official' correlation between different regional systems on the basis of a single shared value. However, as we are going to demonstrate, different local systems happen to match each other at many different values, thus representing a very real difficulty in determining, on the basis of the empirical evidence alone, which system any given 'standard' weight properly belonged to.

Ongoing metrological research has produced a substantial advancement in our understanding of weight systems in the Near East and the Aegean between the third and the second millennia BC (Alberti *et al.* 2006; Chambon 2011; Parise 1970/71; Petruso 1978; 1992; Powell 1979; Rahmstorf 2003; 2006; 2010; Zaccagnini 1984). The fortunate co-occurrence of texts and inscribed weights has provided the ideal framework for the identification of rather 'exact' arrays of multiples of given theoretical 'units'. On the analytical side, the reconstruction of weight systems has been backed by the application of mathematical/statistical methods, thus determining the definition of common procedures, characterised by the adoption of the 'cosine quantogram analysis', or 'Kendall formula' (Kendall 1974), a mathematical tool for identifying 'quanta', or hypothetical units.

Following the success of eastern Mediterranean and Aegean metrologies, research on Bronze Age Europe has begun in relatively recent times to adopt similar analytical tools: such approaches were in effect successful in identifying small sets of likely balance weights (Pare 1999; Rahmstorf 2010). However, the samples are generally too small to provide statistically reliable results (Pakkanen 2011). Since actual balance weights are generally scarce in Bronze Age contexts, European metrologists have often focused on the search for regularities in the weights of disparate classes of metal finds, such as specific object categories (Malmer 1992; Peroni 1966; Primas 1997; Sperber 1993; Sommerfeld 1994), fragmented items and scrap (Peroni 1998; Primas 1997; Sommerfeld 1994), funerary goods (Wiegel 1994), gold objects (Eiwanger 1989; Sperber 1993) and the overall weight of hoards (Tirabassi 1997). Such studies succeeded in highlighting the existence of recurrent weight quantities. While authors recognised that in these cases the object under study was 'weighed metal' and not actual balance weights, an appropriate theoretical framework was never developed to address such differences and to properly interpret significant regularities.

We propose that concentrations of weighed metal quantities can be conceptualised as 'Standard Average Quantities' (SAQ), which generally conform to the practice of 'portioning' goods (Ialongo and Vanzetti 2016); portions are characterised by an inherent approximation and are not necessarily exact multiples of official weight units. Simply put, metal objects and hoards are not balance weights: while the latter are 'exact' tools employed to assess and to assign a 'value' against an objective 'norm' and have a 'quantal' (theoretical) sequence, the former are items made of definite quantities of metal, whose weights are not straightforwardly related to the same quantal sequence. While it can be legitimately assumed that the frequent concentrations of weight values of metal objects and of whole hoards should be related to some sort of normative system, it is not to be taken for granted that these concentrations are directly linked to simple multiples of one unit. Even in 'international' exchange, conversion on specific weights does not imply a single shared standard scale, nor strict exactness. Let us imagine two traders, each with his own set of balance weights (e.g. one in pounds and the other in grams); conversions can conveniently take place by agreeing on quantities that approximately correspond to 'round' multiples of both units. In the case of pounds and grams, they could agree upon using 1lb ≅ 450g as a possible link or as a basic incremental unit (1lb = 453,592g and 450g = 0,992lb), thus limiting the theoretical error in both systems of account to less than 1%. It is clear that, based on the material evidence alone, it would be very difficult to determine whether this transaction was made in pounds or in grams, as well as if a single system was shared by traders or not. The intersection between normative conditioning and simple convenience can, in fact, produce ambiguous results; at the same time, however, both these aspects are crucial in the understanding of economic behaviour. The concept of SAQ has been specifically developed in order to address this ambiguity, which we think is linked to the concept of portioning.

This paper comprises four parts. The Ancient Near East is addressed first, showing that, even in high-control contexts, approximation and indeterminacy should be considered together with the definition of exact theoretical weight units; the discussion is supported by the analysis of three different sets of balance weights found at Troy, Byblos and Ebla, dating to the third millennium BC. The European context is approached next. We focus on Pare's (1999) analysis of European balance weights, which provides the opportunity to address interpretive problems of the convergence of different weight systems. We then shift the focus away from the supposed 'exactness' of balance weights and address the problem of 'weighed metal'. We introduce the notion of Standard Average Quantity (SAQ) as a middle-range tool for the comprehension of shared, 'culturally significant' attitudes in assembling quantities of traded goods (portions). Therefore, SAQs allow to address the relation between routine behaviour and theoretical standard scales in transactions where goods are traded in portions. As a contemporary case study to explore the concept of SAQs, we analyze the weights of portioned goods in modern supermarkets.

Finally, we test our assumptions empirically on a sample of weighed metal objects from several Bronze Age hoards from Italy. It is then proposed that it is possible to use approximate values, without relying on exact weight systems, in order to draw significant conclusions about economic interactions in Late Bronze Age Europe.

Materials and methods

The study is based on the statistical analysis of three different sets of material evidence, drawn from diverse historical contexts.

A. The sample of Ancient Near Eastern balance weights was picked from the third-millennium layers at Troy (western Anatolia; 52 items), Byblos (Lebanon; 95 items) and Ebla (inland Syria; 73 items); weight values were derived from Ascalone and Peyronel (2006).

B. The sample of selected Italian hoards comprises 2195 items in total, taken from 62 hoards divided into coherent chrono-geographical groups and dating between c. 1200–800 BC (Final Bronze Age–Early Iron Age). Eight distinct sample groups are singled out (Figure 1). The sample groups are composed as follows:[2]

- Madriolo, single hoard sample group; NE area; FBA; 92 items (Borgna 1992)
- Poggio Berni, single hoard sample group; centre-E area; FBA; 93 items (Morico 1984)
- S. Francesco, single hoard sample group; centre-N area; EIA; 247 items (Montelius 1893: 335; Sorda 1975)
- Tuscany, four hoards sample group; centre-W area; FBA; 279 items (Cateni 1977; Peroni 1961)
- Contigliano, single hoard sample group; centre area; FBA–EIA; 107 items (Ponzi Bonomi 1970)
- Sardinia, 43 hoards sample group; W area; FBA–EIA; 457 items (Ialongo 2011)
- Ardea, single hoard sample group; centre-S area; EIA; 293 items (Peroni 1967)
- SE Sicily, ten hoards sample group; S area; FBA–EIA; 627 items (Albanese Procelli 1993)

[2] Chronological periods are defined according to the Italian chronology (Pacciarelli 2000): Final Bronze Age=FBA; Early Iron Age=EIA. Cardinal directions are abbreviated as capital letters.

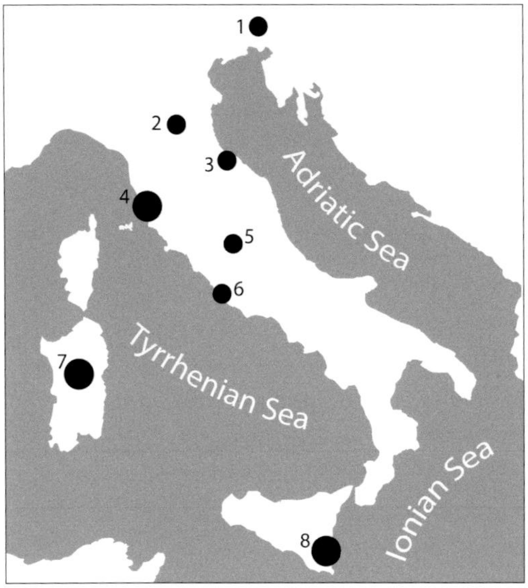

Figure 1. Italian hoards considered in this study. Small circles: single contexts; large circles: groups of contexts. 1 Madriolo; 2 San Francesco; 3 Poggio Berni; 4 Tuscany; 5 Contigliano; 6 Ardea; 7 Sardinia; 8 south-east Sicily.

C. The supermarket 'portions' sample was gathered in four different shops (three in Rome; one in Trebisacce, Calabria) and comprises 421 weight measurements of packaged items in total (Ialongo and Vanzetti 2016).

The analytical method employed here is designed to address multimodality in frequency distributions of weight values. In fact, archaeological data are often quantitatively limited, thus making it difficult to conduct accurate statistical tests. While some contexts, if considered individually, may suffer from limited numbers, our total sample has an adequate size.

The datasets have been interpolated via the smoothing-spline method to a standard total size of 2048 points for each sample group.[3] Interpolation is a mathematical method to identify new points on the Cartesian plane, assuming that the distribution conforms to a given function. This provides two advantages: 1) it is possible to obtain large datasets that are more easily processed through statistical software (see below); 2) all sample groups achieve exactly the same size, which makes them easily comparable. Following interpolation, data are arranged in a binned distribution; each sample group is divided into two separate but overlapping analytical series, in order for the analysis to be run on consistent orders of magnitude, and the bin width is set accordingly, that is: series 1: 7.5g–403g, bin width=1.9775; series 2: 54g–3000g, bin width=14.73.

[3] The interpolated distribution only serves as an aid for the statistical algorithm and is therefore not displayed in graphs.

The binned distributions highlight a sequence of clusters, i.e. 'peaks'. In order for a peak to be 'validated', it is required that the measurements inside it are normally distributed. The normal (or Gaussian) distribution is here assumed to signal the repeated attempts to obtain a predetermined amount, its mean corresponding approximately to the intended value. The multimodal distributions are processed via a statistical software package (Igor Pro 6.05; WaveMetrics Inc., Lake Oswego, OR, USA), through a specific module which detects concentrations that conform to the Gaussian function ('multi-peak fitting'). The output displays several Gaussian curves over the binned distribution (e.g. Figures 2, 7). The position and width of the curves are consistent with the distribution of non-interpolated data, unlike their height, which is disproportionately enhanced by interpolation; since width and position are the only parameters relevant to our analysis, the height has no scale and can also be displayed as 'floating' over bins if required (e.g. Figure 2).

When analyzing the variability of ancient weights, two separate, yet intertwined problems are in question: 1) the 'margin of tolerance', indicating the perception of ancient people; 2) the statistical concept of 'dispersion', which is an analytical problem resulting from empirical evidence. The coefficient of variation (hereafter CV, i.e. relative standard deviation) is used here as a measure of dispersion in order to address analytically the problem of the 'margin of tolerance' of ancient weights, well knowing that other possible causes may contribute to uncertainty (e.g. corrosion, retrieval and preservation biases etc.). The cumulative CV of all the values in a distribution is assumed as an overall measure of normality. Normality is visually assessed, based on the shape of the graph (e.g. Figures 3, 6, 8).

In our interpretive framework, the normally-distributed concentrations of weight values highlighted by the analysis are ultimately taken as an approximation of SAQs, as formerly defined. The method, therefore, was designed to address analytically the repetitive behaviour occurring in economic transactions, where objects are portioned and/or weighed in order to assess their value.

Indeterminacy and approximation in Near Eastern metrology

The seminal works of Thureau-Dangin (1907), Belaiew (1929) and Hemmy (1935) focused on the identification of the Mesopotamian weighing system through mathematical/statistical methods. Without going into the methodological limitations of these early works (cf. Ascalone and Peyronel 2006: 44–6), it can be stated that one of their main results was the acknowledgment that a certain dispersion is always implicit in the empirical distribution of supposedly 'exact' weights; dispersion would mainly depend on the lack of technological precision and on the consequent errors in reproducing standardized balance weights. Hemmy (1935) recognised that the Mesopotamian *shekel* ranged between 8.08 and 8.53g, whereas Belaiew (1929) identified three clusters of values for the *mina* of the Ur III period, respectively 484.8–498g, 502.2g and 511.8g. Powell (1979) would later refine this argument, stating, based on a total sample of 950 weights, that 'Mesopotamian precision weights tolerated an inaccuracy of about 3% of the mass of the object being weighed, which accords closely with the range of accuracy indicated for ancient balances' (Powell 1979: 83). A similar error margin appears, in fact, to have been taken into account even by ancient operators, as can be concluded from ancient texts (Joannès 1989: 127). However, as we are going to illustrate further below, the actual dispersion of balance weights can attain even higher values.

The concept of the 'propagation of uncertainty' is generally advocated by scholars dealing with Ancient Near Eastern weight systems. The common approach implies considering units as merely conventional (i.e. theoretical) and recognising that a certain fluctuation is always present (Alberti *et al.* 2006; Ascalone and Peyronel 2006; Parise 1970/71; Rahmstorf 2010). Sometimes the fluctuation may result in two overlapping distributions, pertaining to two distinct conventional values; such a case represents a common source of indeterminacy. Uncertainty is raised in particular by the impossibility to know *a priori* whether a given unmarked weight is either a multiple or a fraction of whatever known unit, and often results in the doubtful attribution of certain balance weights to two or more different systems. This can happen particularly when the mass value of a balance weight falls within the 'margin of tolerance' of multiples belonging to more than one system. In this respect the analysis of the Aegean and Anatolian Early Bronze Age weights undertaken by Rahmstorf (2010) serves as a typical example. The author analyses a total amount of c. 230 weights from c. 50 sites. Rahmstorf uses the 'Kendall formula' in order to detect 'quanta' in the distribution of balance weights between 5g and 15g, given a fixed dispersion of ±5% (Rahmstorf 2010 uses 'deviation': 89); he also makes use of marked weights to support the identification of possible standards. The detected quanta cluster around certain masses, among which the quantum of c. 9.4g (corresponding to the Levantine *shekel*, see below) is strongly represented (more than 2/3 of the total sample is assigned to this unit; Rahmstorf 2010: fig. 8.4). Besides the unit of 9.4g, other standards are attested as well, leading the author to ask himself 'whether there could already have been various units used in the EBA Aegean that, unfortunately, were lying very close to each other, making definite assignment difficult' (Rahmstorf 2010: 89).

Units

The contemporary use of a multiplicity of units in the Aegean is implied by Rahmstorf's analysis. However, which is less than certain is which theoretical units precisely lay behind each 'quantum'. His tentative attribution of such units to different standards, such as the Mesopotamian *shekel* of 8.3g and the Levantine *shekel* of 9.4g, has been possible thanks to previous studies of Ancient Near Eastern metrology, and in particular the work by Parise (1970/71; 1981; 1984), who first identified the existence of three different *shekel*s, respectively in use in western Anatolia, the Levant and inland Syria.

Parise reconstructed the conversion rates between the different *shekel*s (i.e. the *shekel* 'of Khatti', the *shekel* 'of Ugarit' and the *shekel* 'of Karkemish') and recognised that the three distinct series possessed a common 'standard' multiple in the *mina* with a theoretical value of 470g (the so-called 'western *mina*'), widespread in the Levant alongside the Mesopotamian *daric* of 500g. He was able to calculate, through a comparative analysis of cuneiform texts and inscribed balance weights from Ugarit (late second millennium BC), the ratio between *shekel*s of different systems and the *mina* of 470g. The standard value of the *mina* was defined according to a ratio of 60, 50 or 40 units, characterising, respectively, the Syrian, Levantine and Anatolian systems. During the Late Bronze Age, 60 *shekel*s 'of Karkemish', 50 *shekel*s 'of Ugarit' or 40 *shekel*s 'of Khatti' (with theoretical values of 7.83g, 9.40g and 11.75g) were respectively required in order to obtain a *mina* of 470g (Parise 1984: 129). Indeed, the widespread adoption of the 'western *mina*' in the Syrian and Levantine areas can be dated back to the mid-third millennium BC (Early Bronze Age), as can be inferred from texts and balance weights discovered at Tell Mardikh/Ebla (Syria), where the three systems are already documented, with substantially the same values as those attested in the late second millennium BC (Archi 1987; Ascalone and Peyronel 2006: 23–5; Milano 2003; Pomponio 1980; Zaccagnini 1984; 1999/2001; see below).

Conversion rates

Conversion rates were often applied in order to facilitate economic transactions in interregional trade. The existence of shared units (i.e. *mina* and *talent*) suggests that the *mina* of 470g functioned effectively as a link between different weight systems. While in each region of the eastern Mediterranean the *mina* fractions 'were calculated differently, the bulk quantities of commodity (especially wool and metals) could have circulated without difficulties from one side to another' (Alberti *et al.* 2006: 1). The potential confusion deriving from the coexistence of a multiplicity of unit standards sometimes gave rise to the need for specifying the reference system employed in transactions, such as in the case illustrated by a cuneiform text from Alalakh (AT 33; second millennium BC) (Chambon 2011: 84; Zebb 1991): it is reported that a noblewoman, named Sumunnabi, purchased 135 jars of beer according to the standard 'of Alep', for the price of 135 (silver) *shekels* 'of Alep'. This example hints at the requirement for the reference system to be specified, in order to state that Sumunnabi paid the price according to the standards applicable at that time in the kingdom of Yamḫad (Alep), and not in some other country (Chambon 2011: 85).

Approximation and weight-loss control

The concepts of approximation and margin of tolerance are always to be considered when dealing with ancient weighing systems. These come into play in the weighing practice and are strictly related to both balance technology and weighing procedures (Peyronel 2011). Mari's texts (second millennium BC) report three types of weighing procedures (Joannès 1989) employing equal-arm balances: 1) the object to be weighed was placed on one pan of the balance, while on the other pan weights were added until the equilibrium was reached ('simple weighing'); 2) several weights, exceeding the mass of the object to be weighed, were put on one pan, while on the opposite one other weights were added to the object until the equilibrium was reached ('counterweighing'); 3) when the 'exact' equilibrium was not achieved through the previous methods, the weight was approximated (akk. *sîqum*) and rounded down, within a reasonable margin of error ('approximate weighing'). The term *sîqum* (approximation) is often attested. Written records indicate that the margin of tolerance was about one *shekel* when the object weighed more than one *mina* and in the range of the *shekel*'s fraction when the objects weighed less than one *mina* (Joannès 1989: 139). This implies a perception of the concept of 'order of magnitude', albeit possibly still empirical.

The question of approximation often appears as a primary concern in bureaucratic practice and is deeply intertwined with instances of control by central authorities. Mari's texts report about a specialised officer, named the *ebbum*, who was in charge of controlling the transactions of metals (Durand 1987). The officer supervised the weighing procedures, often in the presence of the King of Mari. Through the weighing procedures the palace controlled the flow of metals, particularly of those allocated to artisans in order to manufacture prestige objects (Arkhipov 2012: 183). Joannès (1989: 127) observes that officers in charge of supervising the weighing and the value conversion of metals were appointed with the duty to supervise the many steps of the whole process (through repeated weight checks) from the 'purchase' of the raw material, through smelting and until the ultimate shaping, in order to certify that the original mass had not undergone undue weight loss. The officer's responsibility was further heightened by his awareness that multiple sets of balance weights (belonging to different systems) were contemporarily in use in the palace: 'La concurrence de plusieurs services de poids pouvait ainsi être source de distorsions, d'où la nécessité de noter leur origine: service du roi, poids du marché' (Joannès 1989: 127).[4]

Official units and the multiplicity of measures

Public administrative institutions, such as palaces or temples, certainly played a major role in the rationalisation of measures by fixing the official standard (Ascalone and Peyronel 2000; 2001). The authority guaranteed the accuracy of measurements through 'official' balance weights, stored in public buildings (such as temples and palaces). In the Royal Palace of Ebla (mid-third millennium BC), in addition to weights pertaining to the Syrian system, several other series are documented, likely including the Levantine, Anatolian, Mesopotamian and Aegean systems; this testifies to a multiplicity of measures, simultaneously employed by the palatial institution, in order to account for economic transactions. In this respect, all the balance weights documented in Palace G at Ebla must be considered as 'official' weights of the local administrative bureau, regardless of the respective reference systems (Ascalone and Peyronel 2006).

One of the first 'official' attempts to reorganise the systems of measures (through metrological linkages of weight, volume and capacity systems) is ascribed to the Akkadian dynasty (2350–2112 BC; Powell 1987/90: 508); however, the first actual metrological reform, leading to the definition of a 'royal' standard proper, is introduced slightly later by king Ur-Namma of the third dynasty of Ur (2112–2095 BC). This reform is not likely to have occurred as an introduction *ex novo* of metrological standards, but rather as an official acknowledgment of already existing ones. In his 'Codex' Ur-Namma provides a 'list of equivalences' and states that he 'fixed' the value of a *shekel* at 1/60 of a *mina* (Wilcke 2002). In a more recent analysis of the text a different interpretation of the term 'fixed' (sum. *hé-ni-ge-en*) has been proposed: Chambon (2011: 38–40) suggests that the term should be understood as 'confirmed' (after Frayne 1997). Therefore, the reform should not be seen as an attempt to impose new standards, but rather to formalise pre-existing ones (Chambon 2011: 41). The reform led to the emission of inscribed weights with royal names, 'warranting' the official metrological standards issued by the central authority (Ascalone and Peyronel 2000; Chambon 2011: 40).

---

[4] 'The concurrence of several sets of weights could hence be a source for distortion, giving rise to the necessity to note their origin: service of the king, weight used in the market' (editors' translation).

Empirical variability

One of the fundamental assumptions of metrological studies is that concentrations of values represent either actual units of measurement or their multiples. However, the straightforward assumption that approximate weight clusters always represent units, or 'round' multiples, can lead to substantially biased interpretations. In order to define our research framework, we empirically tested this assumption against the real distribution of Near Eastern balance weights, and in particular on the rich record provided by the site of Ebla, studied by Ascalone and Peyronel (2006). They attempt a detailed analysis in order to relate each balance weight to its most likely reference system. Ascalone and Peyronel are well aware of the inherent indeterminacy of supposedly 'exact' weights, and in fact often provide different likely references for uncertain specimens. Their caution is further supported by our analyses.

The frequency distribution clearly shows that clusters (i.e. 'peaks') are indeed well recognisable across the whole series (Figure 2). However, if we look closely at what is actually 'inside' the peak, it clearly emerges that almost all significant

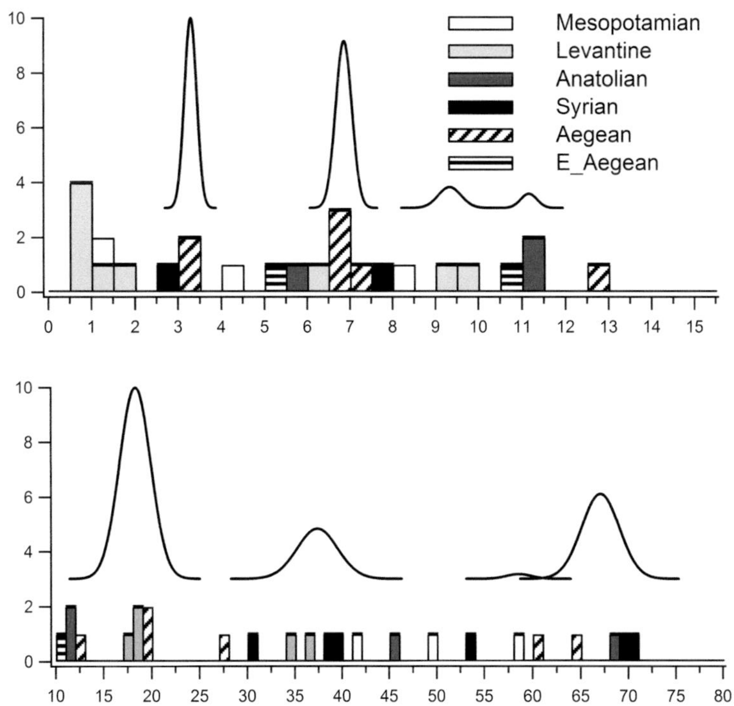

Figure 2. Binned distributions of balance weights from Ebla (third millennium BC). Different bar fills indicate different systems (after Ascalone and Peyronel 2006); overlaid 'peaks' indicate significant concentrations. Top: values between 0–15g; bottom: values between 10–80g.

concentrations are composed of balance weights belonging to two or more different systems of units. As several authors have remarked (Ascalone and Peyronel 2006; Pakkanen 2011; Parise 1970/71; Petruso 1992; Rahmstorf 2010), the confident identification of specific units is possible in Ancient Near Eastern contexts (and it is safe to reiterate: with a certain degree of uncertainty) only by virtue of the conversion factors provided by the correspondences between texts and inscribed weights, which means that the same array of 'precise' weights would be very difficult to identify in other contexts where ancient standard measures are not corroborated by external evidence (e.g. texts). Can we say, then, that clusters represent units? It is clear that the answer is not univocal. In other words: clusters indeed represent units and their multiples, but at the same time each cluster may account for a multiplicity of different systems of measurement.

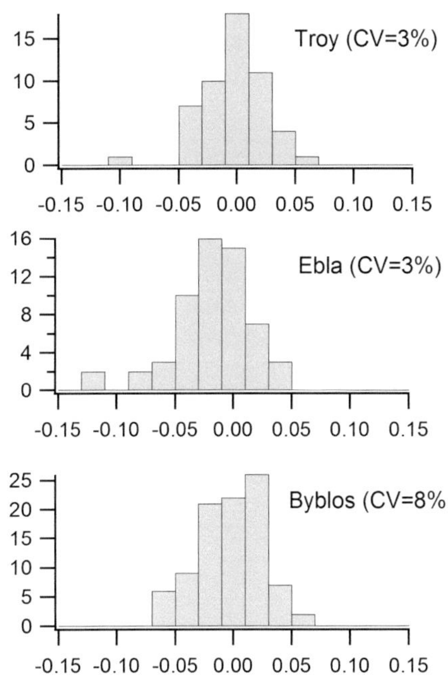

Figure 3. Cumulative binned distributions of CVs of the balance weights from Troy, Ebla and Byblos (third millennium BC; values computed according to the attributions made in Ascalone and Peyronel 2006). The overall CV of each cumulative distribution is reported in the graphs.

The problem of approximate clusters also raises the question of the 'margin of tolerance'. Here, we will use the coefficient of variation (CV) as a measure of dispersion of weight values. While the threshold of ±3% may be assumed as a standard theoretical one (Powell 1979), in practice it may be too restrictive and perhaps not always adequate to address the actual variability of real samples (for instance, Rahmstorf [2010] employed ±5%). The analysis of the weights found in third millennium levels at Ebla, Byblos and Troy will help to clarify this statement. The cumulative CV of the real distributions of balance weights from the three sites (Figure 3), computed according to the standard values identified by Ascalone and Peyronel (2006), shows that: 1) values are normally distributed, which lends strong support to the attributions made by the authors and 2) the real margin of tolerance can attain values of CV as high as ±8%. While the balance weights at Troy and Ebla are in line with the theoretical ±3% threshold, the distribution of the Byblos sample indicates a much higher dispersion. The peculiar position of Byblos as a major port of trade in the eastern Mediterranean might have been responsible for a much higher frequency of conversion operations between different systems of weights than at Troy and Ebla (Schon 2015, for example, has observed that the dispersion of different sets of balance weights tends to vary in relation to both the sampling strategies and the type of use context); this could have caused a higher level of indeterminacy (or even hybridisation?) across different systems. While the Byblos case might be discarded as an 'anomaly', it should nonetheless warn against an overconfident reliance upon strictly predetermined confidence levels.

With this brief aside on Ancient Near Eastern metrology we have attempted to focus on issues of indeterminacy and approximation. What appears to emerge from the discussion is that our uncertainties in identifying the underlying schemes of ancient measures are somehow mirrored in specific issues recurring in ancient practices. While it may be true that 'exactness' was the ultimate purpose of accounting for incomes and expenditures, we must bear in mind that such exactness was almost entirely theoretical and that it did respond, in practice, to the necessity of minimising complaints in public or judicially relevant economic transactions (Schon 2015). We chose to focus on public aspects of weighing practices, but official control was also required in order to regulate different instances of private behaviour. This consideration should suggest further caution towards the over-confident application of 'exact principles' to pre-state societies, like in Bronze Age Europe, where it is uncertain whether central authorities existed to guarantee for the 'officialness' of measures (as already highlighted by Rahmstorf 2010). Furthermore, we have shown how problematic it can be to identify different systems based on balance weights coexisting in the same context. Moving now to Late Bronze Age Europe, we will see the problems related to the widely shared hypothesis that European standard units came into existence at least since the Middle/Late Bronze Age, and that they converged toward the Aegean ones, or were directly borrowed from the Aegean world in a Mediterranean context of increased trade.

Indeterminacy and convergence of weight systems in prehistoric Europe

Premise

Studies on prehistoric European metrology generally attempt to reconstruct system(s) of measurement through the discovery of its (their) basic unit (Lenerz-de Wilde 1995; Malmer 1992; Pare 1999; Peroni 1966; 1998; Primas 1997; Sommerfeld 1994; Sperber 1993; Tirabassi 1997; Wiegel 1994). The rationale behind the 'quest for the unit' follows the assumption that the more or less widespread adoption of a given unit should account for an equally uniform system of measurement. Regardless of the different methods employed, studies on European Bronze Age weights and possible weight systems share a common approach, recently summarised by Peroni (2006): 1) the trade of metal is the main form of commodity exchange in Europe during the Bronze Age; 2) the progressive diffusion of weighing equipment implies a conscious approach to the quantification of economic value; 3) the frequency in mid-to-long range exchange produces a convergence towards the definition of 'standard amounts' of weight, which can be identified in the archaeological record; 4) the convergence towards standard values is the only archaeologically observable parameter that allows to address interconnections between radically different economic systems.

Margin of tolerance: a measure of indeterminacy

Pare (1999) recognises a class of rectangular objects in Late Bronze Age contexts (Br D), with a significant distribution in elite burials in central Europe, which he convincingly identifies as balance weights (Table 1). By applying the 'Kendall formula', he finds at least three values (3.6, 6.9 and 20.1g) which, he suggests, can work as 'units' for the system of measurement to which such weights were meant to conform. Based on intuitive fractional calculations, Pare further proposes a fundamental unit of 61.3g, represented by the weight from Gondelsheim (60.65g). He makes a strong point about his system being substantially analogous to the Aegean one, based on a unit of c. 61g according to Petruso (1992), and argues for an Aegean derivation. This argument seems to be historically deduced, as it fits within the Europe-Mediterranean connections labelled as the 'metallurgical *koiné*' of the Late Bronze Age (Peroni 2004). We will try to describe how approximation and variability come into play in the comparative study of different systems of units by discussing Pare's attempt to connect the central European system to the Aegean one.

The case presents several critical points: 1) the sample (17 items) is far below the required confidence level suggested for quantal analysis (Pakkanen 2011); 2) five weights out of 17 escape the quantal logic and are deliberately left out of the conclusions; 3) the interpretation shows an overconfident reliance on the initial assumption, i.e. that quanta are in fact units, and tends to bypass other possible causes, for instance that quanta can be influenced by clusters in the distribution deriving from the coincidence/closeness of different systems of measurement; 4) this becomes clearer if we consider a simple fact inherent to basic mathematical reasoning, i.e. that 'the same products of pairs of numbers may be obtained by multiplying vastly many different pairs of factors' (M. Lo Schiavo 2009).

Now, let us assume such cautious considerations as a mere list of caveats and admit that the distribution of rectangular weights is in fact strikingly similar to multiples of the Aegean *shekel* (6.69g, according to Zaccagnini 1999/2001). But is the Aegean unit the only possible reference for the central European system? We attempt to tackle this question by approaching the record as a series of distributions, rather than an array of exact values (Table 1). The mass value of each rectangular weight is compared to the closest multiple of every known elementary unit (*shekel*) in use in different areas of the Mediterranean during the second millennium BC (Ascalone and Peyronel 2006; Parise 1970/71; 1981; 1984; Petruso 1992; Rahmstorf 2010; Zaccagnini 1999/2001); individual measures on the same row are considered as if they were part of the same distribution, and the CV is calculated accordingly. The average CV of each distribution on the same row is generally fairly low and tends to decrease as magnitude increases. Whereas the one-to-one comparison with the Aegean system might appear to support a direct derivation, the perspective changes substantially if we consider all Mediterranean *shekel*s, ultimately providing a more nuanced framework: different systems appear quite easily convertible into one another, provided statistical dispersion is taken into account and kept at a tolerable level. We do not question the affinity of the central European system with the Aegean one; nonetheless, our attempt to extend the comparative framework shows that affinities with other contemporary systems also exist. Furthermore, a close look at the average CV of each system, compared individually with the distribution of rectangular weights, clearly indicates that the Aegean series is not even the most akin, 'eastern' Aegean and Levantine series being somewhat 'closer' on average and the Syrian one almost on par (Table 1); in fact, only the Anatolian system seems consistently different. We believe that the nuanced framework emerging from our analysis should suggest caution in applying straightforward diffusion models.

Only historical considerations lend support to the proposed derivation from the Aegean, or from the eastern Mediterranean in general, whereas the empirical distribution of measures and the fractional logic appear insufficient to support the hypothesis of a straightforward and precise derivation from a specific system (e.g. the Aegean one). This raises the question of whether a specific diffusion model is the only option to interpret the apparent convergence of the different weight systems throughout the Mediterranean, and even Europe.

'Convergence' of different systems of units: an ill-posed problem

The above analysis has shown that different Mediterranean systems appear to converge on similar values, or fractional values, and we have also illustrated the case of the convergence/conversion of the *shekel* and the *mina* in the Ancient

	Mediterranean units														
	E-Aegean			Aegean			Anatolian			Levantine			Syrian		
rectangular weights	factor	value	CV	factor	value	CV	factor	value	CV	factor	value	CV	factor	value	CV
3.83															
6.5				1	6.69	2.0%							1	7.8	12.9%
6.7				1	6.69	0.1%							1	7.8	10.7%
7.45				1	6.69	7.6%							1	7.8	3.2%
7.86				1	6.69	11.4%							1	7.8	0.5%
10	2	10.4	2.8%	1	6.69	28.0%	1	11.75	11.4%	1	9.4	17.5%	1	7.8	17.5%
15.01	3	15.6	2.7%	2	13.38	8.1%	1	11.75	17.2%	2	18.8	2.7%	2	15.6	2.7%
15.55	3	15.6	0.2%	2	13.38	10.6%	1	11.75	19.7%	2	18.8	0.2%	2	15.6	0.2%
19.89	4	20.8	3.2%	3	20.07	0.6%	2	23.5	11.8%	2	18.8	11.5%	3	23.4	11.5%
20.8	4	20.8	0.0%	3	20.07	2.5%	2	23.5	8.6%	2	18.8	8.3%	3	23.4	8.3%
21.4	4	20.8	2.0%	3	20.07	4.5%	2	23.5	6.6%	2	18.8	6.3%	3	23.4	6.3%
21.45	4	20.8	2.2%	3	20.07	4.7%	2	23.5	6.4%	2	18.8	6.1%	3	23.4	6.1%
39.27	8	41.6	4.1%	6	40.14	1.5%	3	35.25	7.6%	4	37.6	0.5%	5	39	0.5%
41	8	41.6	1.0%	6	40.14	1.5%	4	47	9.6%	4	37.6	3.5%	5	39	3.5%
43	8	41.6	2.3%	6	40.14	4.9%	4	47	6.3%	5	47	6.0%	6	46.8	6.0%
55.02	11	57.2	2.7%	8	53.52	2.0%	5	58.75	4.6%	6	56.4	0.5%	7	54.6	0.5%
60.65	12	62.4	2.0%	9	60.21	0.5%	5	58.75	2.3%	6	56.4	2.0%	8	62.4	2.0%
average CV			2.1%			5.7%			9.3%			5.4%			5.8%

Table 1. The mass values of rectangular weights from central Europe (first column on the left, values in grams; after Pare 1999) are compared to the 'closest' multiples of each known Mediterranean *shekel*. For each Mediterranean system, a separate column indicates the CV of each multiple of a given *shekel* in relation to the 'closest' rectangular weight. In the bottom row, the average CV of each series is calculated.

Near East. The question of the convergence of different systems, if tackled from its basic principles, can be explained empirically as a simple consequence of the mathematical properties of different series of discrete units, and might even imply a limited relevance of cultural factors.

We have tried to illustrate a synthetic conceptualisation of how multiples of the different Mediterranean units can apparently converge around approximate common values (Figure 4). The Aegean unit of 6.69g is used as the main reference to which other units will be compared and a series of its multiples from ×1 to ×60 is calculated; for each remaining unit, the 'round multiple' closest to the obtained Aegean multiples is then calculated and the CV of the values on the same row is computed. It is strikingly apparent that the CV falls very sharply through the lowest multiples (between ×1 and ×3) and stabilises at very low values from multiple ×6 onward. Of course, if fractions were included in the calculations the CV would have stabilised on very low values from the start of the distribution. The following 'rule of thumb' can be derived: given the set of Mediterranean units, any value above 40g can always be indefinitely attributed to any system of units, without using fractions. It is safe to reiterate here that such indeterminacy can be dealt with, to a fair extent, in Aegean and Near Eastern contexts, where theoretical systems of fractions and equivalences are known *a priori* through texts and their identification is facilitated in practice by the occurrence of marked and inscribed weights. In particular for the Bronze Age Aegean, several studies remark that the validation of mathematically reconstructed series of exact values can only occur if both conditions (i.e. marked weights and the availability of texts as reference) are met in the same array of sample balance weights. Such cases gain strength through the observation of the occurrence of clusters of weight values around the proposed units, fractions and multiples; however, empirical data do not conform to exactness, and interpretation (based on texts etc.) is crucial (Pakkanen 2011; Petruso 1992: 63). It follows that the same indeterminacy can stand as an inextricable puzzle in prehistoric Europe if we try to infer systems of units only through mathematical and comparative means.

Mediterranean units

factors of 6.69g	Aegean	Eastern Aegean	Anatolian	Levantine	Syrian	CV
	6.69	**5.2**	**11.5**	**9.4**	**7.8**	
1	6.69	5.20	11.75	9.40	7.80	30.9%
2	13.38	15.60	11.75	9.40	15.60	20.2%
3	20.07	20.80	23.50	18.80	23.40	9.7%
4	26.76	26.00	23.50	28.20	23.40	8.2%
5	33.45	31.20	35.25	37.60	31.20	8.1%
6	40.14	41.60	35.25	37.60	39.00	6.3%
7	46.83	46.80	47.00	47.00	46.80	0.2%
8	53.52	52.00	58.75	56.40	54.60	4.8%
9	60.21	62.40	58.75	56.40	62.40	4.3%
10	66.90	67.60	70.50	65.80	70.20	3.0%
	...					
20	133.80	135.20	129.25	131.60	132.60	1.7%
	...					
30	200.70	202.80	199.75	197.40	202.80	1.1%
	...					
40	267.60	265.20	270.25	263.20	265.20	1.0%
	...					
50	334.50	332.80	329.00	338.40	335.40	1.0%
	...					
60	401.40	400.40	399.50	404.20	397.80	0.6%

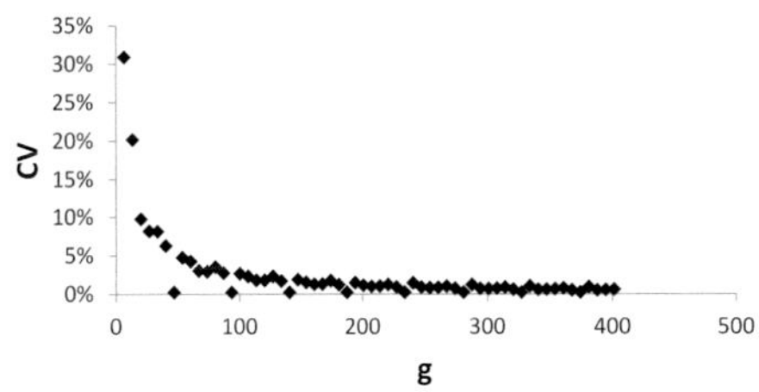

Figure 4. Top: multiples of the 'Aegean' *shekel* (after Zaccagnini 1999/2001) compared to the 'closest' multiples of other Mediterranean *shekels*; in the right column, the CV is computed for all values in the same row. Bottom: the CV of each row is plotted against each distribution mean.

The general affinities emerging from the comparison of different Mediterranean series suggest a more complex framework than simply the transmission of a system of account from one 'country' to another. As we have shown, the reasons for such affinities can be largely independent from any cultural/historical situation. Simply put, any paired series of units will 'get close' to each other indefinite times, in correspondence with *approximate* common multiples; this is to say that, even if not *exactly* matching, the two multiples will be 'close enough' to be considered within the same margin of tolerance (M. Lo Schiavo 2009; Rahmstorf 2010: 89). The only way to validate the fractional logic would be to find strict and recurrent correspondences between 'relevant' multiples, and possibly full series of multiples (cf. Schon 2015), but the European sample does not yet allow for the required levels of statistical significance. A typical case of good correspondence is that already discussed for the Ancient Near Eastern *mina*, where, however, the interpretation is highly reliant on textual evidence.

Constructing an alternative frame of reference: approximation, convergence and Standard Average Quantities

Standard Average Quantities: a middle-range tool

Having clarified our critical remarks and cleared the path of what we consider potential sources of bias, we base our enquiry upon the third of the four key points made by Peroni (2006, quoted above), that is, that 'standard amounts' of weight are effectively recognisable in the archaeological record. Metrological research on Bronze Age Europe has demonstrated beyond reasonable doubt that a vast array of metal objects, other than balance weights, tend to cluster around recurrent approximate values. Clusters are recognisable not only within the same classes of artefacts (Lenerz-de Wilde 1995; Malmer 1992; Peroni 1966; Primas 1997; Sommerfeld 1994; Sperber 1993), but also across different object categories (Ialongo *et al.* 2015; Peroni 1998; Wiegel 1994), as well as in fragmented items (Ialongo *et al.* 2015; Peroni 1998; Primas 1997) and even whole hoards (Ialongo *et al.* 2015; Tirabassi 1997). Correspondences of values are so frequent, even across wide geographical areas, that they can be best interpreted as the result of intentional behaviour that aims at achieving a predetermined weight quantity.

Our analysis aims at addressing the apparent convergence of different systems of measurement around recurrent values, and is based on the hypothesis that different systems of measurement show convergence around those quantities which, for practical reasons, are most frequently employed in exchange activities. On empirical grounds, it is then assumed that convergence phenomena produce arrays of 'portioned goods' whose weight measures tend to cluster in correspondence of such convenient values.

In practical terms, as we have shown, the two aspects cannot be easily separated and distinguished from each other in the archaeological record. On the other hand, the significance of clusters of values in the weight of objects is likely due to both such qualities, and perhaps keeping them separate will not result in a profitable approach. This is all the more true for prehistoric European contexts, where a straightforward identification of exact theoretical units is still highly uncertain. The concept of 'Standard Average Quantity' (SAQ) was designed to account for such a duality and is meant to provide the middle-range tool to connect empirical observations to the broader interpretive framework. A SAQ can be defined as follows: a recurrent, conveniently tradable quantity (of mass), whose adoption is acknowledged within one, or across several different cultural systems. In this respect, a SAQ has a similar function to that of the *mina*, since both are meant to link together different standard systems and to provide utility in conversion operations (Parise 1970/71; 1981; 1984). A SAQ can be measured in terms of any existent system of units, as its utility depends on the agreement between economic actors. A SAQ is, therefore, a 'practical unit' according to which goods are, in effect, portioned and traded. SAQs are ideally represented, on empirical grounds, by the statistically significant concentrations of weight values. In fact, SAQs are not exact, their approximate nature being due to either measure imprecision or inconsistency of different scales of measures. In our model, SAQs are not independent from normative (i.e. theoretical) systems of measurement, but are dynamically involved with them in a dialectical relation, reciprocally shaping each other. In the following paragraph we try to illustrate this process, using a case study different from that of balance weights.

A contemporary case study for the normative qualities of SAQs

To proceed by analogy allows us to extend the framework to more recent times. We will first introduce the role of SAQs with a modern case of weight-related economic behaviour, i.e. the definition of the 'oil barrel' as a unit. The discussion will then focus on the results of recent research on the recurrence of weight values in portioned goods in modern supermarkets (Ialongo and Vanzetti 2016). We attempt to show that, even in modern economies, there is much room left for approximation and ultimately for SAQs to be brought into common use. As a consequence, SAQs have a relevant role in shaping 'customary' economic habits, and this role is at least partly independent from official units sanctioned by central authorities.

In 1866, US oil producers set up an agreement and established the standard quantity of the unit of measure, still employed in the US in present days, commonly known as the oil 'barrel'. Until then, in the early years of oil extraction in the US, a specialised container was yet to be introduced and oil was shipped in reused wooden barrels, originally containing the most disparate goods (from fish to whiskey) and averaging 42 gallons in volume capacity (around 160 litres, allegedly 'as much as a man could reasonably wrestle'). According to the American Oil & Gas Historical Society (AOGHS 2013), the boom of oil production in the early 1860s caused the whole available stock of wooden barrels to be almost wiped from the market: it was in such circumstances that specialised containers were first produced for the oil market, their standard capacity being eventually established at 42 gallons.

This is just an anecdote, yet it provides a suggestive glimpse on how units of measurement can actually come into being out of customary behaviour, even in the industrial era; it renders with a certain precision what SAQs consist of in our model. The first thing one can note is that the 'standard quantity' was already in use before it was officially acknowledged as a unit of measurement proper, similarly to how Ancient Near Eastern reforms ratified pre-existing standards. From an organisational standpoint, the ratification of the 42 gallons barrel was driven by convenience, as sellers and buyers alike were already familiar with the average quantity which the product was shipped in; therefore, making an already customary measure the 'official' one would have likely appeared as the most convenient choice for all the agents involved. Put in other terms, the ratification of the unit of measurement intervened in formally regulating a specific instance of market exchange which already had its customary norms, and which was, in turn, already regulated by a well-established, relational framework of habit and trust. The idea that official units may derive from customary standards is not new. Lenerz-de Wilde (1995, followed by Pare 1999; Peroni 1998; Primas 1997) made a convincing argument about the earliest European standards having derived from widely distributed ingot-like objects, such as rings, torcs and axes, between the Late Copper Age and the Early Bronze Age. For the Ancient Near East, Powell (1987/90) suggests a shared etymology of the term *shekel* and the Sumerian word for 'axe', hinting that the term could have initially referred to axes as approximate standards. Moreover, the Sumerian, Akkadian and Greek words for *talent* would all basically mean 'burden/load' (Powell 1987/90: 510), hinting that a *talent* would stand for 'as much as a man can carry' (Ascalone and Peyronel 2006: 42); this, in turn, closely recalls the origins of the oil barrel, stemming from recycled containers and reportedly selected in order to contain 'as much as a man could reasonably wrestle'. The concept of a relationally defined convergence process is crucial to our model of SAQ and embodies an alternative view in respect to the diffusion model that is often assumed in metrological studies. We have proposed that material evidence provides insufficient support for a straight derivation of European units from central-eastern Mediterranean standards (as proposed by Pare 1999 and Cardarelli *et al.* 2004; see also F. Lo Schiavo 2006; Ruiz-Galvez Priego 2000). The latter interpretation, moreover, owes much to centre-periphery models, which recent research tends to question, suggesting instead a more complex and dynamic framework (e.g. Broodbank 2013; Jones *et al.* 2014; Jung and Mehofer 2013).

An analytical approach to the formation of SAQs requires highly controlled samples in order to avoid the production of *post-hoc* arguments. Our sample is consequently picked from a specific form of economic behaviour very familiar to all of us, which we believe stands as a peculiar example of how customers' desires interact with commercial offer in producing 'customary standards': packaged goods in supermarkets. We assume that groceries are assembled in packages of different quantities in order to meet the preferences/needs of different categories of customers (e.g. singles, couples, large families and so on); therefore, we expect that the distribution of weight values follows an observable multimodal distribution. The full results of the analyses of this supermarket sample have been published elsewhere (Ialongo and Vanzetti 2016); we will focus here on a few specific aspects.

The study was conducted on packaged goods sold in supermarkets in Rome and in Trebisacce (CS, Calabria). The sample is divided into two categories: packages of goods bearing an exact, 'round' nominal weight (with no 'real' weight listed on the label) and portioned goods with their 'real' weight reported on the package. We did not consider any case of goods simply sold by number. To clarify: there is a wide array of packaged goods (e.g. potatoes, onions, carrots) that are sold by a 'round' nominal weight (i.e. 100g, 200g, 500g etc.) and priced accordingly (i.e. with a fixed price), and other goods that are packaged, but priced according to their actual quantity (e.g. meat). Several 'clusters of values' result from the analysis (Table 2). In this case, the results are rather easily obtained: it is sufficient to group the different kinds of packaged goods by their respective labels, and then compute the basic statistics of each grouping.

Calabria_SAQ	Rome_SAQ	nominal value	CV	groceries
	140.09 178.32 178.89	150	13.4%	garlic, entrecôte, ham
442.80	408.00 436.20 458.00 470.83 474.00	400	5.5%	pork steak, turkey breast, chicken breast, sausage, carrot
531.15 540.67 552.00	531.15 538.00	500	1.6%	onion, bacon, pork steak, tomato, sausage
671.63	610.67 691.11 693.50	600	5.8%	sausage, chicken breast, pear
771.87	763.33 771.87	750	0.6%	onion, apple
1021.05	966.86 1021.05 1054.00	1000	3.6%	carrot, apple, tomato

Table 2. Actual weight values (in grams) of SAQs in supermarkets in Calabria and Rome (n=421), compared to the nominal values listed on packages (after Ialongo and Vanzetti 2016); the CV of each SAQ is provided. The right column lists the different types of groceries included in each SAQ.

SAQs in supermarkets indeed show clusters around recurrent values, regardless of the nature of the good being portioned; very different groceries are intentionally assembled in order to match a few recurrent, predetermined quantities, which are in turn very often ascribable to approximate 'round' multiples of either 50g, 100g or 150g (Table 2). The fact that, in each distribution, at least one package with 'nominal' value is always present makes it quite easy to set the indicative equivalence with such round quantities. It is clear that different groceries cluster around the same 'nominal' values: with regard to the behavioural/normative duality of SAQs, we interpret such a state of things as the outcome of the intersection between customers' desires (as they are 'interpreted' by the seller) and a form of 'normative way of thinking', tending to direct the practice of assembling packages towards 'round' amounts, with the simple purpose of facilitating accounting operations for the convenience of both buyers and sellers.

A closer look at the separate distributions of supermarkets in Rome and in Calabria will help clarify how, in our model, SAQs can be strongly influenced by cultural factors that are only loosely constrained, rather than entirely determined by the need to comply with an officially sanctioned normative system. The graph in Figure 5 shows the binned distributions at a very low resolution. 'Small' quantities are far more recurrent in Rome than in Calabria, which should mean that there is less demand for small SAQs in Calabria than there is in Rome, at least in the explored supermarkets. Among all possible causes, one that perhaps appears rather compelling is the different composition of households in the two regions: according to the 2011 census (ISTAT 2011), households in Calabria are c. 1.4 times larger, on average, than they are in Rome. Other causes may also come into play, such as the common habit of storing/hoarding food in southern regions of Italy and, in a broader perspective, a substantially lower GDP. Given the limited scope of the analysis, the validation of such a relationship clearly requires both more insight and a larger sample. However, we believe that the significance of the point at stake is sufficiently clear: the formation of SAQs is uneven, and influenced by convenience, profit and other factors, not only by the official norm. On the other hand, evident connections between the two 'regional series' (Rome and Calabria) also exist. The two different series match at several significant values and also maintain the same approximate 'modules' (one could say 'quanta'), but produce, in practice, two different empirical distributions, which are in turn available for evaluation through simple statistics. Norm-independent factors such as kinship relations (and perhaps social organisation in general, wealth distribution, ritual habits, disposition to warfare etc.) could shape SAQs at any time, while at the same time being rationally organised in order to approximately match official standards.

Further conclusions can be drawn from the sample and serve to better outline the analogy between supermarket SAQs, balance weights and specifically (as we will discuss later on) metals in prehistoric hoards. First of all, the weights of goods belonging to each type of groceries are normally distributed (Figure 6). Secondly, the cumulative CV is rather high even in packages with nominal values (7% for packages *with* nominal values; 15% for those *without*). While this is the consequence of merely practical causes (e.g. grocery SAQs are made of indivisible modules: one cannot sell four and a half tomatoes), it warns us to be cautious in assuming exactness as the only ordering principle, even in our supposedly 'exact' economy. Thirdly, it is ultimately impossible to infer the 'official standard unit' (i.e. '1' or '10') from the empirical distribution alone, but rather the approximate 'quantum' of 50g would appear as significant.

SAQs in Italian hoards: distribution and correspondences

The main body of this article was primarily meant to describe our analytical framework and its interpretive implications; the following outline of our preliminary analysis of Italian hoards will serve to illustrate the possible applications of the method and to suggest further developments.

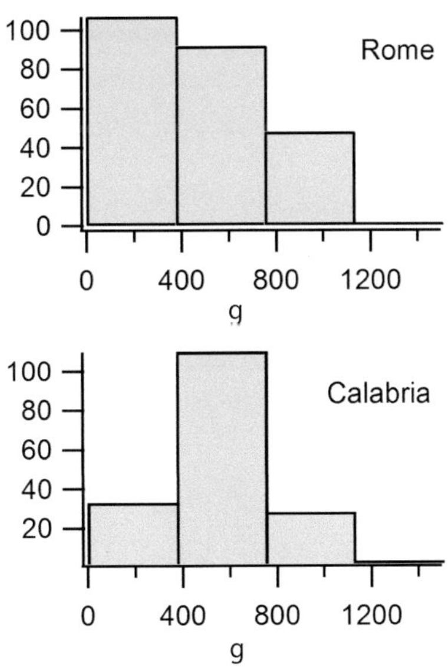

Figure 5. Binned distribution (interval: 380g) of SAQs in supermarkets in Rome and Calabria.

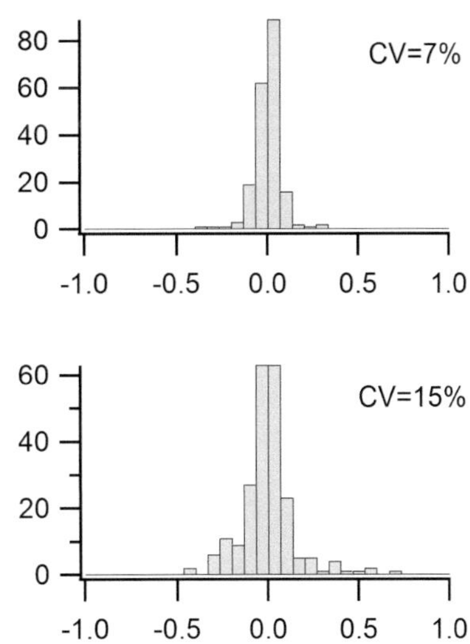

Figure 6. Cumulative binned distributions of CVs of the two different categories of SAQs in supermarkets. Top: goods with exact 'round' nominal weight listed on the package; bottom: portioned goods with real weight listed on the package.

From the analytical perspective, the main points emerging from our discussion support the following hypotheses to be used in the study of Italian hoards: 1) the distribution of weights is expected to be multimodal; 2) significant clusters of weight values, representing SAQs, should be normally distributed; 3) the CV of significant clusters should fall within a tolerable level (i.e. not more than 8%). We matched our hypotheses against eight different sample groups, each representing either a single, important hoard or corresponding to a group of hoards from a well-defined chrono-geographical context. All items contained in hoards were considered in these analyses, without any selection based either on shape or function.

The results of the 'multi-peak' analysis (Figure 7) show that all the distributions are multimodal, and that several 'peaks' match across different contexts (Table 3). Since the distributions are continuous, the boundaries of each peak must be set arbitrarily: the graphs in Figure 8 represent the cumulative CV of the sampled distributions, 'truncated' respectively at ±5%, ±10% and ±15% from the mean value of each peak and corresponding to CVs respectively equal to 3%, 5% and 8%. Graphs 1 and 2 retain a symmetrical, roughly bell-shaped curve, whereas graph 3 shows the incipient emergence of two more peaks on both sides of the central one (i.e. a multimodal distribution), meaning that the range is large enough to encompass adjacent peaks and should therefore be discarded. Graphs 1 and 2 suggest that the sample is organised according to a multimodal distribution of normally distributed clusters whose CV ranges between 3%–5%, which is in line with the expectations; moreover, the sample truncated at ±5% includes 31% of total measurements, while the ±10% one accounts for 49% of total measurements. To summarise, the results match our hypotheses: we can conclude that a large part of the sample (between 30%–50%) can be explained as an array of normally distributed clusters with a CV between 3%–5%. In the light of the

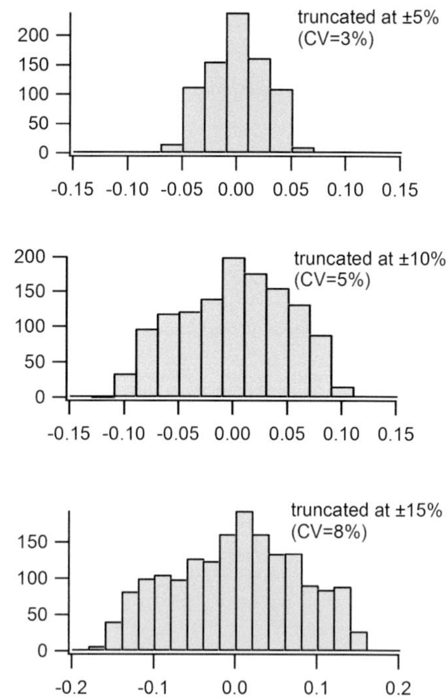

Figure 8. Cumulative binned distributions of CVs of SAQs in Italian hoards, symmetrically truncated at different distances from the mean (±5%, ±10%, ±15%).

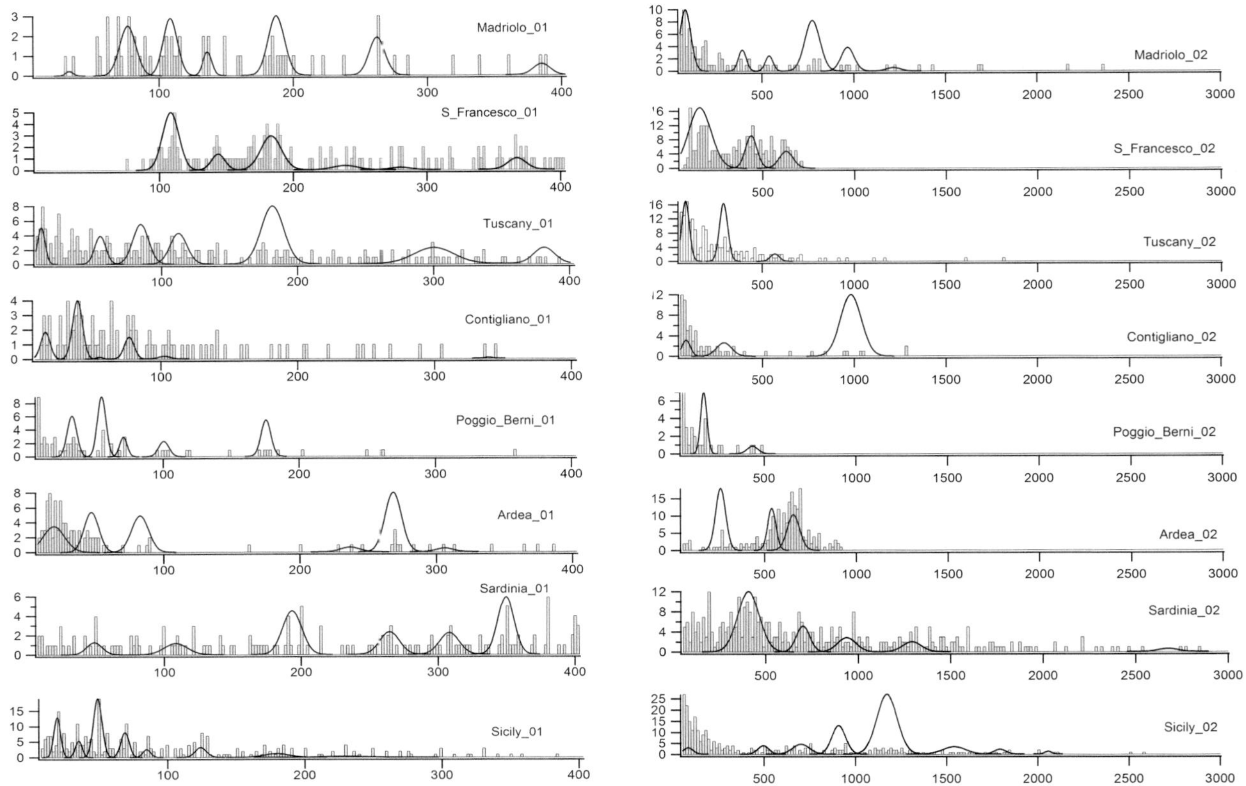

Figure 7. Binned distributions of weight values pertaining to metal objects in selected Italian hoards; overlaid 'peaks' indicate significant distributions. Left: values between 7.5–403g; right: values between 54–3000g (note that the hoard from Crotone lacks items above 400g).

considerations formulated so far in this paper, we could then state that a large part of the metal objects in Italian hoards between the Final Bronze Age and the Early Iron Age were possibly intentionally produced/fragmented in order to obtain a predetermined weight.

The observations on the overall distributions support the idea that the achievement of a predetermined weight was a primary concern, as reflected by objects found in hoards, but provide no information on the weight systems and units in use and on how different systems may possibly have been connected. One could have tried to analyse in more depth the correspondences between different weight series and attempt to devise, by adopting a 'quantal' approach, the 'units' underlying each system. However, we will show that another approach is possible, making use of indeterminacy and approximation, rather than dismissing them as weaknesses. Following the considerations on the relational qualities of SAQs, we set a preliminary framework aimed at quantifying the potential ties between each chrono-geographical context. The mean values are matched in rows (Table 3) in order to obtain a plausible CV for each row. The resulting contingency table was used to run a cluster analysis, in Euclidean distance, choosing the furthest neighbour joining method (the one that most emphasises differences between variables, thus producing more compact clusters; cf. Mooi and Sarstedt 2011: 251–2).

The results are encouraging (Figure 9): the analysis singles out two neat clusters, the first one including hoards from the central Tyrrhenian area (Sardinia, Tuscany and Ardea), and the second one tying together hoards of the central-northern Apennine area (Poggio Berni, S. Francesco and Contigliano) (cf. Figure 1). The clusters appear entirely plausible, grouping together hoards from relatively circumscribed areas; the first cluster, in particular, links together two macro-regions (Sardinia and the central Tyrrhenian area) that are well known to have maintained frequent overseas relationships through the whole of the Late Bronze/Early Iron Age. A third, weaker link is highlighted between south-east Sicily and Madriolo (north-eastern Alps) that may seem to be at odds with the considerable distance separating north-east Italy from the southern Ionian Sea. However, recent research has shown that there is a high probability that a great deal of the metal in use in Adriatic and Ionian Italy (especially in Calabria) during the Late Bronze/Early Iron Age was actually imported from the eastern Alps (Jung *et al.* 2011). We further observed that, by changing the joining method of the cluster analysis, the basic clusters remain substantially unchanged, thus supporting the solidity of the pattern underlying the data. At this stage of research, this can only suggest that weight systems in the Ionian Sea may have converged towards similar

Madriolo	S_Francesco	Poggio Berni	Tuscany	Contigliano	Sardinia	Ardea	Sicily		CV
			11.46						...
				15.41					...
						19.37	19.37		**0%**
33.21		33.21					35.19		**3%**
				39.14					...
		54.96	54.96	54.96	49.03	47.05	49.03		**7%**
							68.80		...
76.71		70.78	84.62	76.71		82.65	84.62		**7%**
108.35	108.35	100.44	112.31	102.42	108.35				**4%**
136.04	143.95						124.17		**7%**
187.45	183.50	175.59	181.52		193.39		179.54		**3%**
	238.87					236.89	230.96		**2%**
262.60					264.58	268.53			**1%**
	280.40		300.17	289.68	308.08	306.10			**4%**
				339.72	349.61				**2%**
385.20	367.41		381.25						**2%**
	436.98	436.98			407.52				**4%**
540.09			569.55			540.09	495.90		**6%**
775.77	628.47				702.12	657.93	702.12		**8%**
967.26				981.99	937.80		908.34		**3%**
1217.67					1291.32		1173.48		**5%**
							1541.73		...
							1792.14		...
							2057.28		...
					2675.94				...

Table 3. Contingency table of the correspondences between the distribution means of each 'peak' from different contexts. The CVs of the distributions in each row are listed in the right column.

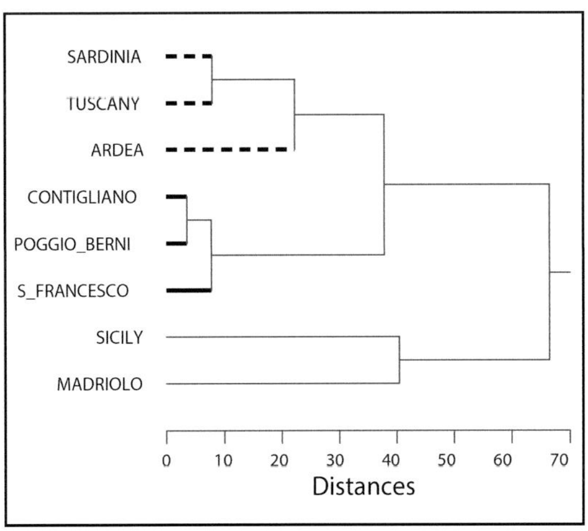

Figure 9. Hierarchical tree-clustering of selected Italian hoards, based on the contingency table in Table 3 (Euclidean distance, furthest neighbour method).

standards to those in north-east Italy, as a consequence of frequent trade along Adriatic routes; in any case, by looking at the whole pattern, results seem to encourage further insight into the possible connections highlighted by the similarities in the distribution of SAQs. To summarise the results of such preliminary analyses, we can conclude that SAQs, as conceptual tools, appear promising in explaining the patterned variation of weight regularities across long distances and in providing interpretive hints that go beyond the mere normative aspects addressed by traditional metrology.

Conclusions

Our discussion of some basic statistical properties of the distributions of weight measures, drawn from Ancient Near Eastern metrology, tested on European samples and discussed against modern proxies, can be summarised in four general statements:

1. a certain dispersion in weight measurements is 'socially accepted' in transactions
2. customary standards exist (SAQs) that are only partly related to 'official' weight systems and units
3. 'official' weight standards (theoretical units) are difficult to recognise through empirical methods alone, while they can be inferred through circumstantial evidence (e.g. texts, marked weights, historical considerations etc.)
4. SAQs are recognisable through empirical methods

If compared to theoretical units (very difficult to determine), SAQs provide an alternative framework in studying the relationships within and across preliterate economic systems, since they can be effectively observed, measured and compared to a much greater extent. But what are we actually observing when we put our focus on SAQs? While theoretical units give us a glimpse on how quantities were *counted*, and ultimately transcribed in official accounts of literate societies, SAQs are sources of information on more practical aspects of trade activities. The process by which a SAQ comes to represent a customary standard is partly independent from officially-sanctioned units. For example, this is the case of portions in supermarkets, ideally assembled in order to match the needs of average kinds of customers, possibly depending on different compositions of households, but also on cultural practices in storing and shipping goods (as in the case of the modern oil barrel), etc. In general, SAQs, while depending on measuring things and even using theoretical units for formal definition, can be independently used as a source of information on society, economy and trade networks.

Our attempt to analyse the geographical distribution of SAQs in hoards from Final Bronze Age/Early Iron Age Italy through cluster analysis seeks to quantify the connections between local contexts, based on the assumption that similar arrays of SAQs should be related to effective trade relations in a network. The analysis would certainly require a wider scope, both geographically and chronologically; however, the preliminary results are encouraging in that they indicate that the distribution of SAQs might correspond to significant exchange networks in Bronze Age Italy. Our analyses based on SAQs have attempted to show that 'substantive', local-level social constraints (in the 'Polanyian' sense) are coherent with the mechanisms of large-scale and long-distance exchange. Customary standards, in the form of SAQs, tend to stem from the intersection between 'social' and 'economic' instances, and their potential to draw observations about large-scale economic networks and trajectories is worth exploring, without necessarily relying on exact weight standards and directional diffusion hypotheses.

Acknowledgements

N. Ialongo devised and coordinated the research, developed the statistical method and performed the analyses; A. Vacca treated Ancient Near Eastern weight systems; A. Vanzetti advised the research process. The theoretical framework was defined by N. Ialongo and A. Vanzetti in previous research and further developed in this study together with A. Vacca. The interpretive framework and the conclusions are a result of the discussion within the research team. We thank M. Ortolani for the support on statistical analyses. We finally thank the editors for providing accurate comments on the manuscript, and giving us relevant suggestions to improve the text; all remaining shortcomings are our own responsibility.

Bibliography

Albanese Procelli, R. M. 1993. *Ripostigli di bronzi della Sicilia nel Museo di Siracusa.* Palermo, Accademia nazionale di Scienze, Lettere e Arti.

Alberti E., Ascalone, E., Parise, N. and Peyronel, L. 2006. Weights in context: current approaches to the study of the ancient weight systems. In E. Alberti, E. Ascalone and L. Peyronel (eds), *Weights in context. Bronze Age weighing systems of the eastern Mediterranean: chronology, typology and archaeological contexts. Proceedings of the International Colloquium, Rome 22nd–24th November 2004*: 1–8. Roma, Istituto Italiano di Numismatica (Studi e Materiali 13).

AOGHS 2013. History of the 42-gallon oil barrel. http://aoghs.org/news/history-of-the-42-gallon-oil-barrel/ (accessed 18 March 2016).

Archi, A. 1987. Reflections on the system of weights from Ebla. In C. H. Gordon, G. A. Rendsburg and N. H. Winter (eds), *Eblaitica: essays on the Ebla archives and Eblaite language, Vol. 1*: 47–83. Winona Lake, Eisenbrauns.

Arkhipov, I. 2012. *Le vocabulaire de la métallurgie et la nomenclature des objets en métal dans les textes de Mari. Matériaux pour le Dictionnaire de Babylonien de Paris, Tome III*. Louvain, Peeters (Archives Royales de Mari 32).

Ascalone, E. and Peyronel, L. 2000. '... secondo la norma del peso del re'. Alalakh e Mari: contesti archeologici palatini e sistemi ponderali in Siria durante la media età del Bronzo. *Quaderni Ticinesi di Numismatica e Antichità Classiche* 29: 7–45.

Ascalone, E. and Peyronel, L. 2001. Two weights from temple N at Tell Mardikh-Ebla, Syria: a link between metrology and cultic activities in the second millennium BC? *Journal of Cuneiform Studies* 53: 1–12.

Ascalone, E. and Peyronel, L. 2006. *I pesi da bilancia dell'età del Bronzo Antico e Medio*. Roma, Università di Roma 'La Sapienza' (Materiali e Studi di Archeologia Orientale 7).

Belaiew, N. T. 1929. Au sujet de la valeur probable de la mine sumérienne. *Revue d'Assyriologie* 26: 115–32.

Borgna, E. 1992. *Il ripostiglio di Madriolo presso Cividale e i pani a piccone del Friuli-Venezia Giulia*. Roma, Quasar.

Broodbank, C. 2013. *The making of the Middle Sea. A history of the Mediterranean from the beginning to the emergence of the Classical World*. London, Thames & Hudson.

Cardarelli A., Pacciarelli, M. and Pallante, P. 2004. Pesi e bilance nell'età del Bronzo italiana: quadro generale e nuovi dati. In E. De Sena and H. Dessales (eds), *Archaeological methods and approaches: industry and commerce in ancient Italy*: 80–8. Oxford, Archaeopress (British Archaeological Reports International Series 1262).

Cateni, G. 1977. Il ripostiglio di Limone (Livorno). *Studi Etruschi* 45: 3–37.

Chambon, G. 2011. *Normes et pratiques: l'homme, la mesure et l'écriture en Mésopotamie. I. Les mesures de capacité et de poids en Syrie Ancienne, d'Ebla à Émar*. Berlin, PeWe (Berliner Beiträge zum Vorderen Orient 21).

Cocchi Genick, D. 1985. Colle Le Banche (Camaiore, Lucca). In D. Cocchi Genick and R. Grifoni Cremonesi (eds), *L'età dei metalli nella Toscana nord-occidentale, catalogo della mostra Viareggio, Maggio-Dicembre 1985*: 324–60. Pisa, Piacini Editore.

Durand, J.-M. 1987. Questions de chiffres. *MARI* 5: 605–10.

Eiwanger, J. 1989. Talanton — Ein bronzezeitlicher Goldstandard zwischen Ägäis und Mitteleuropa. *Germania* 67(2): 443–62.

Frayne, D. R. 1997. *The royal inscriptions of Mesopotamia. Early periods. Vol. 3/2: Ur III period (2112-2004 BC)*. Toronto, University of Toronto Press.

Hemmy, A. S. 1935. The statistical treatment of ancient weights. *Ancient Egypt and the East* 1: 83–93.

Ialongo, N., Di Renzoni, A., Ortolani, M. and Vanzetti, A. 2015. An analytical framework for the research on prehistoric weight systems: a case study from Nuragic Sardinia. *Origini* 37(1): 151–73.

Ialongo, N. 2011. *Il santuario nuragico di Monte S. Antonio di Siligo (SS). Studio analitico dei complessi cultuali della Sardegna protostorica*. PhD thesis, Università di Roma 'La Sapienza'. http://hdl.handle.net/10805/1490 (accessed 30 October 2015).

Ialongo, N. and Vanzetti, A. 2016. The intangible weight of things: approximate nominal weights in modern society. In S. Biagetti and F. Lugli (eds), *The intangible elements of culture in ethnoarchaeological research*: 283–91. Berlin, Springer.

ISTAT 2011. *Censimento della popolazione e delle abitazioni 2011.* http://dati-censimentopopolazione.istat.it (accessed 19 March 2016).

Joannès, F. 1989. Les méthodes de pesée à Mari. *Revue d'Assyriologie et d'Archéologie Orientale* 83: 113–52.

Jones, R., Levi, S. T., Bettelli, M. and Vagnetti, L. (eds) 2014. *Italo-Mycenaean pottery: the archaeological and archaeometric dimension.* Roma, CNR — Istituto di Studi sul Mediterraneo antico (Incunabula Graeca 103).

Jung, R. and Mehofer, M. 2013. Mycenaean Greece and Bronze Age Italy: cooperation, trade or war? *Archäologisches Korrespondenzblatt* 43: 175–93.

Jung, R., Mehofer, M. and Pernicka, E. 2011. Metal exchange in Italy from the Middle to the Final Bronze Age (14th–11th century B.C.E.). In P. Betancourt and S. C. Ferrence (eds), *Metallurgy: understanding how, learning why. Studies in honor of James D. Muhly*: 231–48. Philadelphia, INSTAP Academic Press.

Kendall, D. B. 1974. Hunting quanta. *Philosophical Transactions of the Royal Society of London. Series A, Mathematical and Physical Sciences* 276: 231–66.

Lenerz-de Wilde, M. 1995. Prämonetäre Zahlungsmittel in der Kupfer- und Bronzezeit Mitteleuropas. *Fundberichte aus Baden-Württemberg* 20: 229–327.

Lo Schiavo, F. 2006. Western weights in context. In E. Alberti, E. Ascalone and L. Peyronel (eds), *Weights in context. Bronze Age weighing systems of the Eastern Mediterranean: chronology, typology and archaeological contexts. Proceedings of the International Colloquium, Rome 22nd–24th November 2004*: 359–79. Roma, Istituto Italiano di Numismatica (Studi e Materiali 13).

Lo Schiavo, M. 2009. A threefold ill-posed problem. In F. Lo Schiavo, J. D. Muhly, R. Maddin and A. Giumlia-Mair (eds), *Oxhide ingots in the central Mediterranean*: 449–71. Roma, CNR — Istituto di Studi sulle Civiltà dell'Egeo e del Vicino Oriente (Biblioteca di Antichità Cipriote 8).

Malmer, M. E. 1992. Weight systems in the Scandinavian Bronze Age. *Antiquity* 66: 377–88.

Milano, L. 2003. Sistemi finanziari in Mesopotamia e Siria nel III millennio a.C. In L. Milano and N. Parise (eds), *Il regolamento degli scambi nell'antichità (III–I millennio a.C.)*: 3–58. Roma, Editori Laterza.

Montelius, O. 1893. *La civilisation primitive en Italie depuis l'introduction des métaux.* Stockholm, Imprimerie Royale.

Mooi, E. and Sarstedt, M. 2011. *A concise guide to market research: the process, data, and methods using IBM SPSS Statistics.* Berlin, Springer.

Morico, G. 1984. *Il ripostiglio di Poggio Berni. Catalogo della mostra, Rimini, palazzina delle mostre, dicembre 1984 - aprile 1985.* Roma, Paleani.

Pacciarelli, M. 2000. *Dal villaggio alla città. La svolta protourbana del 1000 a.C. nell'Italia tirrenica.* Firenze, All'Insegna del Giglio (Grandi Contesti e Problemi della Protostoria Italiana 4).

Pakkanen, J. 2011. Aegean Bronze Age weights, *chaînes opératoires* and the detecting of patterns through statistical analyses. In A. Brysbaert (ed.),

Tracing prehistoric social networks through technology: a diachronic perspective on the Aegean: 143–66. London, Routledge.

Pare, C. F. E. 1999. Weights and weighing in Bronze Age central Europe. In V. L. Aravantinos, J. A. Barceló and C. Bockisch-Bräuer (eds), *Eliten in der Bronzezeit: Ergebnisse zweier Kolloquien in Mainz und Athen*: 421–514. Mainz, Römisch-Germanisches Zentralmuseum (RGZM Monographien 43).

Pare, C. F. E. 2013. Weighing, commodification, and money. In H. Fokkens and A. Harding (eds), *The Oxford handbook of the European Bronze Age*: 508–27. Oxford, Oxford University Press.

Parise, N. 1970/71. Per uno studio del sistema ponderale ugaritico. *Dialoghi di Archeologia* 4: 3–36.

Parise, N. 1981. Mina di Ugarit, mina di Karkemish, mina di Khatti. *Dialoghi di Archeologia* 3: 155–60.

Parise, N. 1984. Unità ponderali e rapporti di cambio nella Siria del nord. In A. Archi (ed.), *Circulation of goods in non-palatial context in the Ancient Near East*: 125–38. Roma, Edizioni dell'Ateneo (Incunabula Graeca 82).

Peroni, R. 1961. *Ripostigli delle Età dei Metalli. 2 — ripostigli del Grossetano*. Firenze, Sansoni (Inventaria Archaeologica 2).

Peroni, R. 1966. Considerazioni ed ipotesi sul ripostiglio di Ardea. *Bullettino di Paletnologia Italiana* 75: 175–80.

Peroni, R. 1967. *Ripostigli delle Età dei Metalli. Ripostiglio di Ardea*. Firenze, Sansoni (Inventaria Archaeologica 4).

Peroni, R. 1998. Bronzezeitliche Gewichtssysteme im Metallhandel zwischen Mittelmeer und Ostsee. In B. Hänsel (ed.), *Mensch und Umwelt in der Bronzezeit Europas*: 217–24. Kiel, Oetker-Voges Verlag.

Peroni, R. 2004. Sistemi transculturali nell'economia, nella società, nell'ideologia. In D. Cocchi Genick (ed.), *L'età del bronzo recente in Italia. Atti del congresso nazionale, Lido di Camaiore (LU), 26-29 ottobre 2000*: 411–28. Lucca, Baroni.

Peroni, R. 2006. La circolazione dei beni e le sue motivazioni extraeconomiche ed economiche. In *Atti della XXXIX Riunione Scientifica Istituto Italiano di Preistoria e Protostoria 'Materie prime e scambi nella preistoria italiana', Firenze, 25-27 Novembre 2004*: 169–87. Firenze, Istituto Italiano di Preistoria e Protostoria.

Petruso, K. M. 1978. *Systems of weight in the Bronze Age Aegean*. Unpublished PhD thesis, Indiana University.

Petruso, K. M. 1992. *Ayia Irini. The balance weights: an analysis of weight measurement in prehistoric Crete and the Cycladic Islands*. Mainz, Philipp von Zabern (Keos 8).

Peyronel, L. 2011. *Mašqaltum kittum*. Questioni di equilibrio: bilance e sistemi di pesatura nell'Oriente antico. In E. Ascalone and L. Peyronel (eds), *Studi italiani di metrologia ed economia del Vicino Oriente antico dedicati a Nicola Parise in occasione del suo settantesimo compleanno*: 105–61. Roma, Herder (Studia Asiana 7).

Pomponio, F. 1980. AO 7754 ed il sistema ponderale di Ebla. *Oriens Antiquus* 19: 171–86.

Ponzi Bonomi, L. 1970. Il ripostiglio di Contigliano. *Bullettino di Paletnologia Italiana* 79: 95–154.

Powell, M. A. 1979. Ancient Mesopotamian weight metrology: methods, problems and perspectives. In M. A. Powell and R. H. Sack (eds), *Studies in honour of Tom B. Jones*: 71–109. Neunkirchen, Butzon & Bercker (Alter Orient und Altes Testament 203).

Powell, M. A. 1987/90. Masse und Gewichte. In *Reallexikon der Assyriologie und Vorderasiatischen Archäologie* 7: 457–530. Berlin, Walter De Gruyter.

Powell, M. A. 1996. Money in Mesopotamia. *Journal of the Economic and Social History of the Orient* 39(3): 224–42.

Primas, M. 1997. Bronze Age economy and ideology: central Europe in focus. *Journal of European Archaeology* 5(1): 115–30.

Rahmstorf, L. 2003. The identification of Early Helladic balance weights and their wider implications. In K. Polinger Foster and R. Laffineur (eds), *Metron: measuring the Aegean Bronze Age. Proceedings of the 9th International Aegean Conference / 9e Rencontre égéenne internationale, Yale University 18-21 April 2002*: 293–300. Liège, Université de Liège (Aegeum 24).

Rahmstorf, L. 2006. In search of the earliest balance weights, scales and weighing systems from the east Mediterranean, the Near and Middle East. In E. Alberti, E. Ascalone and L. Peyronel (eds), *Weights in context. Bronze Age weighing systems of the Eastern Mediterranean: chronology, typology and archaeological contexts. Proceedings of the International Colloquium, Rome 22nd-24th November 2004*: 9–48. Roma, Istituto Italiano di Numismatica (Studi e Materiali 13).

Rahmstorf, L. 2010. The concept of weighing during the Bronze Age in the Aegean, the Near East and Europe. In I. Morley and C. Renfrew (eds), *The archaeology of measurement. Comprehending heaven, earth and time in ancient societies*: 88–105. Cambrigde, Cambridge University Press.

Renfrew, C. 2008. Systems of value among material things: the nexus of fungibility and measure. In J. K. Papadopoulos and G. Urton (eds), *The construction of value in the Ancient World*: 249–60. Los Angeles, Cotsen Institute of Archaeology Press (Cotsen Advanced Seminar Series 5).

Ruìz-Gàlvez Priego, M. 2000. Weight system and exchange networks in Bronze Age Europe. In C. F. E. Pare (ed.), *Metals make the world go round: the supply and circulation of metals in Bronze Age Europe. Proceedings of a conference held at the University of Birmingham in June 1997*: 267–79. Oxford, Oxbow Books.

Schon, R. 2015. Weight sets: identification and analysis. *Cambridge Archaeological Journal* 25(2): 477–94.

Sommerfeld, C. 1994. *Gerätegeld Sichel. Studien zur monetären Struktur bronzezeitlicher Horte im nördlichen Mitteleuropa*. Berlin, Walter de Gruyter (Vorgeschichtliche Forschungen 19).

Sorda, S. 1975. I ripostigli di bronzi protostorici dell'Italia centrale. *Annali dell'Istituto Italiano di Numismatica* 22: 61–74.

Sperber, E. 1993. Establishing weight systems in Bronze Age Scandinavia. *Antiquity* 67: 613–19.

Thureau-Dangin, F. 1907. L'U, le Qa et la Mine, leur mesure et leur rapport. *Journal Asiatique* 10: 79–111.

Tirabassi, J. 1997. Valori ponderali nei ripostigli dell'Età del Bronzo Recente e Finale dell'Italia settentrionale: considerazioni e congetture. *Pagine d'Archeologia* 1: 1–23.

Viedebantt, O. 1917. *Forschungen zur Metrologie des Altertums*. Leipzig, Teubner (Abhandlungen der Philologisch-Historischen Klasse der Sächsischen Akademie der Wissenschaften 34).

Viedebantt, O. 1923. *Antike Gewichtsnormen und Münzfüße*. Berlin, Weidmannsche Buchhandlung.

Weissbach, F. H. 1907. Über die babylonischen, assyrischen und alt-persischen Gewichte. *Zeitschrift der Deutschen Morgenländischen Gesellschaft* 61: 379–402, 948–50.

Weissbach, F. H. 1916. Neue Beiträge zur keilinschriftlichen Gewichtskunde. *Zeitschrift der Deutschen Morgenländischen Gesellschaft* 70: 49–91.

Wiegel, B. 1994. *Trachtkreise im südlichen Hügelgräberbereich: Studien zur Beigabensitte der Mittelbronzezeit unter besonderer Berücksichtigung forschungsgeschichtlicher Aspekte*. Espelkamp, Leidorf (Internationale Archäologie 5).

Wilcke, C. 2002. Der Codex Urnamma (CU): Versuch einer Rekonstruktion. In T. Abusch (ed.), *Riches hidden in secret places. Ancient Near Eastern studies in memory of T. Jacobsen*: 191–233. Winona Lake, Eisenbrauns.

Zaccagnini, C. 1984. The terminology of weight measure for wool at Ebla. In P. Fronzaroli (ed.), *Studies on the language of Ebla*: 189–204. Firenze, Istituto di Linguistica e di Lingue Orientali (Quaderni di Semitistica 13).

Zaccagnini, C. 1999/2001. The mina of Karkemiš and other minas. *State Archives of Assyria Bulletin* 13: 39–56.

Zeeb, F. 1991. Studien zu den altbabylonischen Texten aus Alalah, I: Schuldscheine. *Ugarit-Forschungen* 23: 405–38.

Fragmentation patterns revisited: ritual and recycling in Bronze Age depositional practice

Dirk Brandherm

Abstract

In the present contribution we argue for a distinction between two broad categories of fragmentation patterns among metalwork depositions of the European Bronze Age, one stemming from ritual decommissioning for religious purposes, the other from the breaking-up of metal objects for recycling or for use as hackbronze currency. It is further argued that this distinction does not always map neatly onto a dichotomy between the religious and the mundane where the motives behind the subsequent deposition of fragmented metalwork are concerned.

Keywords: Bronze Age, metalwork, hoard, deposition, fragmentation pattern

Résumé

Les formes de fragmentation revisitées: rituel et recyclage dans la pratique des dépôts de l'Âge du Bronze

Dans cet article, nous discutons de la distinction entre deux larges catégories de type de fragmentation des objets métalliques regroupés au sein des dépôts et cachettes de l'Âge du Bronze en Europe. Nous soutenons que le premier type résulte d'une destruction pour des raisons religieuses, tandis que le second type découle du bris des objets métalliques en vue de leur recyclage ou de leur utilisation comme « hackbronze ». Toutefois, cette distinction entre les raisons religieuses et profanes concernant la fragmentation des objets ne correspond pas toujours à la dichotomie entre les motifs religieux des dépôts et profanes des cachettes.

Mots-clés: Âge du Bronze, objet métallique, cachette, pratique des dépôts, forme de fragmentation

Zusammenfassung

Fragmentierungsmuster neu betrachtet: Ritual und Recycling in der bronzezeitlichen Niederlegungspraxis

Der vorliegende Beitrag formuliert Kriterien zur Differenzierung zweier unterschiedlicher Fragmentierungsmuster in Hortfunden der europäischen Bronzezeit, von denen sich das eine mit einer religiös motivierten Votivpraxis, das andere mit dem Portionieren von Metall zu Recyclingzwecken und einer Verwendung als Hackbronzewährung in Verbindung bringen läßt. Diese unterschiedlichen Zerlegungsmotive gehen jedoch keineswegs immer mit einer entsprechenden Unterscheidung zwischen religiösen und profanen Motiven für die letztendliche Deponierung fragmentierter Bronzen einher.

Schlüsselwörter: Bronzezeit, Metall, Hort, Deponierung, Fragmentierungsmuster

Introduction

Ever since the early days of prehistoric archaeology as an academic discipline, the fragmentation of objects in many Bronze Age metalwork hoards has prompted diverse and often seemingly incompatible readings. Hypotheses have varied in accordance with different intellectual traditions and fashions, and for the most part have been linked to conflicting interpretations of the hoarding phenomenon in general as either a purely utilitarian or religiously motivated practice.

As early as 1866, J. J. A. Worsaae advocated a reading of many Bronze Age hoards, and particularly of those assemblages containing intentionally damaged and fragmented objects, as votive offerings (Worsaae 1866: 317–19; 1866/71: 67–8). Especially among northern and central European scholars, this explanation has remained popular ever since, although specific categories of hoards have also been interpreted differently (e.g. Hänsel 1997: 13–15; Hundt 1955: 99–107).

For western Europe, E. Chantre's (1875/76: 68) categorisation of Bronze Age metalwork assemblages according to their perceived function, as either founders' or merchants' hoards, proved seminal and cemented a utilitarian interpretation of metalwork deposition and of intentional object fragmentation that still echoes in the terminologies used in many Romance-language traditions today (e.g. Fernández Rodríguez 2014: 16; Melo 2000: 25–6; Ruiz-Gálvez Priego 1995: 29–32; Silva et al. 1984: 73–4). Through the work of J. Evans (1881: 457–9) Chantre's concepts were introduced into Anglophone archaeology, where his labelling of assemblages containing high percentages of fragmented objects as founder's hoards conditioned a utilitarian reading of much of the hoarding phenomenon until at least the 1980s, when post-processual approaches led to the almost wholesale abandonment of strictly utilitarian explanations, and of the loaded labels introduced by Evans, throughout English-speaking archaeology.

This evidently is not to say that interpretative models remained entirely static and unchangeable prior to the advent of post-processualism. The rise of processual archaeology since the 1960s in particular saw a marked shift away from antiquarian and culture-historical approaches towards a focus on questions of social organisation also in the study of Bronze Age metalwork depositions. However, beyond stereotypical references to wilful destruction and abandonment of accumulated wealth for the presumed purpose of gaining social prestige, this did not entail examining the specific motives behind particular practices of object fragmentation and deposition, generally deemed irrelevant in the larger societal scheme of things (cf. Taylor 1993: 95–104).[1]

[1] One of the most overused and misapplied concepts in this context is probably that of the

A more nuanced understanding of the hoarding phenomenon in general and of the intentional fragmentation of objects in particular over the last thirty years or so has been enabled by essentially two factors: in the first instance by a realisation that the fragmentation of and intentional damage to deposited metalwork rarely are completely random, but tend to follow clear patterns (Rittershofer 1983: 345–7; Sommerfeld 1994: 29–36; *contra* Nebelsick 1997; 2000); secondly, by the recognition that a sharp distinction between the religious and the mundane in a Bronze Age context may not always be entirely appropriate to begin with (Brück 1999: 325–8; Torbrügge 1985: 19 note 30). Especially this second recognition led some authors to call for a wholesale abandonment of these categories when dealing with Bronze Age metalwork deposition (e.g. Ballmer 2010: 129; Bradley 2005: 148; Brück 2001: 157), but while these voices are certainly correct in highlighting the etic character of labels such as 'mundane' or 'religious' when applied to prehistoric practices, and in cautioning against the uncritical use of these categorisations where premodern patterns of thought are concerned, it should be obvious that this does not render them altogether irrelevant.

It is one thing to raise awareness of the limitations of our present terminological apparatus, which are inevitably born from the modern observer's etic perspective; it is an entirely different thing to try and substitute the analytical categories we employ with concepts that aspire to emulate an emic point of view, but in practice remain very much subjectivist in nature and do not really facilitate a better understanding of the multidimensional nature of prehistoric metalwork deposition practice. Acknowledging that this practice may have both utilitarian and non-utilitarian underpinnings, and that these two aspects may even intersect within individual hoard assemblages, cannot mean that the distinction between them should be viewed as immaterial. In an attempt to

---

'potlatch', invoked in many studies trying to make sense of the intentional fragmentation of objects in prehistory, and Bronze Age metalwork in particular (Bradley 1982: 118; 1990: 36; Ruiz-Gálvez 1995: 131). It has to be stressed here that ethnographically attested examples of the potlatch practice, apart from being few and far between (Testart 2012: 299; Testart *et al.* 2012: 384–5), are very much characterised by the distinct lack of any notion of material value being offered to a deity or divine power. In all its varied guises, the potlatch at its core remains a ritualised contest of conspicuous consumption that explicitly serves to initiate and maintain patron–client relationships and, in stark contrast to the practice of votive offerings, thus focuses primarily on ritualised gift giving to other members of the relevant social group (Barnett 1938; Rosman and Rubel 1972). The deliberate destruction of material wealth as part of a potlatch might be a striking and powerful performative act, but the gift-giving component is much more central to its purpose. Possible similarities in the ritual expression of both practices, and the spiritual aspects embedded in some ethnographically documented potlatches, should not distract from the fact that the aims of votive offerings on the one hand and of potlatch ceremonies on the other are fundamentally different (cf. Snyder 1975).

address this issue, a number of authors in the past have tried to come up with more explicit and more nuanced classification systems for hoard assemblages containing a significant proportion of fragmented objects (Falkenstein 2011: 73–4; Huth 1997: 149–52; Maraszek 2006: 248–61; Mörtz 2013: 56; Rittershofer 1983: 344–7; Sommerfeld 1994: 21–36; Stein 1976: 22–30), but none of these proposals have managed to gain universal acceptance, not least due to the fact that most of them were based on very specific samples collected at different geographical and chronological scales.

Apart from issues caused by region or period-specific sampling, another problem plaguing much previous work in this field arises from the – for the most part – unquestioned assumption that a utilitarian or non-utilitarian rationale behind the fragmentation of an object is necessarily congruent with the motives behind its deposition. Here we are going to challenge that assumption.[2]

Making sense of fragmentation patterns

First and foremost, it needs to be stressed that when it comes to the intentional fragmentation of objects and their deposition, we are dealing with two quite distinct processes, which in some cases obviously may have occurred in conjunction, but which in others might also have had little to do with each other. It is entirely conceivable that either one of these may have had quite mundane reasons, while the other one could still have been driven by a religious rationale. Therefore, in order to avoid the pitfalls of circular reasoning, the motives behind the fragmentation and the deposition of metalwork objects in the first instance have to be explored independently.

The most common utilitarian rationale for the fragmentation of bronze objects certainly would have been the portioning of metal for remelting as part of the recycling process. That recycling of scrap metal must have formed an integral part of Bronze Age economy is not only dictated by the survival rate of Bronze Age metalwork in the archaeological record (cf. Needham 2001: 282–4), but is also demonstrated by the rare instances of surviving scrap metal assemblages from settlement contexts, such as the recent finds of collected scrap metal from Must Farm in Cambridgeshire (David Gibson, pers. comm.). Evidently only a tiny fraction of the metal circulating in the Bronze Age ever entered the archaeological record for any significant length of time. The overwhelming majority circulated in a more or less continuous recycling loop and was never

[2] The arguments laid out in the following section were first developed in Brandherm (2016: 85–90). Many thanks go to my co-editors for their patience and thorough revision of the original manuscript, and to Muriel Fily for kindly providing the photograph of the Kergaradec 2 hoard shown in our Figure 2.

permanently deposited (Bradley 1988: 253; Bray and Pollard 2012: 856–62; Falkenstein 2011: 74–5 fig. 2; Jockenhövel 1986: 224; Needham 2001: 282–8). There thus can be absolutely no doubt that portioning scrap metal must have been common practice.

There is also evidence to suggest that fragmented bronze objects may have been used as premonetary[3] currency in a system not entirely unlike that of early medieval hacksilber (Brandherm 2004: 368; Brandherm and Moskal-del Hoyo 2014: 35). That we can assume such a function, at least for certain periods and regions within the European Bronze Age, may be inferred from the fact that the spatial distributions of scrap hoards and of standardised ingot forms within individual chronological horizons tend to be mutually exclusive. Although certain forms of ingot money sometimes do also occur in a fragmented state, this does not invalidate the fundamental difference between premonetary currency systems based on fixed denominations on the one hand and exclusively weight-based hackmetal currencies on the other, which both have quite different implications for the economic and social systems within which they operate (cf. Brandherm 2004: 367). Another likely indicator for a probable function of 'hackbronze' as premonetary currency is the almost complete disappearance of previously quite common small bronze scrap items from the agoras of Greek colonies in Sicily, and the substitution of bullion metal by other categories of object as offerings in sanctuaries from Sicily and Latium, following the introduction of coinage in the respective regions (Baitinger forthcoming; Murgan and Kemmers 2016: 279–83).

In stark contrast to these utilitarian explanations for the occurrence of scrap metal in Bronze Age contexts, many scholars have interpreted the intentional fragmentation of metal objects as a religious practice (e.g. Hansen 2016; Nebelsick 1997; 2000). In this case the main objective behind the act of fragmentation is generally assumed to have been aimed at their removal from the sphere of everyday use and at transferring them to the domain of the supernatural or divine. An alternative reading would view religiously motivated fragmentation of metalwork items as the ritual 'killing' of objects perceived as animated beings by Bronze Age people. The former model, focusing on the objects' removal from human use, draws primarily on Greco-Roman sources, whereas the alternative explanation which focuses on the 'killing' of animated objects is inspired more by early medieval tradition

[3] The term 'premonetary' is of course in itself not without its semantic problems and contradictions (cf. Heymans this volume), but is retained here as conventional shorthand for referring to any physical expression of a currency which, while functioning as a medium of exchange and store of value, is not cast into a scaled system of fixed denominations anchored to a standard unit of account.

and by a comparison with modern ethnographic parallels (Brück 2006: 305–10; Hansen 1996; Metzner-Nebelsick 2012; Sommerfeld 1994: 21–36). With some effort one might certainly be able to envisage hypothetical scenarios where both motives work together to drive the intentional fragmentation of metalwork items, but the available analogies from the historical and ethnographic records suggest that in practice we are dealing with two fundamentally different mechanisms which do not really overlap.

This has important implications also for the distinction between religious and mundane elements involved in these mechanisms. Whereas the intentional destruction of metalwork items as part of a votive offering or sacrifice indisputably constitutes a religious act *per se*, the same does not necessarily hold true where objects are being fragmented in order to break the link between their material existence and a life force that is perceived to inhabit them. The perception of objects as animated beings may invariably be rooted in religious belief, but the act of 'killing', i.e. deanimating these objects – even if performed within a ritual framework – does not have to be motivated by religious purpose. The intensive use of force against such an object may simply have played an important part in ritually transforming 'living' matter into 'dead' raw material that was considered safe for recycling (cf. Metzner-Nebelsick 2012: 161–2; Nebelsick 1997: 40–1). This applies especially in those cases where the animate nature of an object may have been viewed as potentially dangerous, a perception frequently attested for weapons in particular, both in medieval literature and in ethnographic sources, and for whose currency in the Bronze Age a case can also be made based on archaeological evidence (Cowen 1966: 294; Pearce 2013: 64–5). We shall return to this issue further below, but first must briefly examine the possible motives behind the deposition of fragmented metalwork.

The most commonly cited likely utilitarian rationale for the deposition of fragmented metal objects is the accumulation and safe storage of material value (e.g. Pauli 1985: 201). For regions and time periods where scrap metal represented a socially recognised medium for accumulating and storing material value, or where it even served as a form of premonetary hackbronze currency, it stands to reason that safekeeping might have been one of the principal motives for the deposition of fragmented metalwork in the ground. This applies not only, but especially in times of war or social upheaval and unrest, when stores of material value are always in danger, due to the suspension of social norms which would otherwise ensure their protection from illegitimate access. Here it is worth remembering, for example, the numerous coin hoards from the time of the Thirty Years' War, and also the caches of religious paraphernalia hidden away by Jewish families and congregations in times of anti-Jewish pogroms, which in the archaeological record show up as chronologically and geographically well-defined 'hoard horizons' (cf. Randsborg 2002: 416–17).

The most frequently suggested religious motivation behind the deposition of metalwork items is their sacrifice as votive offering (e.g. Hänsel 1997; Hansen 1994; 1996). Such an offering may have been made in expectation of a reciprocal benefit bestowed by the recipient of the sacrifice, or in acknowledgement of a benefit already received. In either case one is dealing with part of a *do ut des* transaction between the party offering the sacrifice and the party receiving it. Needless to say, this mechanism is fundamentally different from the placing of hidden material value under the protection of a deity or divine power for safekeeping.

With votive offerings one also has to keep in mind that the place in which objects were eventually deposited does not have to coincide with the location where the offering originally took place. Greco-Roman sources provide ample testimony of the secondary deposition below ground of votive offerings which previously had been openly on display, not necessarily in exactly the same spot (cf. Mandera 1985: 187–9). In such a case, the fragmentation of votive objects may have occurred only at the time of this secondary deposition, and thus may not represent the original act of sacrifice or the transfer into the possession of its divine recipient.

Objects may also have been deposited in accordance with religious beliefs so they would be available to a deceased person in their afterlife. Such depositions may have been undertaken by the owner himself prior to his/her passing, or by another party following the owner's death. For pagan northern Europe we have written testimony from the early medieval period that this did not necessarily require proximity of the relevant items to the final resting place of the deceased person's mortal remains (Hundt 1955: 108; Lund 2017: 99). Here also, the fragmentation of objects might have formed part of a ritual that served to facilitate their transition into the Otherworld.

Despite the various caveats expressed above, and also despite the fact that in some instances pragmatic considerations might have overruled any original motivation and that priorities may have shifted subsequently to the original act of deposition (Needham 2001: 287–9), a systematic analysis of the siting of metalwork hoards would still appear to provide the most promising avenue for trying to distinguish between these different categories of deposition (Hansen 2012: 39–43; Scholz 2012: 70–81; Soroceanu 1995: 35–46; 2011: 271–8; Taylor 1993: 78–89). However, conducting such an analysis is beyond the remit of the present contribution. Instead, here we are going to focus on what different fragmentation patterns may tell us about the likely motivation behind the intentional breaking-up of metal objects, and how this might relate to the motives behind their deposition.

Among Bronze Age hoards containing a significant proportion of fragmented items, two main classes of assemblage are generally discernible, differing from each other both in their composition and in the peri-depositional treatment of the deposited objects.

On the one hand we have assemblages composed of items that display evidence of considerable physical force having been used against them, but which show a degree of fragmentation which falls very much short of what one would expect from objects cut up into crucible-sized portions for purposes of recycling (Figure 1).[4] Here we seem to be looking at a distinct process of decommissioning, aimed primarily at putting the items in question beyond any practical use. Normally, the assemblages in this class contain most of the fragments from the deposited objects, although *pars pro toto* elements may also be present, and mostly they comprise objects from only one or two functional categories. In the majority of cases these are weapons or personal ornaments. Specific examples for this class of assemblages are the Duddingston Loch (Coles 1959/60: 117), Ría de Huelva (Ruiz-Gálvez Priego 1995: 185–227) and Wylye (PAS: WILT-038191) hoards.

The second class of assemblages is characterised by a much higher degree of fragmentation, i.e. by the breaking-up of objects into more numerous and proportionally smaller fragments. The incidence of intentional damage not directly related to the fragmentation process among these assemblages is recognisably lower than in the previous class (cf. Boulud and Mélin 2009: 190–

[4] Occasionally the term 'degree of fragmentation' (*Fragmentierungsgrad*) has been employed to refer to the proportion of broken-up bronze objects within a given hoard, or to the proportion of fragmented specimens of a specific object category within different hoard assemblages (Maraszek 2006: 259; Sommerfeld 1994: 31; Vachta 2008: 57). We consider this usage to be misleading and prefer to apply this term solely when referring to the degree of fragmentation of individual objects. The relevant criterion for determining the degree of fragmentation therefore is the number of fragments into which an object has been broken up, rather than the proportion of fragmented objects within a hoard, which would better be termed 'fragmentation index'. Since in most cases not all fragments from a broken-up object will be present in a given assemblage, the exact value for the latter is often difficult to determine through a simple object count. A more reliable and meaningful approach has been suggested by Gabillot (2004: 194–8), who employed the ratio between the median weight of all fragments from a given object type included in a hoard and the median total weight of a complete specimen of the same type as a measure to determine what she referred to as 'indice de métal déposé'. Her study of the Breton hoard record has demonstrated the validity of this approach, both for individual object types represented within specific hoards and for complete hoard assemblages.

Figure 1. Class 1 assemblage from the Ría de Huelva (Huelva), representative selection of objects (photograph Miguel Hermoso Cuesta, Wikimedia Commons CC BY-SA 4.0).

2). In addition to a higher degree of fragmentation of individual objects, these assemblages also tend to include a larger proportion of fragmented items. On the other hand, in this class the majority of fragments from any one object are rarely present in the same assemblage, which is why there are normally far fewer matching fragments per assemblage than in the previous class. Finally, hoards in this second class usually comprise items from multiple object categories, with a higher proportion of tools, casting debris and ingot metal (Figure 2). The hoards of the Boughton-Vénat complex of the Atlantic Late Bronze Age are probably among the most striking examples of this type of assemblage (Brandherm and Moskal-del Hoyo 2014: 32–5), as are the tool-dominated hoards of the Middle Bronze Age in parts of central Europe (Sommerfeld 1994: 103–16) and also some of the Late Bronze Age scrap metal hoards of the central Mediterranean (Giardino 1995: 191–225; Lo Schiavo 1991: 213–14; Ruiz-Gálvez Priego 1986: 12–17).

The distinction between the two classes of assemblage outlined above is not entirely new. Sommerfeld (1994: 31–3 fig. 3) had first observed a differentiation along similar lines within the central European hoard record, and specifically for the weapon hoards of the British Late Bronze Age. Mörtz (2013: 59–60) recently advocated a distinction between different damage and fragmentation

Figure 2. Class 2 assemblage from Kergaradec (Gouesnac'h, Finistère), hoard 2 (photograph Muriel Fily).

patterns that mirror our own observations. Particularly with smaller hoards, attribution to either one of these two classes may not always be unambiguous, but they still constitute two very different types of assemblage and thus should not indiscriminately be labelled as scrap metal or hackbronze. If these terms are to be meaningfully employed at all, their use would appear justified only for the assemblages falling within our second class.

Turning finally to the question of how to interpret these two different types of assemblage, based on the selection and treatment of the objects contained in the relevant hoards, there is a compelling case for interpreting most assemblages included in our first class as the material remains of votive offerings. Since the inclusion of objects here seems to be governed primarily by a symbolic significance derived from their practical function as weapons or ornaments, we shall refer to these as symbolic-value assemblages. The question to what extent their role as symbols in these offerings might relate primarily to the party making the offering, to its addressee or to the event that provided the cause for the sacrifice shall not concern us here, but it is important not to confound their symbolic significance in the transaction between a sacrificant and a deity or numen with the symbolic significance some of them may hold in the interaction between members of society. While concepts underpinning the former may be modelled on the practice of the latter, both are still fundamentally different in nature.

For metal objects, their symbolic significance in societal interactions, as argued e.g. by Heymans (this volume), may derive at least partially from their inherent material value, as, inversely, bullion metal carries in it the potential to be transformed into objects with different symbolic meanings. In contrast, where the symbolic potency of a votive offering derives primarily from the practical function or physical form of the relevant object, its material value may be of little concern. To illustrate this notion through an example from more recent religious practice: if an *ex voto* limb offered in hope or in grateful recognition of recovery from a physical ailment consists of wood, wax, terracotta or metal is entirely immaterial as far as its religious purpose is concerned. In the social practice of publicly performed sacrifices, an *ex voto* may of course also serve purposes of social display, and consequently at a material level in such cases things may not be quite so clear-cut, but it is an *ex voto*'s symbolic significance at the level of the religious transaction on which we want to focus here, not social practice.

As an alternative to an interpretation as votive offerings, in those instances where we are dealing with the deposition of personal sets of weapons and/or ornaments, and regardless of any damage to or fragmentation of the objects in question, there is of course also the possibility that such assemblages might have been deposited not as a sacrifice to a deity, but for use in a person's afterlife. The practice of equipping oneself for the hereafter through the deposition of personal effects in liminal locations is well attested in early medieval Scandinavian literature, and to distinguish between such 'funerary' depositions and votive offerings directed at a deity may prove difficult in practice, even taking into account criteria such as the siting and concomitant circumstances of a deposition (cf. Hansen 1994: 43–58). In no case does the simple differentiation between 'wet' and 'dry' depositions on its own suffice for distinguishing between the different religious motives that may underpin metalwork depositions, a caveat that is supported by the identical treatment of multi-piece sword depositions from 'wet' and 'dry' contexts across large parts of Late Bronze Age Europe (Brandherm and Horn 2012: 124; Torbrügge 1970/71: 87–8). Overall, however, clearly identifiable personal sets of items that might qualify as 'funerary' hoards only constitute a relatively small minority among metalwork assemblages comprising fragmented objects. The bulk of this class, then, is still best understood as votive offerings to a deity.

For the assemblages in the second class, i.e. scrap metal or hackbronze assemblages *sensu stricto*, the question of how to interpret them is a more complex one. The presence in these assemblages of objects from a broad range of different functional categories and the high degree of fragmentation observed among them are still best explained in terms of the utilitarian mechanisms underpinning metal supply management and raw material recycling. The fact that objects from this second class of assemblages may also show signs of intentional damage which clearly exceed what one would expect as a consequence of portioning in and by itself does not preclude a mundane motivation for the deposition of such assemblages. As already highlighted above, if the use of excessive violence against objects perceived as animate indeed served the purpose of depriving them of any remaining life force, it might only be expected that such a treatment would have formed part of normal recycling practice, particularly where this life force may have been viewed as potentially dangerous. However, the relatively systematic fragmentation of objects and the small fragment size that can be observed among the assemblages from our second class clearly contradicts the idea that they were subjected to unpremeditated, haphazard violence during fits of ecstatic frenzy (Brandherm 2004: 368). For different reasons, Mörtz (2013: 63) dismissed this notion of haphazard violence also for the assemblages in our first class.

Consequently, some types of damage observed on objects circulating as raw material, and potentially deposited for entirely mundane reasons, may have been caused by a type of violent treatment which from a modern secular perspective we would not readily recognise as utilitarian, but which — from a Bronze Age health-and-safety point of view — may have had a very practical background, even if ultimately rooted in religious beliefs. However, the degree of damage and fragmentation observed in objects subjected to such 'ritual' treatment as part of the recycling process statistically should be readily distinguishable from fragmentation patterns found among assemblages where both the fragmentation process and the eventual deposition were driven by votive or funerary purposes.

On the other hand, even if metal objects displaying a high degree of fragmentation may be interpreted as mundane recycling stock, this does not imply that their deposition necessarily also occurred due to mundane motives. Where hackbronze functioned as a socially accepted means for storing material wealth, or even as premonetary currency, it evidently could also have been used as a medium for votive offerings, as in the case of the bullion metal depositions from Sicilian and Latian Iron Age sanctuaries (Murgan and Kemmers 2016: 279–83). In contrast to those votive offerings whose potency relied primarily on their agency as symbols, here it would have been their material value which informed the potency of the sacrifice. The practice of sacrificing 'abstract' material value for votive purposes is well attested in monetary and also in some developed premonetary economies (cf. Gates 1987: 266–74; Hansen 1996: 264 note 38).[5]

In order better to distinguish between these two different categories of votive offerings (Figure 3), we will formally refer to the first as symbolic-value votive offerings (SVVOs) and to the latter as material-value votive offerings (MVVOs). This distinction does not imply that the composition of MVVO assemblages invariably is entirely random, and that no criteria other than their bullion value may have influenced the selection of metalwork items included in such assemblages. In practice, some overlap might well exist between these categories, and even if we accept a function of hackbonze as premonetary currency, the inclusion of certain categories of object in material-value votive offerings, or exclusion from them, may still be significant. That said, in such cases one might expect any symbolic connotations involved in the selection process to differ from those found with express symbolic-value votive offerings (cf. Brandherm and Moskal-del Hoyo 2014: 40–1).

In contrast to the category of hoards interpreted here as SVVOs, whose deposition invariably would have been driven by religious beliefs, for hackbronze depositions, apart from their potential role as religiously motivated MVVOs, one cannot dismiss out of hand that at least part of them might simply represent accumulated material wealth hidden for very mundane reasons. In order to determine if a specific hackbronze assemblage was deposited as a votive offering or if it was removed from circulation out of more practical considerations, further criteria need to be employed. Both individually and at a regional level, the composition of such assemblages needs to be tested for patterns that cannot be explained as arising from utilitarian portioning or the inherent mechanisms of a metal economy. Location and siting characteristics likewise need to be examined and cross-checked with other types of deposition at a regional level. The fact that only a minute percentage of hackbronze assemblages has been retrieved from 'wet' locations seems to indicate very different priorities in the siting of these depositions compared to those governing the siting of many SVVOs, but this particular criterion on its own does not provide conclusive evidence for assigning either a religious or utilitarian character to this category as a whole.

[5] It could of course be argued that the concept of quantifiable material value, and even more so that of a currency, premonetary or otherwise, very much depends on the use of symbols, but the symbolism involved in this does operate on a very different semiotic level from the one involved in what here we have chosen to label as symbolic-value votive offerings (cf. Ingham 2004: 15–19).

Symbolic-value votive offerings	Material-value votive offerings
– typically comprising one or two object categories	– typically comprising multiple object categories
– low degree of fragmentation	– high degree of fragmentation
– majority of fragments from individual objects present	– majority of fragments from individual objects missing
– damage and fragmentation targeted at rendering objects unusable	– damage and fragmentation targeted at portioning of metal

Figure 3. Criteria for distinguishing between symbolic-value votive offerings (SVVOs) and material-value votive offerings (MVVOs).

Conclusions

Close scrutiny of fragmentation and damage patterns in Bronze Age metalwork deposited as part of hoard assemblages provides clear evidence that the fragmentation of metal objects on the one hand and the deposition of broken-up metal items on the other in many cases may have been occasioned by largely unrelated motives. Two main classes of assemblages containing fragmented metalwork can be distinguished based on fragmentation and selection patterns. The first of these is consistent with religiously motivated decommissioning of objects for votive or funerary purposes. The second class of assemblage is better explained as resulting from utilitarian scrapping, and in some instances seems to indicate the use of hackbronze as a socially accepted means for storing material wealth, potentially functioning as premonetary currency. The ritual infliction of excessive damage to some scrapped metalwork items can possibly be explained as an attempt to convert animate objects into non-animate raw material that was considered safe to recycle.

It is important to note that the two aforementioned classes of assemblage do not strictly correspond to religious and utilitarian categories of deposition. While hoards comprising assemblages from our first class may be interpreted as votive depositions carrying a distinct symbolic significance that is intimately related to the function of the deposited object types, hoard assemblages from our second class may constitute either utilitarian depositions or religiously motivated votive offerings of abstract material value, with no or little symbolic links between the original function of the scrapped items and the purpose or the recipient of the offering. In other words, the mundane or religious rationale driving the fragmentation of an object particularly in our second class of assemblages does not by itself imply a corresponding background for its ultimate deposition.

This realisation also serves to underline the multidimensional nature of the Bronze Age hoarding phenomenon. One of the main arguments for assigning Bronze Age metalwork hoards to the religious sphere wholesale has generally been that a significant proportion of them, as far as the rationale for their deposition was concerned, is of an undisputably religious nature, and that the assumption that both religiously motivated votive deposits and hoards assembled and hidden for mundane purposes should disappear from the archaeological record coevally around the time of the Bronze Age/Iron Age transition was implausible. If, however, the general restructuring of the metal economy which followed this transition means that hackbronze lost its function as a socially accepted medium for the storage and exchange of material value, it is not only plausible, but entirely logical that it should cease to be deposited both as a mundane store of temporarily hidden material value and as material-value-based votive offering. It really is the widespread, although not ubiquitous disappearance of symbolic-value votive deposits during the Early Iron Age which is more challenging to explain.

Finally, the insights gained from distinguishing between different types of fragmentation patterns and from disentangling votive offerings based on symbolic value from those based on material value serve as a reminder that calls to simply abandon the distinction between categories such as 'religious' and 'mundane' are unhelpful and ultimately hinder a better understanding of Bronze Age economics and value systems. It is of course a truism that modern labels carry connotations shaped by the modern world, and it is certainly important to remember that some of these connotations may be potentially misleading when examining prehistoric practices and value systems. However, the labels used by prehistoric societies per definition are irretrievably lost to us, and the categorisations behind these labels are accessible to us only through indirect means, which inevitably require an analysis that has to employ our own analytical categories.

Postscript

Only after this contribution had been submitted, Wiseman (2018) published a highly relevant study in which he examines the composition of Bronze Age scrap hoards in England and Wales on a statistical basis. The results from his work corroborate some of the points also made here: fragmentation in hackbronze assemblages was driven primarily by the utilitarian necessities of metal recycling, and the content of these assemblages constitutes a more or less representative cross-section of bronze objects from the total pool of metal available for recycling, with no real evidence of purposeful selection. However, Wiseman's study also challenges the interpretation of any significant proportion of hackbronze assemblages as material-value votive offerings, as it suggests that the bulk of these would have been deposited with the explicit intention of retrieval. The study's findings do not necessarily have to be considered final, and more detailed statistical work that includes further parameters needs to be undertaken. In any case, it serves as a welcome reality check for some of the more philosophical interpretations of the hoarding phenomenon.

Bibliography

Baitinger, H. forthcoming. The metal objects from the agora of Selinunte (Prov. Trapani, Sicily). In B. Toune and E. Warmenbol (eds), *Pezzi scelti. Distruzione e manipolazione di beni tra età del Bronzo e del Ferro: dal riciclo al sacrificio / Choice pieces. The destruction and manipulation of goods in the Later Bronze Age: from reuse to sacrifice. Atti del Convegno internazionale, Roma, 16–18 febbraio 2012 / Proceedings of the International Conference, Rome, 16–18 February 2012.*

Ballmer, A. 2010. Zur Topologie des bronzezeitlichen Deponierens. Von der Handlungstheorie zur Raumanalyse. *Prähistorische Zeitschrift* 85: 120–31.

Barnett, H. G. 1938. The nature of the potlatch. *American Anthropologist* 40: 349–58.

Boulud, S. and Melin, M. 2009. Étude comparative des modalités de dépôt en milieu terrestre et en milieux humides en région armoricaine á l'âge du Bronze final. In S. Bonnardin, C. Hamon, M. Lauwers and B. Quilliec (eds), *Du matériel au spirituel. Réalités arquéologiques et historiques des 'dépôts' de la préhistoire à nos jours. Actes des XXIXe rencontres internationales d'archéologie et d'histoire d'Antibes, 16–18 octobre 2008*: 183–94. Antibes, APDCA.

Bradley, R. 1982. The destruction of wealth in later prehistory. *Man* 17: 108–22.

Bradley, R. 1988. Hoarding, recycling and the consumption of prehistoric metalwork: technological change in western Europe. *World Archaeology* 20: 249–60.

Bradley, R. 1990. *The passage of arms: archaeological analysis of prehistoric hoards and votive deposits*. Oxford, Oxbow Books.

Bradley, R. 2005. *Ritual and domestic life in prehistoric Europe*. London, Routledge.

Brandherm, D. 2004. Ein neuer Fund eines Langquaidbeils und einer Lanzenspitze aus Speyer. Zum Beginn und zur Deutung der Brucherzdeponierungssitte in Süddeutschland. *Archäologisches Korrespondenzblatt* 34: 357–74.

Brandherm, D. 2016. Zur Deutung der endbronzezeitlichen Waffendeponierung aus der Ría de Huelva – eine Fallstudie zur Mustererkennung und -deutung in multifunktionstypisch zusammengesetzten Mehrstückdeponierungen der europäischen Bronzezeit. In U. L. Dietz and A. Jockenhövel (eds), *50 Jahre „Prähistorische Bronzefunde" — Bilanz und Perspektiven. Beiträge zum internationalen Kolloquium vom 24. bis 26. September 2014 in Mainz*: 61–98. Stuttgart, Steiner (Prähistorische Bronzefunde XX 14).

Brandherm, D. and Horn, C. 2012. Die Zwei in der Drei, oder: Ein Zwilling kommt selten allein. In B. Ramminger and H. Lasch (eds), *Hunde – Menschen – Artefakte. Gedenkschrift für Gretel Gallay*: 99–141. Rahden, Marie Leidorf (Internationale Archäologie, Studia honoraria 32).

Brandherm, D. and Moskal-del Hoyo, M. 2014. Both sides now: the carp's-tongue complex revisited. *Antiquaries Journal* 94: 1–47.

Bray, P. J. and Pollard, A. M. 2012. A new interpretative approach to the chemistry of copper-alloy objects: source, recycling and technology. *Antiquity* 86: 853–67.

Brück, J. 1999. Ritual and rationality: some problems of interpretation in European archaeology. *European Journal of Archaeology* 2: 313–44.

Brück, J. 2001. Body metaphors and technologies of transformation in the English Middle and Late Bronze Age. In J. Brück (eds), *Bronze Age landscapes. Tradition and transformation*: 149–60. Oxford, Oxbow Books.

Brück, J. 2006. Fragmentation, personhood and the social construction of technology in Middle and Late Bronze Age Britain. *Cambridge Archaeological Journal* 16: 297–315.

Chantre, E. 1875/76. *Études paléoethnologiques dans le bassin du Rhône II. Âge du bronze: recherches sur l'origine de la métallurgie en France. Deuxième partie: gisements de l'âge du bronze*. Paris, J. Baudry.

Coles, J. M. 1959/60. Scottish Late Bronze Age metalwork: typology, distributions and chronology. *Proceedings of the Society of Antiquaries of Scotland* 93: 16–134.

Cowen, J. D. 1966. The origins of the flange-hilted sword of bronze in continental Europe. *Proceedings of the Prehistoric Society* 32: 262–312.

Evans, J. 1881. *The ancient bronze implements, weapons and ornaments of Great Britain and Ireland*. London, Longman, Greens & Co.

Falkenstein, F. 2011. Zu Struktur und Deutung älterurnenfelderzeitlicher Hortfunde im nordalpinen Raum. In U. L. Dietz and A. Jockenhövel (eds), *Bronzen im Spannungsfeld zwischen praktischer Nutzung und symbolischer Bedeutung. Beiträge zum internationalen Kolloquium am 9. und 10. Oktober 2008 in Münster*: 71–105. Stuttgart, Franz Steiner (Prähistorische Bronzefunde XX 13).

Fernández Rodríguez, J. M. 2014. Los depósitos de la Ría de Huelva. En busca del barco perdido. *Onoba* 2: 3–26.

Gabillot, M. 2004. La fragmentation des objets: critère d'étude des dépôts de l'âge du Bronze. In C. Constantin and P. Bodu (eds), *Approches fonctionnelles en Préhistoire. Actes du XXVe congrès préhistorique de France, Nanterre, 24-26 novembre 2000*: 193–201. Paris, Société Préhistorique Française.

Gates, H. 1987. Money for the gods. *Modern China* 13: 259–77.

Giardino, C. 1995. *Il Mediterraneo occidentale fra XIV ed VIII secolo a. C. Cercie minerarie e metallurgice*. Oxford, Tempus Reparatum (British Archaeological Reports International Series 612).

Hänsel, B. 1997. Gaben an die Götter – Schätze der Bronzezeit Europas – eine Einführung. In A. Hänsel and B. Hänsel (eds), *Gaben an die Götter – Schätze der Bronzezeit Europas*: 11–22. Berlin, Staatliche Museen und Freie Universität (Bestandskataloge des Museums für Vor- und Frühgeschichte 4).

Hansen, S. 1994. *Studien zu den Metalldeponierungen während der älteren Urnenfelderzeit zwischen Rhônetal und Karpatenbecken.* Bonn, Rudolf Habelt (Universitätsforschungen zur prähistorischen Archäologie 21).

Hansen, S. 1996. Weihegaben zwischen System und Lebenswelt. In H.-J. Gehrke and A. Müller (eds), *Vergangenheit und Lebenswelt. Soziale Kommunikation, Traditionsbildung und historisches Bewußtsein*: 257–76. Tübingen, Narr (ScriptOralia 90).

Hansen, S. 2012. Bronzezeitliche Horte. Zeitliche und räumliche Rekontextualisierungen. In S. Hansen, D. Neumann and T. Vachta (eds), *Hort und Raum. Aktuelle Forschungen zu bronzezeitlichen Deponierungen in Mitteleuropa*: 23–48. Berlin, Topoi.

Hansen, S. 2016. A short history of fragments in hoards in the Bronze Age. In H. Baitinger (ed.), *Materielle Kultur und Identität im Spannungsfeld zwischen mediterraner Welt und Mitteleuropa. Akten der Internationalen Tagung am Römisch-Germanischen Zentralmuseum Mainz, 22.–24. Oktober 2014*: 185–208. Mainz, Verlag des Römisch-Germanischen Zentralmuseums (RGZM-Tagungen 27).

Hundt, H.-J. 1955. Versuch zur Deutung der Depotfunde der nordischen jüngeren Bronzezeit unter besonderer Berücksichtigung Mecklenburgs. *Jahrbuch des Römisch-Germanischen Zentralmuseums* 2: 95–140.

Huth, C. 1997. *Westeuropäische Horte der Spätbronzezeit. Fundbild und Funktion.* Regensburg, Universitätsverlag Regensburg (Regensburger Beiträge zur prähistorischen Archäologie 3).

Ingham, G. 2004. *The nature of money*. Cambridge, Polity.

Jockenhövel, A. 1986. Struktur und Organisation der Metallverarbeitung in urnenfelderzeitlichen Siedlungen Süddeutschlands. In D.-W. Buck and B. Gramsch (eds), *Siedlung, Wirtschaft und Gesellschaft während der jüngeren Bronze- und Hallstattzeit in Mitteleuropa. Internationales Symposium Potsdam, 25. bis 29. April 1983*: 213–34. Berlin, Deutscher Verlag der Wissenschaften (Veröffentlichungen des Museums für Ur- und Frühgeschichte Potsdam 20).

Lo Schiavo, F. 1991. La Sardaigne et ses relations avec le Bronze final atlantique. In C. Chevillot and A. Coffyn (eds), *L'Âge du Bronze atlantique: ses faciès, de l'Écosse à l'Andalousie et leurs relations avec le bronze continental et la Méditerranée. Actes du 1er Colloque du Parc Archéologique de Beynac*: 213–26. Beynac-et-Cazenac, Association des Musées du Sarladais.

Lund, J. 2017. Connectedness with things. Animated objects of Viking Age Scandinavia and early medieval Europe. *Archaeological Dialogues* 24: 89–108.

Mandera, H.-E. 1985. Einige Bemerkungen zur Deutung bronzezeitlicher Horte. *Archäologisches Korrespondenzblatt* 15: 187–93.

Maraszek, R. 2006. *Spätbronzezeitliche Hortfundlandschaften in atlantischer und nordischer Metalltradition.* Halle, Landesmuseum fur Vorgeschichte (Veröffentlichungen des Landesamtes für Denkmalpflege und Archäologie Sachsen-Anhalt 60).

Melo, A. A. 2000. Armas, utensílios e esconderijos. Alguns aspectos da metalurgia do Bronze Final: o depósito do Casal dos Fiéis de Deus. *Revista Portuguesa de Arqueologia* 3(1): 15–120.

Metzner-Nebelsick, C. 2012. Das Opfer. Betrachtungen aus archäologischer Sicht. In A. Lang and P. Marinković (eds), *Bios — Cultus — (Im)mortalitas. Zu Religion und Kultur — Von den biologischen Grundlagen bis zu Jenseitsvorstellungen. Beiträge der interdisziplinären Kolloquien vom 10.-11. März 2006 und 24.-25. Juli 2009 in der Ludwig-Maximilians-Universität München*: 157–79. Rahden, Marie Leidorf (Internationale Archäologie — Arbeitsgemeinschaft, Symposium, Tagung, Kongress 16).

Mörtz, T. 2013. Zerteiltes Leid. Anmerkungen zur Deutung mutwilliger Beschädigungen von Metalldeponierungen der späten Bronzezeit. *Mitteilungen der Berliner Gesellschaft für Anthropologie, Ethnologie und Urgeschichte* 34: 55–66.

Murgan, A. and Kemmers, F. 2016. Temples, hoards and pre(?)monetary practices - Case studies from mainland Italy and Sicily in the 1st millennium B.C. In H. Baitinger (ed.), *Materielle Kultur und Identität im Spannungsfeld zwischen mediterraner Welt und Mitteleuropa. Akten der Internationalen Tagung am Römisch-Germanischen Zentralmuseum Mainz, 22.-24. Oktober 2014*: 277–90. Mainz, Verlag des Römisch-Germanischen Zentralmuseums (RGZM-Tagungen 27).

Nebelsick, L. D. 1997. Auf Biegen und Brechen. Ekstatische Elemente bronzezeitlicher Materialopfer — Ein Deutungsversuch. In A. Hänsel and B. Hänsel (eds), *Gaben an die Götter — Schätze der Bronzezeit Europas*: 35–41. Berlin, Staatliche Museen und Freie Universität (Bestandskataloge des Museums für Vor- und Frühgeschichte 4).

Nebelsick, L. D. 2000. Rent asunder: ritual violence in Late Bronze Age hoards. In C. F. E. Pare (ed.), *Metals make the world go round. The supply and circulation of metals in Bronze Age Europe. Proceedings of a conference held at the University of Birmingham in June 1997*: 160–75. Oxford, Oxbow Books.

Needham, S. 2001. When expediency broaches ritual intention: the flow of metal between systemic and buried domains. *Journal of the Royal Anthropological Institute of Great Britain and Ireland* 7: 275–98.

Pauli, L. 1985. Einige Anmerkungen zum Problem der Hortfunde. *Archäologisches Korrespondenzblatt* 15: 195–206.

Pearce, M. 2013. The spirit of the sword and spear. *Cambridge Archaeological Journal* 23: 55–67.

Randsborg, K. 2002. Wetland hoards. *Oxford Journal of Archaeology* 21: 415–18.

Rittershofer, K.-F. 1983. Der Hortfund von Bühl und seine Beziehungen. *Bericht der Römisch-Germanischen Kommission* 64: 139–415.

Rosman, A. and Rubel, P. G. 1972. The potlatch: a structural analysis. *American Anthropologist* 74: 658–71.

Ruiz-Gálvez Priego, M. 1986. Navegación y comercio entre el Atlántico y el Mediterráneo a fines de la Edad del Bronce. *Trabajos de Prehistoria* 43: 9–42.

Ruiz-Gálvez Priego, M. 1995. Depósitos del Bronce Final: ¿Sagrado o profano? ¿Sagrado y, a la vez, profano? In M. Ruiz-Gálvez Priego (ed.), *Ritos de paso y puntos de paso. La Ría de Huelva en el mundo del Bronce Final europeo*: 21–32. Madrid, Universidad Complutense (Complutum Extra 5).

Scholz, H. 2012. Lageuntersuchungen als Mittel zur Hortbeschreibung und -interpretation. In S. Hansen, D. Neumann and T. Vachta (eds), *Hort und Raum. Aktuelle Forschungen zu bronzezeitlichen Deponierungen in Mitteleuropa*: 69–91. Berlin, Topoi.

Silva, A. C. F., Silva, C. T. and Lopes, A. B. 1984. Depósito de fundidor do final da Idade do Bronze do Castro da Senhora da Guia (Baiões, S. Pedro do Sul, Viseu). In *Lucerna: colectânea de estudos de homenagem a D. Domingos de Pinho Brandão*: 73–109. Porto, Centro de Estudos Humanísticos.

Snyder, S. 1975. Quest for the sacred in northern Puget Sound: an interpretation of potlatch. *Ethnology* 14: 149–61.

Sommerfeld, C. 1994. *Gerätegeld Sichel. Studien zur monetären Struktur bronzezeitlicher Horte im nördlichen Mitteleuropa*. Berlin, Walter de Gruyter (Vorgeschichtliche Forschungen 19).

Soroceanu, T. 1995. Die Fundumstände bronzezeitlicher Deponierungen. Ein Beitrag zur Hortdeutung beiderseits der Karpaten. In T. Soroceanu (ed.), *Bronzefunde aus Rumänien*: 15–80. Berlin, Spiess (Prähistorische Archäologie in Südosteuropa 10).

Soroceanu, T. 2011. Zweigeteilte Einheit oder geeinte Zweiheit? Zur Frage der Dualität in den bronzezeitlichen Deponierungen. In S. Berecki, R. E. Németh and B. Rezi (eds), *Bronze Age rites and rituals in the Carpathian Basin. Proceedings of the International Colloquium from Târgu Mureş, 8-10 October 2010*: 269–94. Târgu Mureş, Mega.

Stein, F. 1976. *Bronzezeitliche Hortfunde in Süddeutschland. Beiträge zur Interpretation einer Quellengattung*. Bonn, Rudolf Habelt (Saarbrücker Beiträge zur Altertumskunde 23).

Taylor, R. J. 1993. *Hoards of the Bronze Age in southern Britain: analysis and interpretation*. Oxford, Tempus Reparatum (British Archaeological Reports British Series 228).

Testart, A. 2012. Les hypothèses. In A. Testart (ed.), *Les armes dans les eaux. Questions d'interprétation en archéologie*: 277–302. Paris, Editions Errance.

Testart, A., Boulestin, B. and Deyber, A. 2012. Arguments et contre-arguments. In A. Testart (ed.), *Les armes dans les eaux. Questions d'interprétation en archéologie*: 303–405. Paris, Editions Errance.

Torbrügge, W. 1970/71. Vor- und frühgeschichtliche Flußfunde. Zur Ordnung und Bestimmung einer Denkmälergruppe. *Bericht der Römisch-Germanischen Kommission* 51/52: 1–146.

Torbrügge, W. 1985. Über Horte und Hortdeutung. *Archäologisches Korrespondenzblatt* 15: 17–23.

Vachta, T. E. F. 2008. *Studien zu den bronzezeitlichen Hortfunden des oberen Theissgebietes*. Bonn, Rudolf Habelt (Universitätsforschungen zur prähistorischen Archäologie 159).

Wiseman, R. 2018. Random accumulation and breaking: the formation of Bronze Age scrap hoards in England and Wales. *Journal of Archaeological Science* 90: 39–49.

Worsaae, J. J. A. 1866. Om nogle Mosefund fra Broncealderen. *Aarbøger for nordisk oldkyndighed og historie* 1866: 313–26.

Worsaae, J. J. A. 1866/71. Sur quelques trouvailles de l'âge de bronze faites dans les tourbières. *Mémoires de la Société Royale des Antiquaries du Nord, New Series 1866–71*: 61–75.

Weight units and the transformation of value: approaching premonetary currency systems in the Nordic Bronze Age

Lene Melheim

Abstract

Various strands of evidence indicate that there was an ongoing process of commodification in the Nordic realm in the second millennium BC. Despite this, no urban centres or ports of trade have yet been identified in Bronze Age Scandinavia, and little is known about means of exchange and practices for the transformation of value. This article discusses sites with evidence of specialised bronze casting and other types of craft production, interpreted by the author as early ports of trade. It is argued that at such regional centres, imported metal was recast to meet local demands, and from there distributed further inland as preforms. This discussion evolves from Malmer's (1992) theory of a standardised metal weight unit, and focusses on the clay refractories used to produce the metal: crucibles and moulds. It is argued that in the process of commodification, metal took centre-stage both as a convertible store of value and at the same time as a nominator for the maintenance of cultural boundaries.

Keywords: Bronze Age, Scandinavia, ports of trade, weight units, clay refractories

Résumé

Unités de poids et transformation de la valeur : approcher les systèmes prémonétaires de l'Âge du Bronze nordique

Plusieurs évidences indiquent un processus croissant de marchandisation dans le domaine nordique du 2ème millénaire BC. Et cela malgré le fait qu'aucun centre urbain ou port de commerce n'ai été encore identifié à ce jour en Scandinavie durant l'Âge du Bronze et qu'il y a peu de données disponibles concernant les échanges et les pratiques de transformation. Le but de cet article est de présenter une série de sites ayant livré des traces de fonte d'alliage cuivreux ainsi que d'autres productions artisanales nous permettant d'y voir les tout premiers ports de commerce. Nous pensons que sur certains centres, le métal importé était refondu pour fournir la demande locale et de là, le métal était redistribué à l'intérieur sous la forme d'ébauche. Cette présentation prolonge la théorie des unités de poids standardisés en métal proposée par Malmer (1992) et en se concentrant sur les productions en argile réfractaire utilisées en métallurgie à l'instar des moules et des creusets. Nous pensons que dans le processus de marchandisation, le métal avait une place centrale comme stock de valeur transformable et jouait également un rôle comme marqueur dans le maintien des frontières culturelles.

Mots clé: Âge du Bronze, Scandinavie, ports de commerce, unités de poids, productions en argile réfractaire

Zusammenfassung

Gewichtseinheiten und Werttransformierung: eine Annäherung an prämonetäre Währungssysteme in der Nordischen Bronzezeit

Verschiedene Indizienketten weisen darauf hin, dass der Nordische Kreis während des 2. Jahrtausends v. Chr. einem kontinuierlichen Prozess der Vermarktlichung unterworfen war. Dennoch konnten bisher keine städtischen Zentren oder Seehandelsplätze im bronzezeitlichen Skandinavien identifiziert werden und es ist nur wenig über die Art der Tauschmedien und die Praxis der Werttransformierung bekannt. Der vorliegende Beitrag behandelt Fundstellen mit Belegen für spezialisierten Bronzeguss und andere Handwerkstätigkeiten, die von der Verfasserin als frühe Seehandelsplätze gedeutet werden. Es wird argumentiert, dass in derartigen regionalen Zentren importiertes Metall zur Befriedigung einer lokalen Nachfrage umgegossen und von dort aus in Form von Halbfabrikaten ins Landesinnere weiterverhandelt wurde. Diese Argumentation fußt auf der von Malmer (1992) vertretenen Theorie einer standardisierten Gewichtseinheit für Metall und konzentriert sich auf die in der Metallverarbeitung verwendete technische Keramik, Gusstiegel und Gießformen. Demnach spielte Metall im Prozess der Vermarktlichung eine zentrale Rolle, sowohl als konvertierbare Thesaurierungsform von Wert wie zugleich auch zur Kennzeichnung kultureller Grenzen.

Schlüsselwörter: Bronzezeit, Skandinavien, Seehandelsplätze, Gewichtseinheiten, technische Keramik

Introduction

Different yet interacting economies existed in Eurasia in the second millennium BC. Whilst the chiefdoms of the Nordic sphere have been classified as ranked systems of exchange (Kristiansen 2012), the Mediterranean world was characterised to a larger extent by urban centres practicing true commerce, including proto-currencies and mass production of goods. Indeed, although gift exchange remained an important political and social phenomenon, it seems that a process of increased commodification was spurred in the Nordic realm around 1600–1500 BC. A steep increase in retrieved metal objects occurred at the transition from Montelius Period Ia to Ib, around 1600 BC (Vandkilde 1996: fig. 279). It seems that from this point in time, objects and raw materials gained through long-distance exchange were increasingly treated as commercial products. Locally-made metal objects by far outnumbered imported objects, and at the same time a distinguished Nordic stylistic repertoire was developed. This, and the fact that metal workshops increase in number and size from c. 1500 BC, suggests that local metal workshops were now the main providers of bronze objects to the Nordic societies. On the other hand, the lead isotopes signatures of recently analysed objects (e.g. Ling *et al.* 2014) indicate that metal was imported from ore sources outside the regional sphere of interaction. This is likely to imply that a transformation of value took place from one system to the other.

Very little is known, however, about how and where this occurred. It is proposed here that in the Nordic region, centralised metal workshops, often maritime sites, served as landing and market places and loci for the transformation of value. This is based on the theory of a local weight standard (perhaps even a proto-currency), which was convertible with other, more widely spread weight standards and monetary systems and enabled transactions to take place. An indicator for the existence of a common weight standard is found in, among other things, the standardized size of the crucibles at Nordic workshop sites. Another significant trait is the occurrence on these sites of unalloyed copper and tin. This indicates that the metal reached the workshops not primarily as already alloyed and finished objects, but in ingot form.

Revamping gifts and commodities

Following the anthropologically-derived distinction between gifts and commodities and the strong emphasis on gift exchange in the archaeologies of the 1980s and 1990s, the traditional concept of trade was nearly abolished from the Scandinavian Bronze Age discourse. Instead, the dominant model became that of hierarchical societies based on allocation of goods and redistribution of resources, nurtured by reciprocal gift-giving between peer polities at the interregional and regional levels (e.g. Kristiansen 1987; Larsson 1986). In the extreme version of this model a bipolar division is implied, where gift exchange is understood as first and foremost a social institution, creating unequal relationships and tying people together in future obligations and loyalties, while the exchange of commodities is understood first and foremost as profit-driven, involving free partners and no further obligations. I here advocate a middle position, seeing trade and gift exchange as coexistent and often interlinked (e.g. Kilger 2008; Oka and Kusimba 2008; Skre 2008). This also implies that gifts and commodities cannot be strictly separated (e.g. Vandkilde 2005). Although social and cultural distinctions may be tied to objects' material properties, such as colour, durability, malleability, availability or distance from the source, the idea that objects have inherent social qualities (e.g. Binford 1962) is a dead end. Current approaches to Bronze Age goods typically interpreted as commodities suggest that objects can shift from alienable to inalienable, from commodity to gift, or vice versa. Often, this occurs when objects move across a cultural boundary. A loss of cultural value seems to have occurred, for example, when Hallstatt B winged axes were imported to Scandinavia (Bradley 1985: 700). When it comes to the Ösenringe, an opposite process is argued for, i.e. that a change from commodity to gift occurred outside their main area of distribution (Vandkilde 2005).

Given that the maintenance of cultural boundaries is considered to rely on a constant flow of goods across them rather than splendid isolation (Barth

1969), these shifts may be interpreted not primarily as ignorance of other value systems, but as a willed transformation. Different currencies can perfectly well be interchangeable, despite being tied to different systems of value. For example, in the Nordic Viking Age, silver was valued as a medium of exchange in three different forms: rings/ingots of standardized weights, fragmented silver and imported coinage. Coins, hack-silver and ingots served the same or very similar functions and were interchangeable, despite belonging to different spheres of exchange and different systems of value (Kilger 2008; 2011; cf. Skre 2011).

Premonetary currencies may, like money, appear in the form of copper alloys or precious metals. Apparently, the universal usage and significance of metal as value denominator relate to its material properties, its very versatility (or liquidity). Metal has the capacity of retaining value when being remelted and transformed. This ensures a potential anonymity and lack of cultural bias in economical transactions. The same material properties may explain the plasticity of metals as exchange objects, making them able to move easily along the gift-commodity-currency axis.

In a Bronze Age Europe characterised by a mix of ritualised gift-giving systems and urban trading systems, metals entered all these spheres and moved between them. Objects interpreted as representing weight standards and proto-currencies developed in central Europe a little before 2000 BC, as exemplified by the Alpine ring and rib ingots, understood as an intermediary between ingot and money (Lenerz-de Wilde 1995; 2002). This evolved towards the expression found c. 1300 BC, when metals seem to be treated as all-purpose money, a notion that is based on the presence of stamped marks and the breakage of objects like sickles and ingots into basic units (Primas 1997).

An interesting parallel to the Early Bronze Age ring-money is represented by the copper ingots of pre-colonial Africa (Herbert 1984). They filled a range of functions from currency and raw material to gifts and grave goods and circulated widely in different spheres: from the market to primarily religious and social/prestige spheres. They were not just used, but intentionally produced for various spheres, for commercial purposes – that is as currency and as a means to store wealth – *and* for ceremonial purposes. Ingot shapes varied from crosses to jewellery and rods. The latter were easily transformed into wire bracelets or necklaces and would, when cut up, retain their potential as currency for smaller purchases. An example from Nigeria shows how inflation was counteracted by chiefs who withdrew large quantities of *manillas* (bracelet-shaped ingots) from circulation for longer periods of time (Herbert 1984: 200–5). In addition to the ingots, copper could serve as currency in many other shapes, as buttons, beads, daggers and axes.

Imported metal and trade routes

In the Eurasian Bronze Age, the quest for sources of raw materials seems to have been a constant concern and a driving force in the dispersal of cultural traits and knowledge (Melheim *et al.* 2016). Despite numerous occurrences of expedient ore sources in Sweden, Norway and Finland, a high degree of importation has been demonstrated. Proponents of Montelius's (1885) theory of importation have claimed that most Bronze Age metal was imported to Scandinavia from ore sources in the eastern Alpine area, Erzgebirge or the Carpathian mountains. With the recent application of lead isotope analysis, a much more complex picture has emerged of Scandinavia's role in wider European socio-economic systems, which forces us to rethink questions related to trade, exchange networks, metal supplies and means of transportation. With the exception of one piece of slag from the Late Bronze Age metal workshop at Hallunda in Sweden, all analyses point toward imported copper. More than 200 lead isotope analyses have so far been conducted on Swedish (Ling *et al.* 2014; Vandkilde 2017), Danish (Melheim *et al.* forthcoming a) and Norwegian bronzes (Melheim *et al.* forthcoming b). While this data set represents a permille of all retrieved metalwork in Scandinavia and is currently too small to draw general conclusions from, the results invigorate a renewed discussion about copper sources and trade. A significant proportion of the analyses show consistency with copper ores in Slovakia, the UK, the Austrian Alps, the Italian Alps, the Iberian Peninsula and Sardinia. While these conclusions may be calibrated in the future, there is a strong indication that metal reached Scandinavia from a wide range of sources all over Europe, and not exclusively from the Alpine or Carpathian copper regions, as was assumed earlier. Indeed, a new focus on the role of northern populations in an Atlantic-Mediterranean trade network is warranted.

The strong predilection for central and eastern European ore sources in traditional interpretations must be understood against the backdrop of stylistic similarities between metalwork from these areas and Scandinavia, which is likely to reflect close contact and strong cultural bonds. We can already conclude that when it comes to the origin of ores and the origin of metalworking styles, in many cases these do not overlap (Earle *et al.* 2015). It is interesting to note that it was what he saw as strong evidence for trade that made Montelius argue for copper importation to Scandinavia, rather than a lack of abilities to produce copper from local ores (Melheim 2015a: 155–8). He considered the Nordic metalworkers to be highly skilled and was (to some extent) aware of the rich indigenous copper ore sources in the middle and northern parts of the region. Instead he stressed the lack of tin occurrences on the Scandinavian peninsula and the demand for Baltic amber in the south as driving forces (Montelius

1878; 1919). The potential link to an Atlantic-Mediterranean network forces us to reconsider received truths about trade routes and adds to the picture of a dominant movement of metals following the major European rivers. Quite possibly, we are speaking about a North Sea Channel-Atlantic seaways connection (Earle *et al.* 2015; Needham 2009).

Early ports of trade in the far north?

The British Isles have the Salcombe wrecks, or rather their cargoes, as clear evidence of contact with the Mediterranean (Needham *et al.* 2013). What about the far north? Let us consider a ship sailing northwards on the Atlantic-Channel-North Sea route, or ships returning from an expedition to, let us say, Spain: where would they have landed to unload and exchange their cargo? It seems very likely, based, among other things, on evidence from overseas imports, that the large Bronze Age metal workshop sites in Scandinavia and around the Baltic Sea functioned as market places and aggregation sites, which gathered people from far and near at certain times of the year (Bradley 1985). This is for instance likely to be the case for sites like Asva on Sareema (Estonia), Hallunda in Mälaren (Sweden) and Hunn in Fredrikstad (Norway). These sites are typically situated at locations easily accessible by boat and show abundant evidence of local craft production.

Here, I will use the example from Hunn, Norway (Figure 1), to illustrate my point. Hunn, with its two workshop areas dated to c. 1300–700 BC and evidence of specialised bronze production, was probably a regional centre for craft production and trade in outer Østfold (Melheim *et al.* 2016). The presence here of unalloyed copper hints at a trade in raw metals, as indicated also by evidence from other Scandinavian workshop sites such as Hallunda (Jaanusson 1981) and the Kristineberg site near Malmö (Högberg 2011). Clay mould assemblages show that metal preforms were among the products that were cast, strongly suggesting that a further transformation of raw materials into locally accepted artefact forms took place (Melheim 2015b).

The interregional Bronze Age trade created new needs to aggregate, quite likely on a seasonal basis, at maritime locations along the coast which could facilitate communication. Hunn lies at the heart of one of the densest rock art areas in southern Norway, in the rock art region of Tanum-Østfold, and is assumed to have functioned as an aggregation site and a landing place for boats. Quite likely, people from a larger catchment area visited the rock art areas in order to maintain, reproduce or initiate socio-ritual structures (Melheim and Ling 2017). The exchange of commodities and gifts may be just one aspect of these gatherings. Hunn has good conditions for embarking inland on rivers

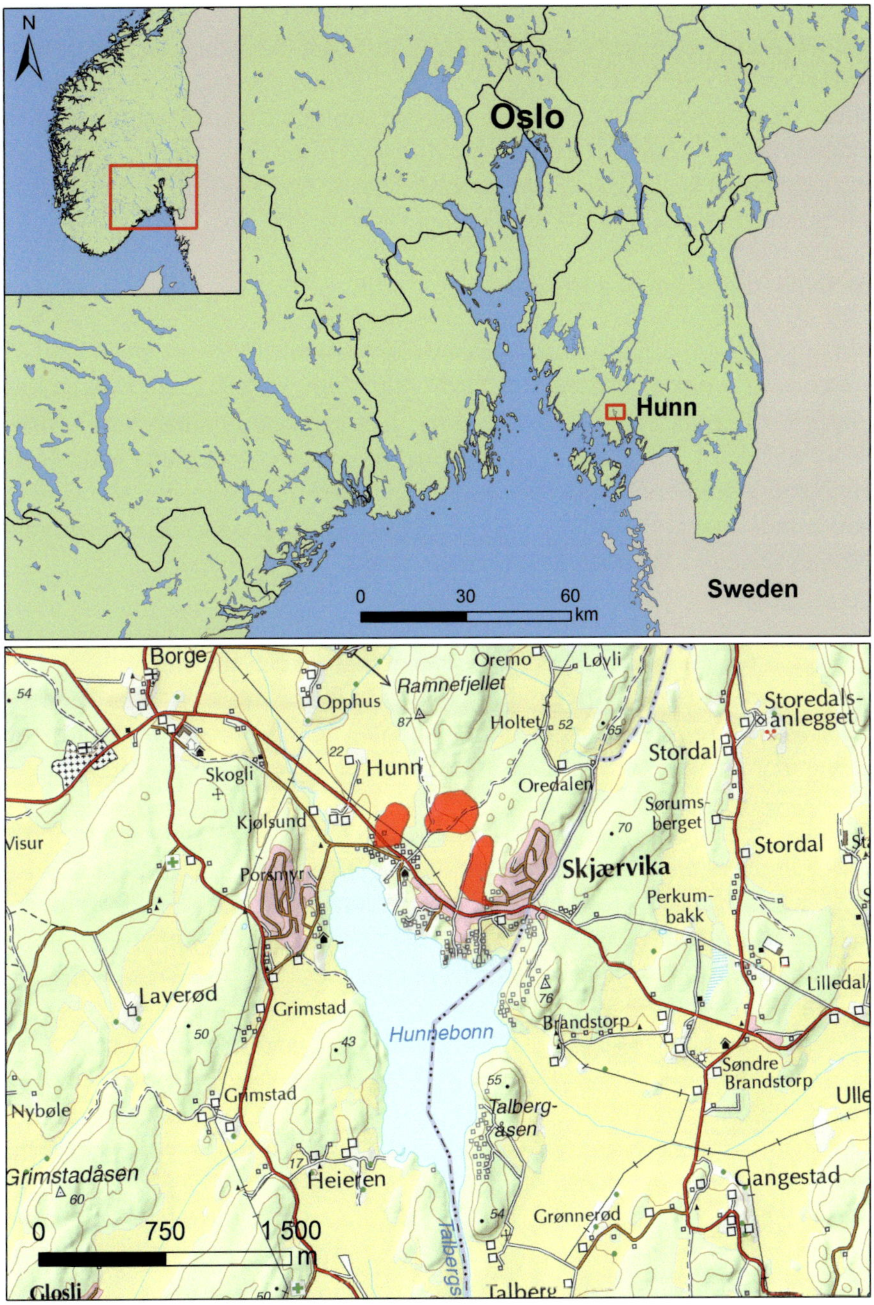

Figure 1. Map of Norway with the area of Hunn indicated.
Ravneberget (Ramnefjellet) is indicated with an arrow.
Map: Steinar Kristensen.
Map data: Kartverket (norgeskart.no).

and prehistoric tracks and is situated by a protected natural harbour. The bay (Hunnebunn) is connected with the sea through a 2km long narrow passage, which could be monitored from the nearby cliff Ravneberget, later to become a hillfort. The significance of Hunn developed through time, beginning with the establishment of sites in the area when the land dried up in the Mesolithic and continuing with farms and burials around 2000 BC and a as locus for specialised craft production around 1300 BC (Melheim *et al.* 2016).

Crucibles indicative of a Nordic weight unit

Malmer (1992) identified a local Nordic weight unit of 107.7g, based on analyses of metalwork (bronze statuettes and gold oath rings) and cross-cultural comparison. Arguably, as maintained by other scholars building on Malmer, this weight unit tied in with a wider monetary system convertible with weight units used elsewhere in Europe, e.g. in the Mediterranean region, where it corresponded roughly with the weight of four *uncia* in the Roman system, again based on the older Egyptian *beqa* (Eriksson 2008: 218–24; Sperber 1993).

Using this standard in interpretations of the material from the Nordic workshop sites, an interesting correspondence occurs. It seems that an indication of the existence of common weight standards is found in the standardized size of Nordic Bronze Age crucibles (Melheim 2015a; 2015b). I will discuss this by looking more closely into the crucible assemblage from the Hunn site.

In total, a little more than 3kg of crucible fragments were retrieved from this site (Melheim *et al.* 2016). Calculation of crucible volume was one means used in order to approach the volume of production at the site. Two more or less intact pear-shaped crucibles were used as a basis for the estimate (Figure 2). With the exception of eleven sherds from crucibles of a somewhat larger type, the bulk of crucible fragments belongs to this category (Melheim 2015a: 100). First, maximum figures were reached using the formula $\Pi r^2 h$, adapted to the oval shape (r replaced by ½ l and ½ b). The result varied from 0.75 to 0.83dl (crucible I = 74.5cm^3, i.e. 74.5ml; crucible II = 82.7cm^3, i.e. 82.7ml). In addition, an experiment was conducted with water filled in a plastic bag (bread bag) that was placed in the reconstructed crucible, to a level below the limit of the red-glazed part, and then measured. These somehow lower figures (crucible I: 0.45–0.5dl; crucible II: 0.55–0.6dl) were considered the more reliable. Thus, 0.5–0.6dl, or 50–60ml, is a realistic estimate of the volume of a Bronze Age crucible of the type found at Hunn. Similar results have been provided by Danish evidence (Jantzen 2008: 197), although here the capacity of three different crucible sizes was calculated (Table 1).

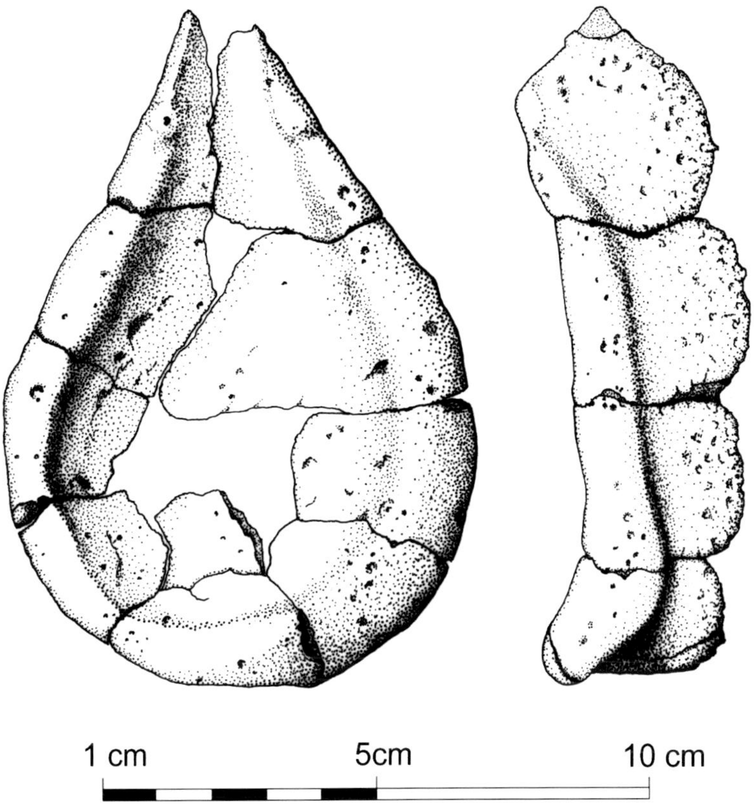

Figure 2. Ordinary-sized crucible (Crucible II) from Hunn (Midtfeltet).
Drawing: Hege Vatnaland.

Calculations suggest that 1ml bronze corresponds to c. 8.8–8.9g/cm^3 (Koch 2000: 23; cf. Engedal 2010: 147). The contents of an ordinary crucible, 50–60ml, would on this basis correspond to a maximum of 534g of bronze.

Against this background it is clear that the Hunn crucibles were easily large enough for the casting of the most typical tool of the period. The weight of a socketed axe, as exemplified by a study from western Norway, ranges from 26 to 376g, yet only rarely exceeding 250g (Eilertsen 2007: 71–7, app. 1: II, XV, tab. 10). When it comes to other artefact categories, swords, as studied in an overview from Bronze Age Denmark, seem to be the heaviest and most demanding artefacts in terms of the amount of bronze, weighing 256–924g (Koch 2000: 23–6, 49–51). In contrast, rings weigh 10–128g, women's belt gear varies between 40 and 450g and only the heaviest hanging bowls approach the upper limit of an ordinary

	ml/cm³	Bronze (g)
Hunn	50–60	409–534
Jantzen I	25–40	225–350
Jantzen II	40–120	350–1070
Jantzen III	>120	>1070

Table 1. Crucible capacity based on ordinary-sized crucibles from Hunn (Midtfeltet) compared with three different crucible sizes in Denmark (after Jantzen 2008 and Melheim 2015a).

crucible's capacity. This means that the ordinary crucibles from Hunn could be used for producing anything from the smallest ring to a hanging bowl, whereas artefacts like large swords, mostly confined to the earliest part of the Nordic Bronze Age, and solid shaft-hole axes would probably require crucibles of the larger type (Engedal 2010: 147; cf. Malmer 1992: 385) and/or several crucibles operated simultaneously.

A conclusion that may be drawn from this is that the capacity of an ordinarily-sized crucible from Hunn compares to the weight unit system proposed by Malmer. In fact, the upper limit for a crucible's estimated capacity, 534g, corresponds to five times a weight unit of 107.07g (=535g). The largest crucibles with an estimated capacity of 1070g (Jantzen 2008: 197) — occurring in lower numbers at Hunn and other Nordic workshop sites — correspond to almost exactly ten times this unit (Table 1).

In consideration of the theory that metal was recast at central metal workshops and redistributed (Weiler 1996), a logical conclusion to be drawn from the above is that metal arrived to Hunn in the form of convertible weight units and/or that weight units were produced here. The frequent presence of clay moulds, made to produce simple rods, at Hunn and other Scandinavian metal workshops confirms that preforms were produced, probably to be distributed further inland through regional networks using the same basic weight unit (Figure 3). The occurrence of ring/rod moulds at Hunn ties in with the theory of production of standardized preforms based on a weight standard and suggests that Hunn was a central workshop from which raw material was redistributed. The half-melted rings/rods from a smith's hoard at Bjørnstad in Halden, c. 25km from Hunn, further underscore this scenario of redistribution from central workshops (Figure 4). They are of a type assumed to be preforms for manually twisted rings (Jantzen 2008: 74). The hoard contained a twisted neck ring of the *Wendelringe* type, which may very well have been made from such ring/rod preforms, too. Focussing on patterns in the weights of rings/rods and broken ('hack') tools and weapons, Weiler (1994; 1996) argued for the existence of lesser weight units that represented localised metal standards adhered to in the redistribution of raw material. In this system, a rod, for example, could correspond to the amount of metal needed to cast a pair of tweezers or two razors (Weiler 1994: 142–5; 1996: 18–19).

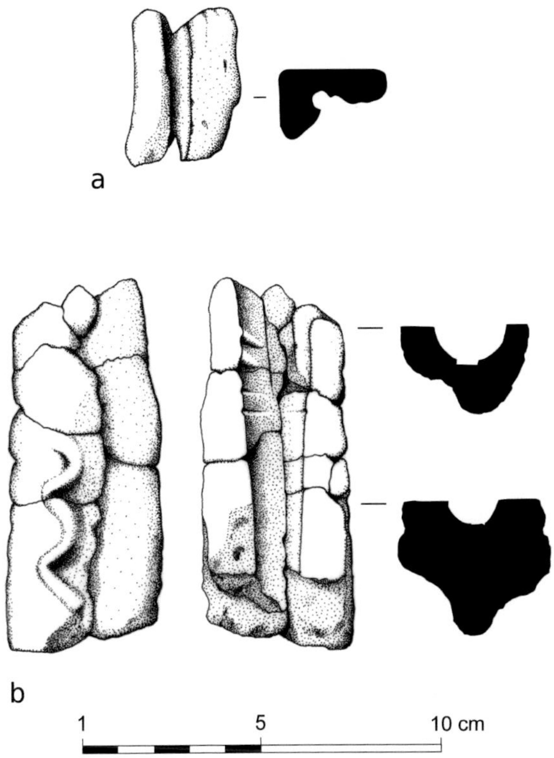

Figure 3. Mould fragments from the metal workshop at Hunn (Midtfeltet): a) for the casting of rods; b) for a spearhead of the West Baltic type. Drawings: Hege Vatnaland (after Melheim 2015a).

The Uluburun example

In order to follow a piece of raw copper from a mine on the Iberian Peninsula, in the UK, Sardinia or Italy to Scandinavia, we must allow for the coexistence of several different systems of exchange working simultaneously (cf. Sherratt 1993). It is this author's view that ritualised gift giving and trade indeed coexisted in Scandinavia in the second millennium BC, as they did in the Mediterranean world. The main difference between these regions and their interlinked economies lies in the organisational levels. Wengrow (2011), looking at the economies of Eurasia, draws a distinction between archival and sacrificial economies; where archival systems practise true commerce and use seals to secure and authenticate mass-produced goods, sacrificial economies are ranked systems of exchange. The latter is exactly what we find in Scandinavia in the Bronze Age. The Nordic model is described as contingent on horizontal and vertical transactions (Kristiansen 2007; 2012). Vertical transactions involve the

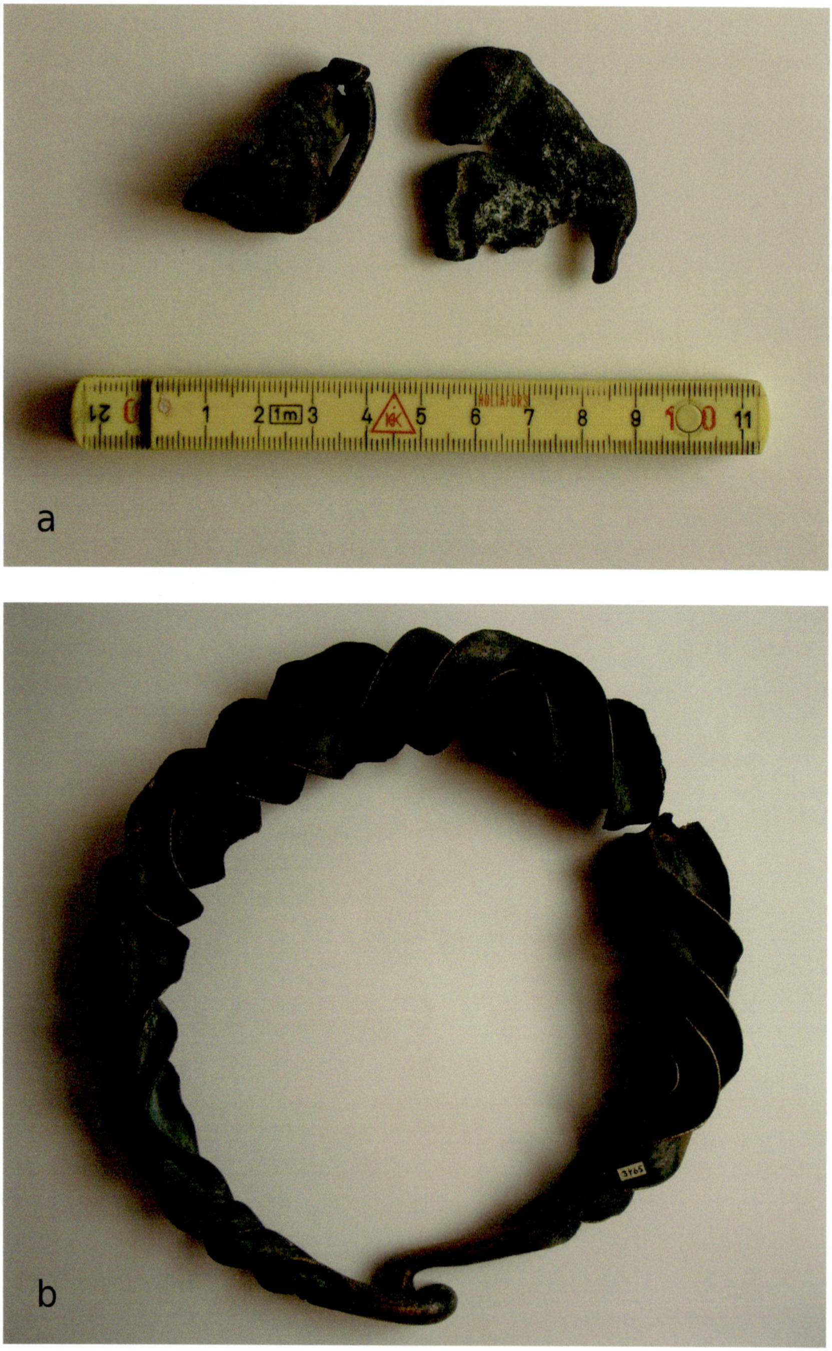

Figure 4. Scrap hoard from Bjørnstad with a) two half-melted rods; b) a neck ring of the *Wendelringe* type (photo: Lene Melheim, not to scale).

removal of things from circulation, for instance through the burial of wealth and ritual depositions. These transactions provide the basis for participation in the horizontal transactions: political alliances and trade.

The amount of metal circulating in the Mediterranean in the later part of the second millennium BC is perhaps best illustrated by the Uluburun and Cape Gelidonya shipwrecks, which sunk around the same time as the metal workshop at Hunn was at its peak. From just one oxhide ingot from the Uluburun shipwreck, typically weighing about 20–25 kilos, one hundred Nordic axes could be produced. While the Uluburun ship's mission was first seen as driven by prestige exchange or tribute between palaces — since the cargo matches lists of dowries and gifts in the Amarna letters (Kristiansen and Larsson 2005; Pulak 1998) — attention was later drawn to the commercial aspects of the cargo (Bachuber 2006; Monroe 2011). The distinction between gifts and commodities is indeed blurry: bulk metals are listed in the gift inventories along with other raw materials, while prestige objects are listed with their weight and thus appear as commodities. To explain this, it is argued that palatial gift exchange was a complex procedure, politically and economically motivated at the same time (Bachuber 2006). In the ongoing process of commodification, which may have represented a threat in some areas, the mariners and merchants were liminal agents — always at the margins of society and free to pursue profit and accept risk (Monroe 2011).

The identification of various sorts of weight units can be used to trace traders and metalworkers operating across the Mediterranean. Such mobility is indicated by the presence on the Iberian peninsula of the Syrian *shekel* of 9.3g, which was widely used in the eastern Mediterranean and is present among the weights of the Uluburun cargo, as well as occurrences of the Microasiatic half-*shekel* of 5.5/5.8g at Frattesina in the Po valley and even as far north as Switzerland (e.g. Horeijs 2009; Ruiz-Gálvez Priego 2008).

Wengrow (2011) argues, in line with Barth (1969), that the upkeep of cultural boundaries in Bronze Age Europe relied on a constant flow of goods across them, and that metal played a central role in the maintenance of boundaries between these systems. However, the character of these transactions changed according to social distance between the participants. Possibly, if the metal trade in the Atlantic and Mediterranean networks was commodity-based, the cultural influence was less strong. This may be exactly why we find evidence of a willed transformation of value at the centralised metal workshop sites in the Nordic sphere.

Conclusion

The fact that the Atlantic-Mediterranean network has sailed up as one of the main deliverers of copper to the Nordic region has seriously challenged the notion of exchange networks solely based on personal ties and alliances, and urged a consideration of other possible scenarios. Weight units have been explored in this article as one proxy for trade and trade routes. Calculations were made not on the basis of the metal objects themselves, but on the basis of the volume of crucibles. The capacity of an ordinary crucible is five times Malmer's Nordic weight unit, and the capacity of the larger crucibles is ten times this unit. When paired with evidence for the production of prefabricated metal rods/rings, it seems that workshops like Hunn in Norway should be considered as locations for the transformation of value, where foreign material forms were recast, so to speak, to meet local demands.

Bibliography

Barth, F. 1969. *Ethnic groups and boundaries.* Boston, Little, Brown & Company.

Binford, L. 1962. Archaeology as anthropology. *American Antiquity* 28(2): 217–25.

Bachuber, C. 2006. Aegean interest in the Uluburun ship. *American Journal of Archaeology* 110: 345–63.

Bradley, R. 1985. Exchange and social distance: the structure of Bronze Age artefact distributions. *Man* 20(4): 692–704.

Earle, T., Ling, J., Uhner, C. O. J., Stos-Gale, Z. and Melheim, L. 2015. The political economy and metal trade in Bronze Age Europe: understanding regional variability in terms of comparative advantages and articulations. *European Journal of Archaeology* 18(4): 633–57.

Eilertsen, K. 2007. *Holkøksene fra Vestlandet. Tid, rom og funksjon.* Unpublished MA thesis, Universitetet i Bergen.

Engedal, Ø. 2010. *The Bronze Age of northwestern Scandinavia.* Unpublished PhD thesis, Universitetet i Bergen.

Eriksson, T. 2008. Guld som glimmar. In E. Hjärthner-Holdar, T. Eriksson and A. Östling (eds), *Mellan himmel och jord. Ryssgärdet, en guldskimrande bronsåldersmiljö i centrala Uppland*: 211–24. Uppsala, Riksantikvarieämbetet.

Herbert, E. 1984. *Red gold of Africa: copper in precolonial history and culture.* Madison, University of Wisconsin Press.

Horejs, B. 2009. Metalworkers at the Çukuriçi Höyük? An Early Bronze Age mould and a 'Near Eastern weight' from western Anatolia. In T. L. Kienlin and B. W. Roberts (eds), *Metals and societies. Studies in honour of Barbara S. Ottaway*: 358–68. Bonn, Rudolf Habelt (Universitätsforschungen zur prähistorischen Archäologie 169).

Högberg, A. (ed.) 2011. *Södra Kristineberg — hantverk i fokus. Arkeologiska slutundersökningar 2001-2006 Oxie socken i Malmö stad, Skåne län.* Kristianstad, Sydsvensk Arkeologi AB.

Jaanusson, H. 1981. *Hallunda: a study of pottery from a Late Bronze Age settlement in central Sweden.* Stockholm, The Museum of National Antiquities.

Jantzen, D. 2008. *Quellen zur Metallverarbeitung im Nordischen Kreis der Bronzezeit.* Stuttgart, Franz Steiner Verlag (Prähistorische Bronzefunde XIX 2).

Kilger, C. 2008. Wholeness and holiness: counting, weighing and valuing silver at Kaupang in the early Viking period. In D. Skre (ed.), *Means of exchange: dealing with silver in the Viking Age*: 253–325. Århus, Aarhus University Press.

Kilger, C. 2011. Hack-silver, weights and coinage: the Anglo-Scandinavian bullion coinages and their use in late Viking-Age society. In J. Graham-Campbell, S. M. Sindbæk and G. Williams (eds), *Silver economies, monetization and society in Scandinavia, AD 800–1100*: 259–81. Århus, Aarhus University Press.

Koch, E. 2000. Bijagt, biavl og biprodukter fra Nordeuropas bronzealder. *Aarbøger for Nordisk Oldkyndighed og Historie* 2000: 7–54.

Kristiansen, K. 1987. From stone to bronze — the evolution of social complexity in northern Europe, 2300–1200 BC. In E. Brumfield and T. Earle (eds), *Specialization, exchange and complex societies*: 30–51. Cambridge, Cambridge University Press.

Kristiansen, K. 2007. The rules of the game: decentralized complexity and power structures. In S. Kohring and S. Wynne-Jones (eds), *Socialising complexity: approaches to power and interaction in archaeological discourse*: 60–75. Oxford, Oxbow Books.

Kristiansen, K. 2012. Bronze Age dialectics: Ritual economies and the consolidation of social divisions. In T. L. Kienlin and A. Zimmermann (eds), *Beyond elites: alternatives to hierarchical systems in modelling social formations*: 1–12. Bonn, Rudolf Habelt (Universitätsforschungen zur prähistorischen Archäologie 215).

Kristiansen, K. and Larsson, T. B. 2005. *The rise of Bronze Age society: travels, transmissions and transformations.* Cambridge, Cambridge University Press.

Larsson, T. B. 1986. *The Bronze Age metalwork in southern Sweden. Aspects of social and spatial organization 1800–500 BC.* Umeå, Universitetet i Umeå (Archaeology and Environment 6).

Lenerz-de Wilde, M. 1995. Prämonetäre Zahlungsmittel in der Kupfer- und Bronzezeit Mitteleuropas. *Fundberichte aus Baden-Württemberg* 20: 229–327.

Lenerz-de Wilde, M. 2002. Bronzezeitliche Zahlungsmittel. *Mitteilungen der Anthropologischen Gesellschaft in Wien* 132: 1–23.

Ling, J., Stos-Gale, Z., Grandin, L., Billström, K., Hjärthner-Holdar, E. and Persson, P.-O. 2014. Moving metals II: provenancing Scandinavian Bronze Age artefacts by lead isotope and elemental analyses. *Journal of Archaeological Science* 41(1): 106–32.

Malmer, M. 1992. Weight systems in the Scandinavian Bronze Age. *Antiquity* 66: 377–88.

Melheim, L. 2015a. *Recycling ideas. Bronze Age metal production in southern Norway.* Oxford, Archaeopress (British Archaeological Reports International Series 2715).

Melheim, L. 2015b. Støpeplasser og handelsplasser – to sider av samme sak? In N. Terkildsen, M. Mikkelsen and S. Bodum (eds), *Bronzestøbning i yngre bronzealders lokale kulturlandskab*: 15–30. Viborg, Holsterbro.

Melheim, L. and Ling, L. 2017. Taking the stranger on board: the two maritime legacies of Bronze Age rock art. In P. Skoglund, J. Ling and U. Bertilsson (eds), *North meets south. Theoretical aspects on the northern and southern rock art traditions in Scandinavia*: 59–86. Oxford, Oxbow Books (Swedish Rock Art Series 6).

Melheim, L., Anfinset, N. and Prescott, C. 2016. Bronze casting and cultural connections: Bronze Age workshops at Hunn, Norway. *Prähistorische Zeitschrift* 91(1): 42–66.

Melheim, L., Grandin, L., Billström, K., Persson, P.-O., Stos-Gale, Z., Ling, J., Kristiansen, K. and Hjärthner-Holdar, E. forthcoming a. Moving metals III: Possible origins for copper in Bronze Age Denmark based on lead isotopes and geochemistry.

Melheim, L., Andersen, T. and Simonsen, S. L. forthcoming b. The first lead isotope data on Norwegian copper-alloys from the Bronze Age.

Monroe, C. 2011. From luxuries to anxieties: a liminal view of the Late Bronze Age world-system. In T. Wilkinson, S. Sherratt and J. Bennet (eds), *Interweaving worlds: systemic interaction in Eurasia, 7th to 1st millennia BC*: 87–99. Oxford, Oxbow Books.

Montelius, O. 1878. *Om lifvet i Sverige under hednatiden.* 2nd edition. Stockholm, P. A. Norstedt & Söner Förlag.

Montelius, O. 1885. *Om tidsbestämning inom bronsåldern med särskildt afseende på Scandinavien.* Stockholm, Kongl. Boktryckeriet.

Montelius, O. 1919. *Vår forntid.* Stockholm, P. A. Norstedt & Söner Förlag (Sveriges historia 1).

Needham, S. 2009. Encompassing the sea: 'maritories' and Bronze Age maritime interactions. In P. Clark (ed.), *Bronze Age connections: cultural contact in prehistoric Europe*: 12–37. Oxford, Oxbow Books.

Needham, S. and Giardino, C. 2008. From Sicily to Salcombe: a Mediterranean Bronze Age object from British coastal waters. *Antiquity* 82: 60–72.

Needham, S., Parham, D. and Frieman, C. 2013. *Claimed by the sea: Salcombe, Langdon Bay, and other marine finds of the Bronze Age.* Bootham, CBA Books.

Oka, R. and Kusimba, C. M. 2008. The archaeology of trading systems, part 1: towards a new trade synthesis. *Journal of Archaeological Research* 16: 339–95.

Primas, M. 1997. Bronze Age economy and ideology: central Europe in focus. *Journal of European Archaeology* 5(1): 115–30.

Pulak, C. 1998. The Uluburun shipwreck: an overview. *International Journal of Nautical Archaeology* 27(3): 188–224.

Ruiz-Gálvez Priego, M. 2008. Writing, counting, self-awareness, experiencing distant worlds: identity processes and free-lance trade in the Bronze Age/ Iron Age transition. In S. Celestino, N. Rafel and X-L. Armada (eds), *Contacto cultural entre el Mediterráneo y el Atlántico (siglos XII–VII ane). La precolonización a debate*: 27–40. Madrid, CSIC.

Sherratt, A. G. 1993. What would a Bronze Age world system look like? Relations between temperate Europe and the Mediterranean in later prehistory. *Journal of European Archaeology* 1(2): 1–57.

Skre, D. 2008. Dealing with silver: economic agency in south-western Scandinavia AD 600–1000. In D. Skre (ed.), *Means of exchange: dealing with silver in the Viking Age*: 345–55. Århus, Aarhus University Press.

Skre, D. 2011. Commodity money, silver and coinage in Viking-Age Scandinavia. In J. Graham-Campbell, S. M. Sindbæk and G. Williams (eds), *Silver economies, monetization and society in Scandinavia, AD 800–1100*: 67–91. Århus, Aarhus University Press.

Sperber, E. 1993. Establishing weight systems in Bronze Age Scandinavia. *Antiquity* 67: 613–19.

Vandkilde, H. 1996. *From stone to bronze: the metalwork of the Late Neolithic and Earliest Bronze Age in Denmark*. Århus, Jutland Archaeological Society (Jutland Archaeological Society Publications 32).

Vandkilde, H. 2005. A biographical perspective on Ösenringe from the Early Bronze Age. In T. Kienlin (ed.), *Die Dinge als Zeichen: Kulturelles Wissen und materielle Kultur. Internationale Fachtagung an der Johann Wolfgang Goethe-Universität, Frankfurt am Main 3.-5. April 2003*: 263–81. Bonn, Rudolf Habelt (Universitätsforschungen zur prähistorischen Archäologie 127).

Vandkilde, H. 2017. *The metal hoard from Pile in Scania, Sweden: place, things, time, metals, and worlds around 2000 BCE*. Århus, Aarhus University Press (The Swedish History Museum Studies 29).

Weiler, E. 1994. *Innovationsmiljöer i bronsålderns sanhälle och idévärld. Kring ny teknologi och begravningsritual i Västergötland*. Umeå, Umeå Universitet (Studia Archaeologica Universitatis Umensis 5).

Weiler, E. 1996. Metal standard during the Bronze Age. *Lund Archaeological Review* 2/1996: 17–30.

Wengrow, D. 2011. 'Archival' and 'sacrificial' economies in Bronze Age Eurasia: an interactionist approach to the hoarding of metals. In T. C. Wilkinson, S. Sherratt and J. Bennet (eds), *Interweaving worlds: systemic interactions in Eurasia, 7th to 1st millennia BC*: 135–44. Oxford, Oxbow Books.

Heads or tails: metal hoards from the Iron Age southern Levant

Elon D. Heymans

Abstract

This paper deals with the monetary nature of the Iron Age silver hoards from the southern Levant. Starting from an approach to money as being always a token and a commodity at the same time, two hoards from Megiddo and Arad are explored as case studies. Based on an extensive discussion with reference to Viking Age silver hoards and literary sources, an interpretation of the silver hoards as both token and commodity is proposed, thereby showing that pre-coinage silver already had the monetary characteristics that are usually only associated with coinage.

Keywords: money, hoards, hacksilber, Levant, Iron Age

Résumé

Pile ou face: dépôts métalliques de l'Âge du Fer dans le Levant du sud

Cet article traite de la nature monétaire des dépôts d'objets fragmentés en argent de l'Âge du Fer au Proche Orient. Partant de l'idée de la monnaie comme symbole et comme marchandise en même temps, nous avons choisi les dépôts de Megiddo et Arad comme cas d'étude. En utilisant les dépôts en argent Viking ainsi que les sources littéraires, une interprétation de ces deux dépôts comme symbole et marchandise est proposée. En conséquence, il est démontré que ces pré-monnaies en argent avaient déjà des caractéristiques monétaires qui sont normalement seulement associées aux monnayages.

Mots-clés: argent, trésors, hacksilber, Levant, Âge du Fer

Zusammenfassung

Kopf oder Zahl: Eisenzeitliche Metallhorte aus der südlichen Levante

Der vorliegende Beitrag thematisiert den monetären Charakter eisenzeitlicher Silberhorte aus der südlichen Levante. Ausgehend von der Prämisse, dass Geld stets gleichermaßen als Zeichen wie als Ware fungiert, werden zwei Horte aus Megiddo und Arad als Fallbeispiele herangezogen. Auf der Grundlage eines Vergleiches mit wikingerzeitlichen Silberhorten und unter Bezugnahme auf schriftliche Quellen wird eine Deutung der beiden Horte sowohl als Zeichen wie auch als Ware verfochten, womit premonetärem Silber dieselben monetären Charakteristika zugesprochen werden, wie man sie üblicherweise erst mit Münzgeld verbindet.

Schlüsselwörter: Geld, Hortfunde, Hacksilber, Levante, Eisenzeit

Introduction

In any strict sense, the concept of premonetary currency is self-contradictory. If by *currency* we mean something that was current (i.e. in general use) as a form of money, and *premonetary* defines something as preceding the phenomenon of money use in any given society, then the latter cannot exist under condition of the former. However, in anthropological and archaeological discourse on money a general notion prevails that differentiates between two types of money: money that is similar to the type of money we use in terms of its social and economic function — modern money; and money that is *not* associated with a developed or commercial economy, and primitive in this sense — primitive money (Einzig 1966 [1949]; Quiggin 1949). Over the course of the past century, different terms reflecting different perspectives have been used to describe this type of money, such as 'special-purpose money' (Bohannan 1959: 492; Dalton 1965; Polanyi 1968a: 166–9; 1968b: 179), or 'social currencies' (Graeber 2011: 129–30). It is this notion of a distinction between the 'modern' and the 'primitive' that seems to underlie the use of the terms *monetary* and *currency* in this context. With currency we awkwardly mean something that seems a bit like money but isn't; and the money implied here and in the term monetary is the money that is part of a developed or commercial economy, going back to the coinage minted by the ancient Greeks.

The introduction of coinage is generally regarded as the manifest start of the history of money (Davies 2002: 23–7; Grierson 1977; Kletter 2003: 149; Kurke 1999: 11–13; Le Rider 2001; Schaps 2004; Seaford 2004: 1–9; Weatherford 1998). Presumably invented in the western Anatolian kingdom of Lydia during the second half of the seventh century BC, and quickly adopted by Greek cities nearby, it spread rapidly, so that by the end of the sixth century independent cities throughout the Greek world had started minting their own coins (Osborne 2009 [1996]: 237ff). Both iconic and recognisable to the present day, it is hardly surprising that coinage and its spread are attributed this historical significance. We should, however, wonder whether a conception of money and monetary history focused on this particular form of money (i.e. coinage) is helpful in understanding either the history of money itself, or ancient society.

It is generally accepted that prior to the introduction of coinage in the eastern Mediterranean, uncoined pieces of precious metal, mostly silver, were performing the functions generally assigned to money (means of exchange, means of payment, store of wealth and standard of value: Polanyi 1968a: 166–9; 1968b: 180–5; Schaps 2004: 12–15). To what extent this 'currency' can actually be regarded as money is the subject of ongoing debate. The current article will attempt to contribute to that debate by looking at silver use prior to the introduction of coinage, and will focus on the characteristics that allowed it to function in the way it did, based on a particular approach to money. In order to do so, two case studies of Iron Age silver hoards from the southern Levant will be presented.

Money as token and commodity

Although it is obvious that coinage is only a particular form of money, the idea that the monetary economy starts with coinage is based on the assumption that only when minted as a coin does precious metal become more than a mere *commodity*, a metal desired for its intrinsic value; it becomes a symbol of value, a *token* issued by the state. This distinction between two fundamental qualities of money has been explored by anthropologist Keith Hart, who describes how the opposition between the concepts of token and commodity has characterised the Western discourse on monetary theory since the mid-nineteenth century. On the one hand, money is primarily understood as a token, issued by the state, and signifying a debt between persons in society. On the other hand, money is perceived as a commodity, something with definite value, endowed by the market (Hart 1986).

However, rather than emphasising one approach over the other, Hart argues that these are two sides of the same coin:

> Look at a coin from your pocket. On one side is 'heads' — the symbol of the political authority which minted the coin; on the other side is 'tails' — the precise specification of the amount the coin is worth as payment in exchange. One side reminds us that states underwrite currencies and that money is originally a relation between persons in society, a token perhaps. The other reveals the coin as a thing, capable of entering into definite relations with other things, as a quantitative ratio independent of the persons engaged in any particular transaction. In this latter respect money is like a commodity and its logic is that of anonymous markets. Heads and tails stand for social organisation from the top down and from the bottom up, epitomised in modern theory by the state and the market respectively (Hart 1986: 638).

It is hardly a coincidence that Hart uses a coin as a metaphor to illustrate money's essential duality; after all, coinage is the historic invention that brings both elements explicitly to expression: originally created as a piece of metal in a standard weight denomination that at the same time carried a seal stamped by the authority (cf. Kim 2001: 20). These seemingly opposing elements, articulating money either as a creation of the market or a creation of the state, are also reflected in the works of Plato and Aristotle. Whereas Plato argues for the use of a 'token money' (*nomisma symbolon*), which should only be acceptable within the community, Aristotle claims that originally a medium of exchange was agreed upon that was useful in itself, such as iron or silver (Pl. *Rep.* 2.371b; *Lg.* 5.742a–b; Arist. *Pol.* 1.1257a 35–8).

Although Hart set out to describe how these opposing approaches have dominated modern monetary theory, this opposition can be regarded as characteristic for Western thinking about money, modern and ancient. His approach can therefore be very useful in understanding early money and the way people have thought about it.

In accepting that money is a token and a commodity at the same time, we can assume that historically, money could only have taken shape by integrating these two elements. But an important question here is whether a token can only be a sign of the state, as it is of course in the context of modern monetary theory. In order to prevent ourselves from identifying money only as the product of state policy,[1] it would be more fitting to understand a token as a representation and agent of social value. Tokens in this sense have often been identified in stateless societies as well, where an important part of social and economic behaviour is understood as revolving around these objects (cf. Douglas 1982 [1967]; Graeber 2011: 125–64). We will stretch Hart's approach in this direction in order to help us understand how silver was valued before the introduction of coinage.

Silver hoards in the southern Levant

As mentioned, prior to the introduction of coinage, uncoined pieces of metal, in particular silver, were used in transactions, valued on the basis of standard weights (Balmuth 2001; Gitin and Golani 2001; Kletter 2003; Kroll 2001; 2008; 2012; Thompson 2003). This material is preserved in the form of silver hoards, around 30 of which, dating roughly to the Iron Age (c. 1200–600 BC), have been excavated in present-day Israel/Palestine since the early twentieth century (Kletter 2003; Thompson 2003). These hoards can contain a variety of objects, such as jewellery, ingots of different sorts, sheet, wire and rods, mostly cut and/or broken. Some hoards also contain non-metal objects, such as stone or paste beads. The general term used for pieces of silver that have been cut or broken is *hacksilber*, and for that reason such silver 'scrap' hoards have often been described as hacksilber hoards.

[1] 'In this view [...] there is money only when [...] tokens of wealth are made into money — when they are named, impersonalised, detached from any relationships with moral, collective or individual persons other than the authority of the state which mints them. [...] The above definition can only cover a secondary type of money — our own' (Mauss 1970 [1925], 93–4).

Initially identified as silver smiths' hoards due to the scrappy nature of the objects and the presence of (broken) jewellery (e.g. M. Aharoni 1980: 40; Herzog 1997: 222; Loud 1948: pl. 229.7–9), in recent decades scholarship has begun to view the hoards as representing economic value based on the weight of the metal (i.e. bullion), leading to the suggestion that it was used as a form of money (Gitin and Golani 2001; Kroll 2001; 2008; 2012; Thompson 2003; contra Kletter 2003). The emphasis on the material's worth, regardless of the objects, reflects an understanding of the silver in the hoards as a commodity.

Christine Thompson argues that the silver hoards indicate a linear development towards coinage. She suggests that the hoards, some of which were wrapped in linen bundles and in a few cases also sealed with stamped bullae, were standardised in weight and the quality of the silver regulated, and thus supposes a direct link with coinage (Balmuth 1976; Gitler 2012: 7–8; Haselgrove and Krmnicek 2012: 239; Thompson 2003). After all, a coin is a piece of metal of a standard weight, stamped with a device. However, whether the bundles were indeed of a set, let alone standard, weight is doubtful, and it is equally unsure whether the few stamped bullae actually represented a known authority, instead of a symbolic association with authority.[2]

What is relevant for our current purpose is that by drawing attention to the stamped bullae as a token of authority, Thompson identifies the token quality as added externally, rather than inherent to the silver. The silver itself is still primarily regarded as a commodity. An alternative understanding of the silver will be suggested based on the following case studies and discussion.

Case study 1: the Megiddo locus 2012 hoard (Rockefeller)

Tel Megiddo is one of the most prominent settlement sites in the region from the late fourth millennium (Early Bronze I) down to the middle of the first millennium BC. Located strategically along the Via Maris on the south-western edge of the Jezreel valley, it is well connected to the coastal plain (Figure 1). The site has been excavated by four expeditions since the early twentieth century, most extensively by the Oriental Institute of the University of Chicago in the 1920s and 1930s.

The hoard currently under discussion was excavated by the Oriental Institute expedition on the northern edge of the site near the area of the palace (area

2 N.b. only in two hoards were such bullae discovered. A bulla stamped with a Middle Bronze Age device with interlocking spirals was found in a hoard from Tel Dor (Stern 2001: 22–4), and three Iron Age types (one geometric, two figurative) were found in a hoard from Tel Keisan (Keel 1980: 282).

AA, locus 2012). It was found buried under the floor in stratum VI A,[3] which dates to the latter part of the Iron I period. The destruction of this stratum has been dated on the basis of an extensive study of radiocarbon samples to the middle of the tenth century cal BC (Toffolo *et al.* 2014). The hoard itself consisted of three lumps of corroded silver pieces wrapped in linen (field numbers a133 A–C). After the corrosion was cleaned off, the hoard was divided: the contents of two of the bundles were sent to the Oriental Institute (a133 A, C; Loud 1948: pl. 229.7, 9), while the contents of the remaining bundle remained under the administration of the Department of Antiquities, the current Israel Antiquities Authority (a133 B; Loud 1948: pl. 229.8). This material is currently on display at the Rockefeller Museum in east Jerusalem. Since the hoard was only published as a plate without further information (cf. Harrison 2004: 78), I have undertaken a study of the material; a preliminary study of the Rockefeller bundle is presented here.[4]

The Rockefeller material consists of 149 objects with a total weight of 87.99 grams.[5] Four of these objects are complete, such as a bracelet and an electrum lunate earring, nine objects are almost complete, and the rest consists of smaller fragments of objects that have been cut or broken up (Figure 2). This high extent of fragmentation of the objects is also observed in a graph that plots each individual object, arranged by weight (Figure 3). Here we see a gradual increase in weight, with c. 85% of the objects weighing under one gram, above which the weight differentiation increases up to three grams. The bracelet (6.78 grams) forms a heavy exception. The gradual increase in weight and high percentage under one gram suggest a dynamic use of the silver, whereby the silver in the hoards was fragmented and used in exchange over a longer period of time, rather than being the result of a single transaction, or having been prepared for a single purpose.

Additionally, a histogram of all objects under one gram shows no distinct clustering of objects (Figure 4), which would have been expected had the objects been 'prepared' in order to belong to standard weight classes (cf. Bivar 1971: 105–7; Thompson 2003: 71–3), as in the case of (early) coin hoards (e.g. Kim and

[3] This information was recorded in the unpublished excavation diary of Gordon Loud, preserved in the archive of the Oriental Institute. See also note 4.

[4] This material is currently kept under IAA no. 1936–1888. I thank Alegre Savariego and Fawzi Ibrahim of the IAA and Rockefeller Museum for allowing me to study the material. Additionally, I thank Dr Jack Green and Helen McDonald of the Oriental Institute Museum for allowing access to the material in Chicago, the study of which was made possible by the Collections Research Grant from the Oriental Institute. I hope to publish a detailed report on the hoard as a whole at a later opportunity.

[5] A bronze arrowhead, visible on the publication photo (Loud 1948: pl. 229.8), is currently missing: neither the staff at the Rockefeller nor at the OI were able to locate it.

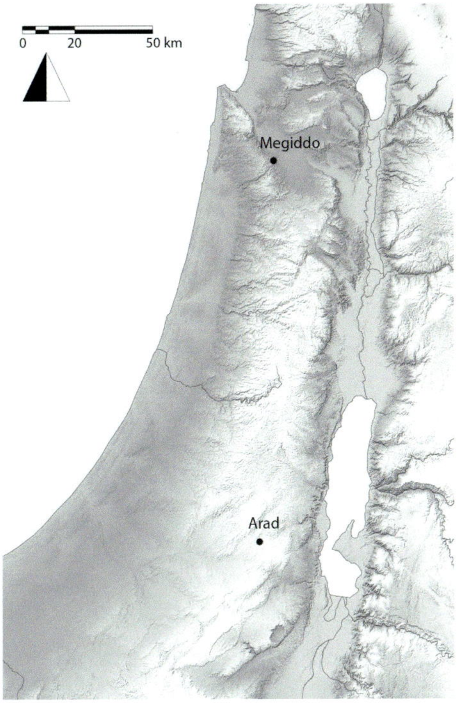

Figure 1. Map of main sites mentioned in the text.

Figure 2. Objects from the Megiddo hoard (courtesy of the Israel Antiquities Authority).

Kroll 2008: fig. 1). It rather appears that the objects were cut up or broken at random, whereby the combination of different objects in the scale pan would enable one to balance the counterweight. It can be noted, however, that the largest part of the objects fall in the range of the smallest denominations of later known weight standards, suggesting that they might have been used in similar size transactions (Kim 2001).

Since most objects are indeed fragmentary already, the breakdown into typological categories was based as much as possible on what type of artefact the object in question had once belonged to. This was done in order to obtain a better insight into what type of objects entered the hoards, and the sphere of use and exchange of which these were a part. That means that a fragment of a lunate earring is counted under jewellery. Rod fragments, a substantial category in the Rockefeller bundle, were cut off from larger strands of bent rod, but it is unclear whether these were (part of) bracelets, or larger coils used as raw silver. This material ambiguity is, however, not out of line with the argument made further below.

When looking at the typological composition of the bundle (Figure 5), we see that around half the objects either are or were objects with a use or display function: 15% are categorised as jewellery, most of which are earrings, and 32% as sheet, a large part of which is decorated. Alternatively, over 30% of the objects (13% course ingots, 13% rods and 6% tokens) can be understood as primarily representing silver as a material, either for exchange or as raw material for the production of other artefacts.

Case study 2: the Arad hoard

The site of Tel Arad is located in the Judean desert, on the north-eastern end of the Beersheba valley (Figure 1). A fortress dating to the Iron Age served as border protection for the kingdom of Juda and safeguarded the caravan-trade routes from the south to the north and the coastal plain in the west. Evidence for these connections has been noted in the ceramic assemblage (Singer-Avitz 2002: 160). The Iron Age fortress was excavated in five seasons between 1962 and 1967 by an expedition of the Hebrew University in Jerusalem, mainly under Yohanan Aharoni. Extensive interim reports have been published after careful restudy at Tel Aviv University (Herzog 2002; Singer-Avitz 2002) and a final report is planned. A renewed study of the hoard, of which preliminary results are presented here, was undertaken in that framework.[6]

[6] I am grateful to Prof. Ze'ev Herzog and Dr Assaf Nativ of Tel Aviv University for inviting me to study the material and for their assistance.

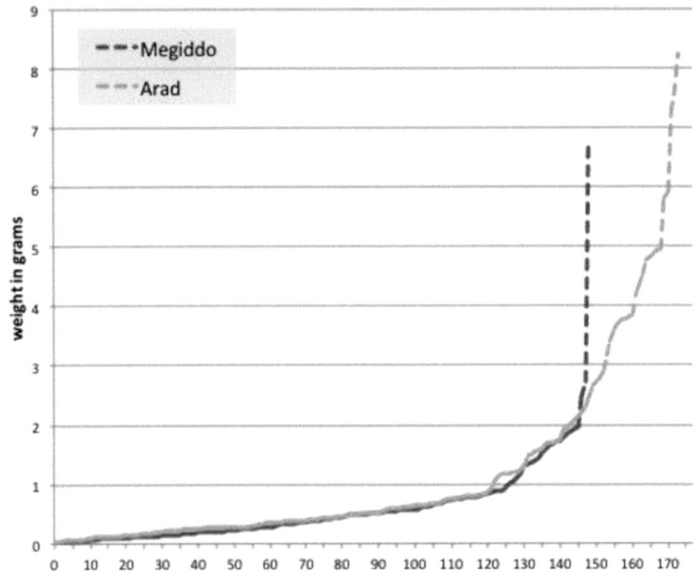

Figure 3. Weight distribution graph, Megiddo and Arad (the four heaviest objects of the Arad hoard, of 10, 12, 20 and 38 grams, have been excluded for clarity).

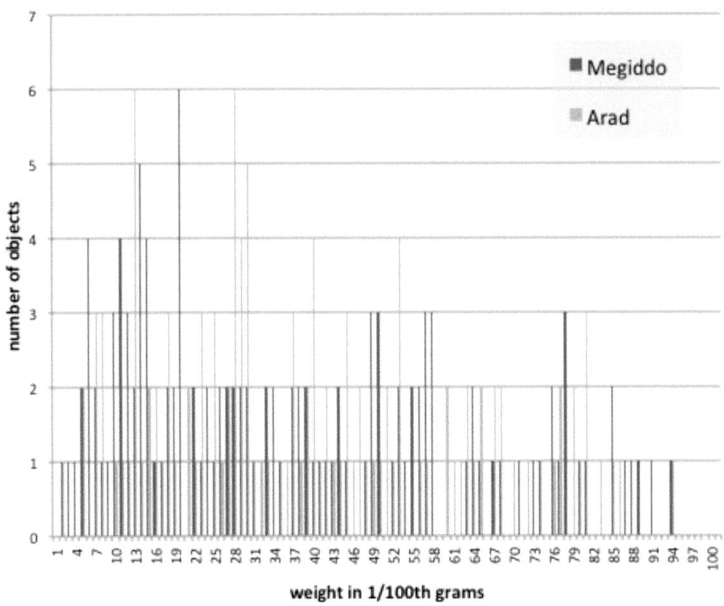

Figure 4. Histogram of weights under 1 gram, Megiddo and Arad.

Found in the south-western quarter of the fortress (locus 979), and initially assigned to stratum XI (Y. Aharoni 1968; M. Aharoni 1980), later study revealed that the hoard was found in a depression under the floor of stratum X. This interpretation is warranted by the level of the find in relation to the floor and the fact that the cooking pot in which the hoard was found is of a type exclusive to the stratum X assemblage (Herzog 2002: 33; Singer-Avitz 2002: 141, 161). Arad stratum X represents the first phase of the Iron II B period and is dated to the mid-eighth century BC. The hoard consisted of two corroded lumps of silver pieces wrapped in linen that were placed in a cooking pot. A dome-shaped stone weight of 11.3736 grams (approximately one Judahite *shekel*; not listed in Kletter 1998) was found in relative proximity to the hoard (apparently not inside the pot), suggesting that the silver was used in exchange (Herzog 2002: 33, 80; Singer-Avitz 2002: 161; contra M. Aharoni 1980: 40; Herzog 1997: 222).

After previous study of the hoard in the 1970s, for which both lumps were broken up and a small portion of the objects was cleaned, all material was put together without recording to which bundle the individual object had belonged. It is thus no longer possible to differentiate between the bundles. In the framework of the current study, 117 objects were selected for conservation, in addition to the 61 objects (of a total of 51.13 grams) that had been cleaned at an earlier stage, leaving aside a smaller portion of 28 untreated fragments (44.56 grams) for future research. After treatment a total weight of 328.09 grams (206 objects) was recorded.[7]

Leaving aside the untreated portion, the current study focuses on 178 objects, weighing a total of 283.53 grams. Of these, three objects were complete and four almost complete, mostly earrings and tokens. The remainder was broken or cut (Figure 6). This high extent of fragmentation is comparable to that of the Megiddo material, as is reflected by the weight distribution graph (Figure 3). The shape of the graph is roughly similar, demonstrating a gradual increase in weight, with 69% of the objects under one gram. After the one gram mark the weight increases exponentially, with four objects weighing over ten grams and the heaviest reaching a weight of 37.53 grams. The histogram also shows a pattern roughly similar to that of the Megiddo material (Figure 4). We can conclude that the weight distribution and fragmentation suggest a dynamic use of the silver, suited for carrying out small-scale transactions of high precision.

[7] At the outset of the current study, prior to the treatment of the additional 117 objects, a total weight of 363.75 grams was recorded. The difference is accounted for by the corrosion products. N.b.: all preliminary publications so far record a total weight of c. 200 grams (M. Aharoni 1980; Y. Aharoni 1968; Herzog 1997: 222–3; 2002: 33; Kletter 2003; Thompson 2003: 97). The basis for this number is unclear, but apparently only part of the hoard (perhaps one of the bundles?) was weighed initially, and the incorrect weight was copied without further scrutiny.

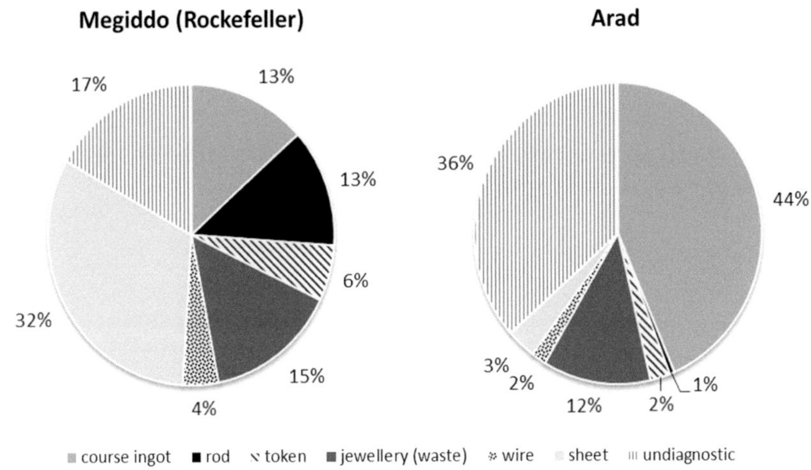

Figure 5. Typology of hoard material, Megiddo and Arad.

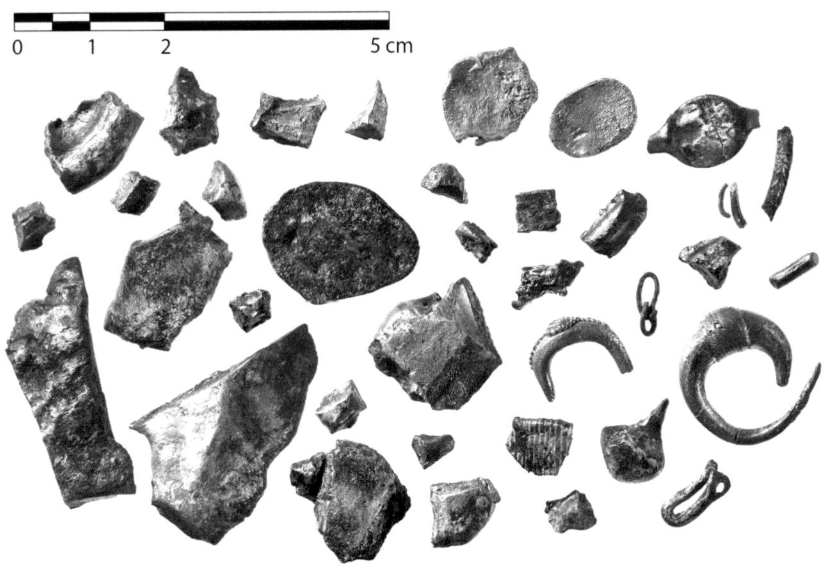

Figure 6. Objects from the Arad hoard (Photo: author).

The typological composition is less diverse than that of the Megiddo hoard (Figure 5). Although the percentage of jewellery (12%) is comparable to that of the Megiddo hoard, the relative amount of sheet and rod is very low. The largest category concerns course ingots (44%), and the large quantity of undiagnostic scrap (36%) is also notable. Despite the difference to the Megiddo material, the amount of objects associated with display and finished objects (jewellery 12%; wire 2%; sheet 3%) is still substantial.

Interpreting silver hoards

These two case studies present us with evidence for the dynamic use of silver, whereby the assemblage of silver pieces within a hoard is shaped as a result of exchange and manipulation (fragmentation) over time and its suitability for carrying out relatively simple transactions, for which only a set of scales and counterweights would be needed. The remaining question is how we can interpret the presence of different types of objects in these hoards. When trying to deal with typological diversity in such hacksilber hoards, it could be instructive to turn to the scholarship on Viking Age silver hoards (c. AD 800–1050) for ideas. The large amount and diversity of silver hoards have produced a growing body of scholarship in recent decades, where different approaches have been employed to gain a better insight into the hoards and the social economy of which they were a part (Graham-Campbell and Williams 2007; Graham-Campbell *et al.* 2011; Hårdh 1996; Skre 2008). These hoards variously contain ornamental objects, weapons, ingots, hacksilber and coins (Figure 7).

Generally, scholarship on these Viking hoards distinguishes between a status or prestige economy and a monetary economy. The prestige economy was characterised by the circulation of whole objects, mostly jewellery, weapons and other prestige items, used in display or exchanged as gifts, while the monetary economy was characterised by silver coinage, used to facilitate commodity trade. A bullion economy, based on the use of ingots and hacksilber, is thought to have formed a transitional stage in the development towards a full monetary economy. At that stage, the social significance and prestige value of the objects as such was disappearing, causing people to cut and break them up, whereby the silver was valued for its weight (Gaimster 2007; Graham-Campbell 2007: 215; Graham-Campbell and Williams 2007; Hårdh 1996; Williams 2007: 178–80, 205–7; cf. Kilger 2008: 259; Metcalf 2007: 1; Sheehan 2007: 160; Sindbæk 2011).

The underlying idea here is that prestige objects were valued not primarily for their material in weight (indicated by the fact that they were not cut up), but for the status associated with them and their role in social discourse. In an important sense, they were valued for their token quality. Alternatively,

Figure 7. Example of a Viking Age silver hoard: Westerklief I from Wieringen, the Netherlands (courtesy of the Rijksmuseum van Oudheden, Leiden).

when being cut up these objects would no longer be able to perform their social function as token; reduced to material, the silver would be primarily valued as a commodity.

However, the way in which different perceptions of the silver's value are emphasised as representing discrete economies, possibly separated in time (cf. Williams 2007: 181–5), seems problematic. Not only does it reflect an evolutionary understanding of economic history, whereby the modern economic practice naturally develops out of the primitive social one; it also considers these economies as belonging to different social realities, one where silver has a strict social significance, and another where silver is a cold disinterested tool of economic exchange (cf. Appadurai 1986). It would perhaps be more appropriate to consider the qualities of token and commodity in such hoards not as static categories, but rather as dynamically integrated.

This can be illustrated on the basis of literary evidence offering an insight into the use of silver in both the Viking Age and the Ancient Near East. Most interesting is a passage from the *Heimskringla*, composed around AD 1230 by the Icelandic poet Snorri Sturluson. It describes the reward paid to the tenth century Norwegian *skald*, or bard, Eyvindr Skaldaspillir:

> Eyvind composed a poem about the people of Iceland, for which they rewarded him by each bonde giving him three silver pennies, of full weight and white in the fracture. And when the silver was brought together at the General Thing,[8] the people resolved to have it purified, and made into a shoulder-pin, and after the workmanship of the silver was paid, the shoulder-pin weighed some fifty marks. This they sent to Eyvind; but Eyvind had the shoulder-pin broken into pieces, and with the silver he bought a farmstead for himself.[9]

Although hacksilber presumably disappeared from circulation in the course of the eleventh century AD, the passage is generally interpreted as reflecting the transition between a prestige economy and a bullion and monetary economy. However, the fact that ornamental objects, appropriate for use as payment, could at will be converted back into bullion could also be understood as reflecting the fluidity between object and material, inherent to the use of silver during the period.

This perception of silver as being used and valued for the quality of being a potential object and material at the same time can be identified in Ancient

[8] This is the Icelandic general assembly, also translated as the *Althing*.
[9] Quoted and discussed by Graham-Campbell 1982: 32–3; 2007: 216; Williams 2007: 182–3.

Near Eastern sources as well. A letter from Karum Kanesh, the Old Assyrian trade colony at Kültepe in central Anatolia (c. eighteenth century BC), records the desperation of an Assyrian woman, Taram Kubi, in financial trouble. She complains to her husband, the merchant Innaya: 'You wrote to me as follows: "Keep the bracelets and the rings that you have, they will be needed to buy you food." It is true that you sent me half a pound of gold through Ili-bani but where are the bracelets that you have left behind? When you left, you didn't leave me one shekel of silver. You cleaned out the house and took everything with you' (Michel 2001: 466; Van de Mieroop 2004: 92). It is significant here that, apparently, references to silver money in weight denomination (*shekel*) and in standard object form (bracelet, ring) are used interchangeably.

Evidence for the use of precious metal objects such as vessels or rings can also be found in biblical sources (Num 7:13–86; Ezra 1:6–11; Job 28:17), and the payment of royal tribute could also take the form of precious metal in weight and objects alike, as we know for example from the tribute paid to the Neo-Assyrian king Shalmaneser III by the Israelite king Jehu. Inscribed on the Black Obelisk around 825 BC, it notes: 'the tribute of Jehu, of the house of Omri: silver, gold, a golden bowl, a golden goblet, golden cups, golden buckets, tin, a staff of the king's hand, (and) javelins' (after Lawson Younger 2000, 270).

Additionally, silver used for exchange and payment was sometimes also converted into finished objects, as an interesting biblical passage reveals. 2 Kings 12 dictates that the silver (*kẹsẹp̄*, the biblical term for silver, as well as money) collected as tax in the temple (Oppenheim 1947) and kept in the cash-box, is designated to pay for maintenance and 'was not used for making[10] silver basins, wick trimmers, sprinkling bowls, trumpets or any other articles of gold or silver for the temple' (2 Kings 12:14). Apparently, it was not uncommon to transform silver acquired through exchange or payment into prestige objects or, in this case, religious paraphernalia. And as is noted in many instances, if needed, the temple would be emptied of these objects as tribute payment or loot (e.g. 1 Kings 14:26, 15:18; 2 Kings 12:19, 14:14, 16:8, 24:13, 25:13–17).

Rather than testifying to the existence of discrete economic spheres between which silver could move, these sources could be understood as pointing to an appreciation of silver as being both object and material at the same time. As they suggest, these objects were often regarded as conventionally desired artefacts, tokens, valued at the same time for their material worth as commodity, while the material was similarly valued because of its potential to constitute objects

[10] Despite the literal meaning of *yēʿāśẹ̄*, translations and commentaries often incorrectly translate the passage as saying that silver/money is not meant to 'buy' or 'acquire' these objects.

that accorded prestige to its owner (cf. Graeber 1996). Exchanges were neither strictly status-driven or monetary in character, but integrated both elements. In that sense, by representing object and material at the same time, the qualities of token and commodity were tied up in the silver.

Conclusion

When relating this discussion back to the case studies presented on the Iron Age silver hoards from Tel Megiddo and Tel Arad, our understanding of the significance of the silver and its use improves. It was already established that the silver in the hoards was part of a dynamic practice whereby objects were cut up and broken at will in order to facilitate their use in exchange by weight. The presence of different types of objects, ornamental objects as well as small ingots, both fragmentary and complete (albeit in small quantities), is however not explained by the singular interpretation of the silver as bullion, valued only for the weight of the material.

The presence of these different types of objects, complete finished items and fragments, rather suggests that the silver in the hoards was appreciated because of its dynamic quality to move back and forth between form and matter, between object and material. It is this perceived quality of the silver that leads us to resist an interpretation emphasising either one over the other, proposing instead an understanding of the silver as inherently transitive.

This implies that an interpretation of the silver as a commodity valued for its weight is equally one-sided. Being inherently transitive, the material was valued for its token quality as well. The presence of finished objects, conventional tokens of status, and desired for that reason, shows that this token quality constituted an inseparable part of the perceived value of the hoard material and its acceptability as a means of exchange.

The silver in the hoards should thus be regarded as token and commodity at the same time. Although perhaps epitomised by it, this duality was not an innovation of coinage. Neither was the token element added only to the supposed commodity silver by means of a stamped sealing on the bundle. This fundamental quality of money, to be both token and commodity, to be constituted by both the market and by public trust by virtue of social convention or tender, was part of the silver itself in the hoards. They were, in fact, two sides of the same metaphorical coin.

Bibliography

Aharoni, M. 1980. A silver hoard from Arad (Hebrew). *Qadmoniot* 13 (49–50): 39–40.

Aharoni, Y. 1968. Tel Arad. *Revue Biblique* 75: 389–92.

Appadurai, A. 1986. Introduction: commodities and the politics of value. In A. Appadurai (ed.), *The social life of things: commodities in cultural perspective*: 3–63. Cambridge, Cambridge University Press.

Balmuth, M. S. 1976. 'Jewellers'' hoards and the development of early coinage. In H. A. Cahn and G. Le Rider (eds), *Proceedings of the 8th International Congress of Numismatics, New York and Washington, September 1973*: 27–30. Paris, Association Internationale des Numismates Professionnels.

Balmuth, M. S. (ed.). 2001. *Hacksilber to coinage: new insights into the monetary history of the Near East and Greece*. New York, N.Y., The American Numismatic Society (Numismatic Studies 24).

Bivar, A. D. H. 1971. A hoard of ingot-currency of the Median Period from Nūsh-i Jān, near Malayir. *Iran* 9: 97–111.

Bohannan, P. 1959. The impact of money on an African subsistence economy. *The Journal of Economic History* 19(4): 491–503.

Dalton, G. 1965. Primitive money. *American Anthropologist* 67(1): 44–65.

Davies, G. 2002. *A history of money: from ancient times to the present day*. 3rd rev. edition. Cardiff, University of Wales Press.

Douglas, M. 1982 [1967]. Primitive rationing. In M. Douglas (ed.), *In the active voice*: 57–81. London, Routledge & Kegan Paul.

Einzig, P. 1966 [1949]. *Primitive money in its ethnological, historical and economic aspects*. 2nd rev. edition. Oxford, Pergamon.

Gaimster, M. 2007. Viking economies: evidence from the silver hoards. In J. Graham-Campbell and G. Williams (eds), *Silver economy in the Viking Age*: 123–33. Walnut Creek, CA, Left Coast Press.

Gitin, S. and Golani, A. 2001. The Tel Miqne-Ekron silver hoards: the Assyrian and Phoenician connections. In M. S. Balmuth (ed.), *Hacksilber to coinage: new insights into the monetary history of the Near East and Greece*: 27–48. New York, N.Y., The American Numismatic Society (Numismatic Studies 24).

Gitler, H. 2012. Introduction. In K. Konuk, C. C. Lorber and H. Gitler (eds), *White gold: revealing the world's earliest coins*: 7–10. Jerusalem, The Israel Museum.

Graeber, D. 1996. Beads and money: notes toward a theory of wealth and power. *American Ethnologist* 23(1): 4–24.

Graeber, D. 2011. *Debt: the first 5,000 years*. Brooklyn, N.Y., Melville House.

Graham-Campbell, J. 1982. Viking silver hoards: an introduction. In R.T. Farrell (ed.), *The Vikings*: 32–41. London, Phillimore & Co.

Graham-Campbell, J., Sindbæk, S. M. and Williams, G. (eds). 2011. *Silver economies, monetisation and society in Scandinavia, AD 800–1100*. Aarhus, Aarhus Universitetsforlag.

Graham-Campbell, J. 2007. Reflections on 'Silver economy in the Viking Age'. In J. Graham-Campbell and G. Williams (eds), *Silver economy in the Viking Age*: 215–23. Walnut Creek, CA, Left Coast Press.

Graham-Campbell, J. and Williams, G. (eds). 2007. *Silver economy in the Viking Age*. Walnut Creek, CA, Left Coast Press.

Grierson, P. 1977. *The origins of money*. London, Athlone Press.

Hårdh, B. 1996. *Silver in the Viking Age: a regional-economic survey*. Stockholm, Almquist & Wiksell.

Harrison, T. P. 2004. *Megiddo 3. Final report on the Stratum VI excavations*. Chicago, Ill., University of Chicago Press (Oriental Institute Publications 62).

Hart, K. 1986. Heads or tails? Two sides of the coin. *Man* 21(4): 637–56.

Haselgrove, C. and Krmnicek, S. 2012. The archaeology of money. *Annual Review of Anthropology* 41(1): 235–50.

Herzog, Z. 1997. The Arad fortresses (Hebrew). In R. Amiran, O. Ilan, M. Sebbane and Z. Herzog, *Arad*: 111–292. Tel Aviv, Hakibbutz Hameuchad Publishing House.

Herzog, Z. 2002. The fortress mound at Tel Arad: an interim report. *Tel Aviv: Journal of the Institute of Archaeology of Tel Aviv University* 2002 (1): 3–109.

Keel, O. 1980. La glyptique. In J. Briend and J.-B. Humbert (eds), *Tell Keisan (1971-1976): Une cité phénicienne en Galilée*: 257–95. Fribourg: Editions universitaires (Orbis biblicus et orientalis, Series Archaeologica 1).

Kilger, C. 2008. Wholeness and holiness: counting, weighing and valuing silver in the early Viking Period. In D. Skre (ed.), *Means of exchange: dealing with silver in the Viking Age*: 253–326. Aarhus, Aarhus University Press (Kaupang Excavation Project Publication Series 2, Norske Oldfunn 23).

Kim, H. S. and Kroll, J. H. 2008. A hoard of Archaic coins of Colophon and unminted silver (CH I. 3). *American Journal of Numismatics* 20: 53–104.

Kim, H. S. 2001. Archaic coinage as evidence for the use of money. In A. Meadows and K. M. W. Shipton (eds), *Money and its uses in the ancient Greek world*: 7–21. Oxford, Oxford University Press.

Kletter, R. 2003. Iron Age hoards of precious metals in Palestine — an 'underground economy'? *Levant* 35(1): 139–52.

Kletter, R. 1998. *Economic keystones: the weight system of the kingdom of Judah. Journal for the Study of the Old Testament, Supplement Series 276*. Sheffield, Sheffield Academic Press.

Kroll, J. H. 2001. Observations on monetary instruments in pre-coinage Greece. In M. S. Balmuth (ed.), *Hacksilber to coinage: new insights into the monetary history of the Near East and Greece*: 77–91. New York, N.Y., The American Numismatic Society (Numismatic Studies 24).

Kroll, J. H. 2008. The monetary use of weighted bullion in Archaic Greece. In W. V. Harris (ed.), *The monetary systems of the Greeks and Romans*: 12–37. Oxford, Oxford University Press.

Kroll, J. H. 2012. The monetary background of early coinage. In W. E. Metcalf (ed.), *The Oxford handbook of Greek and Roman coinage*: 33–42. Oxford, Oxford University Press.

Kurke, L. 1999. *Coins, bodies, games, and gold: the politics of meaning in Archaic Greece*. Princeton, N.J., Princeton University Press.

Lawson Younger Jr., K. 2000. Black obelisk (2.113F). In W. W. Hallo and K. Lawson Younger Jr (eds), *The context of scripture. Vol. II. Monumental inscriptions from the biblical world*: 269–70. Leiden, Brill.

Le Rider, G. 2001. *La naissance de la monnaie: pratiques monétaires de l'Orient ancien.* Paris, Presses universitaires de France.

Loud, G. 1948. *Megiddo II. Seasons of 1935–39.* Chicago, University of Chicago.

Mauss, M. 1970 [1925]. *The gift: forms and functions of exchange in archaic societies.* Reprint with corrections. London: Routledge & Kegan Paul.

Metcalf, D. M. 2007. Regions around the North Sea with a monetised economy in the pre-Viking and Viking Ages. In J. Graham-Campbell and G. Williams (eds), *Silver economy in the Viking Age*: 1–11. Walnut Creek, CA, Left Coast Press.

Michel, C. 2001. *Correspondance des marchands de Kanis au début du IIe millénaire avant J.-C.* Paris, Éditions du Cerf.

Oppenheim, A. L. 1947. A fiscal practice of the Ancient Near East. *Journal of Near Eastern Studies* 6(2): 116–20.

Osborne, R. 2009 [1996]. *Greece in the making, 1200–479 BC.* 2nd edition. London, Routledge.

Polanyi, K. 1968a. The economy as instituted process. In G. Dalton (ed.), *Primitive, archaic, and modern economies: essays of Karl Polanyi*: 139–74. Boston, Beacon Press.

Polanyi, K. 1968b. The semantics of money-uses. In G. Dalton (ed.), *Primitive, archaic, and modern economies: essays of Karl Polanyi*: 175–203. Boston, Beacon Press.

Quiggin, A. H. 1949. *A survey of primitive money: the beginning of currency.* New York/London, Barnes & Noble – Methuen.

Schaps, D. M. 2004. *The invention of coinage and the monetization of Ancient Greece.* Ann Arbor, University of Michigan Press.

Seaford, R. 2004. *Money and the Early Greek mind: Homer, philosophy, tragedy.* Cambridge, Cambridge University Press.

Sheehan, J. 2007. The form and structure of Viking-Age silver hoards: the evidence from Ireland. In J. Graham-Campbell and G. Williams (eds), *Silver economy in the Viking Age*: 149–62. Walnut Creek, CA, Left Coast Press.

Sindbæk, S. M. 2011. Silver economies and social ties: long-distance interaction, long-term investments — and why the Viking Age happened. In J. Graham-Campbell, S. M. Sindbæk and G. Williams (eds), *Silver economies, monetisation and society in Scandinavia, AD 800–1100*: 41–65. Aarhus: Aarhus Universitetsforlag.

Singer-Avitz, L. 2002. Arad: the Iron Age pottery assemblages. *Tel Aviv: Journal of the Institute of Archaeology of Tel Aviv University* 2002 (1): 110–214.

Skre, D. (ed.). 2008. *Means of exchange: dealing with silver in the Viking Age*. Aarhus, Aarhus University Press (Kaupang Excavation Project Publication Series 2, Norske Oldfunn 23).

Stern, E. 2001. The silver hoard from Tel Dor. In M. S. Balmuth (ed.), *Hacksilber to coinage: new insights into the monetary history of the Near East and Greece*: 19–26. New York, N.Y., The American Numismatic Society (Numismatic Studies 24).

Thompson, C. M. 2003. Sealed silver in Iron Age Cisjordan and the 'invention' of coinage. *Oxford Journal of Archaeology* 22(1): 67–107.

Toffolo, M. B., Arie, E., Martin, M. A. S., Boaretto, E., and Finkelstein, I. 2014. Absolute chronology of Megiddo, Israel, in the Late Bronze and Iron Ages: high-resolution radiocarbon dating. *Radiocarbon* 56(1): 221–44.

Van de Mieroop, M. 2004. *A history of the Ancient Near East, ca. 3000–323 BC*. Malden, Mass., Blackwell.

Weatherford, J. M. 1997. *The history of money: from sandstone to cyberspace*. New York, Crown Publishers.

Williams, G. 2007. Kingship, Christianity and coinage: monetary and political perspectives on silver economy in the Viking Age. In J. Graham-Campbell and G. Williams (eds), *Silver economy in the Viking Age*: 177–214. Walnut Creek, CA, Left Coast Press.

Weighing premonetary currency in the Iberian Iron Age

Thibaud Poigt

Abstract

While the practice of weighing is well attested in the archaeological record from later prehistoric Iberia, the context of this practice remains uncertain. Several examples show weight standardisation in the composition of hoard assemblages, both of undamaged and fragmented objects, but we rarely can relate the metrological standards identified in such assemblages with contemporary scale weights. Through a study of the weights discovered in the necropolis of El Cigarralejo (Mula, Spain), it is possible to demonstrate the high level of technical sophistication in the conception of Iberian scale weights and the variation between metrological standards from neighbouring sites. These observations lead us to reflect on the potential role of weighing for conducting transactions in a premonetary currency and the use of metrological standards for their normalisation.

Keywords: weights, Iberia, metrological system, photogrammetry

Résumé

Peser la pré-monnaie à l'Âge du Fer en Ibérie

Si l'usage de la pesée est bien attesté par le registre archéologique pour la péninsule Ibérique protohistorique, ses contextes d'utilisation demeurent incertains. Plusieurs exemples montrent l'utilisation de la normalisation pondérale dans la constitution de dépôts d'objets, entiers ou fragmentés, mais peu des étalons métrologiques repérés peuvent être rapprochés des valeurs des poids de balance contemporains. A travers l'étude de cas des poids découverts dans la nécropole d'El Cigarralejo (Mula, Espagne), nous montrons ici la haute technicité entrant dans la conception des lots de poids de balance ibériques et l'hétérogénéité du partage d'étalons métrologiques entre sites voisins. Ce constat mène à s'interroger sur le rôle possible de la pesée dans les pratiques de contrôle de moyens de paiement prémonétaires et l'utilisation de standards métrologiques pondéraux pour leur normalisation.

Mots-clés: poids, Ibérie, système métrologique, photogrammétrie

Zusammenfassung

Das Abwiegen premonetärer Zahlungsmittel in der iberischen Eisenzeit

Auch wenn die Praxis des Wiegens durch archäologische Funde für die Frühgeschichte der Iberischen Halbinsel eindeutig belegt ist, bleibt ungewiss, in welchen Kontexten sie ausgeübt wurde. Mehrere Beispiele belegen eine Gewichtsstandardisierung in der Zusammensetzung von Hortfunden, sowohl von unbeschädigten als auch von fragmentierten Objekten, aber nur wenige der metrologischen Standards, die in diesen Fällen identifiziert wurden, können mit zeitgleichen Wiegeinstrumenten in Verbindung gebracht werden. Eine Untersuchung der Gewichte, die in der Nekropole von El Cigarralejo (Mula, Spanien) entdeckt wurden, belegt den hohen technischen Stand, welcher der Konzeption der iberischen Gewichtssysteme zugrunde liegt, sowie die Variabilität zwischen metrologischen Standards benachbarter Fundorte. Hieraus ergeben sich Fragen zur möglichen Rolle des Wiegens in prämonetären Währungssystemen und für die Verwendung metrologischer Standards in ihrer Normierung.

Schlüsselwörter: Gewicht, Iberien, metrologisches System, Photogrammetrie

Introduction

The purpose of this paper is to reflect on the link between currency, trade and weighing, based on a case study of a set of ten weights found in grave 200 at El Cigarralejo (Mula, Murcia), published originally by Cuadrado (1964). It dates to the late fifth or early fourth century BC, a period during which the Iberians did not use coinage, but were in contact with Mediterranean merchants (essentially Carthaginians and Greeks) who used monetary systems. Indeed, even if the first coins appeared relatively early in the Iberian Peninsula (fifth to fourth centuries BC, from Greek and Punic cities), the indigenous Iberians only adopted a monetary system during the third century BC, a date that corresponds to the first local coinage (García-Bellido 2011: 133; Gorgues 2010: 69).

Weighed metal was used during Antiquity and this practice is referred to for instance by Aristotle, even if we have to be careful to associate these mentions with the people that we are dealing with here:

> For the natural necessaries are not in every case readily portable; hence for the purpose of barter men made a mutual contract to give and accept some substance of such a sort as being itself a useful commodity that was easy to handle in use for general life, iron for instance, silver and other metals, at the first stage defined merely by size and weight, but finally also by impressing on it a stamp in order that this might relieve them of having to measure it; for the stamp was put on as a token of the amount (Politics, I, 1257a, translated by H. Rackham).

Metal represents a universal symbol during later prehistory as an essential raw material. Copper, gold, tin and later iron had a prominent role in many European and Mediterranean exchange networks. Scholarship has emphasised the part played by metal in a wide range of economic, political and social processes, such as the work of Van Driessche about the slow transition from premonetary standards made of metal to the bronze coinage in Greece during the Bronze and

Iron Ages (Van Driessche 2009). For these reasons, it would not be surprising if the principal medium of currency before the appearance of coinage was metal. Nevertheless, other materials could also have fulfilled this function, for instance salt, textiles or cattle.

The aim here is not to discuss the material form of premonetary currency, but to debate the abstract concepts that this practice involves. In the absence of an independent measure for the value of the exchanged goods, the latter is only determined in function of common equivalences, shared by actors of trade. For example, during the Mycenaean period it seems that a bull equalled five sheep (Van Driessche 2009: 31), a current equivalence applied in barter, without use of an independent means of measuring.

Nevertheless, the determination of a means of payment destined to facilitate trade implies agreement about value and measuring quantity. If an animal can be considered as one unit, the matter is different with bulk goods or raw materials, which need more specific quantification. In that case, talking about premonetary currency implies talking about a system of measurement as a means to exercise control over the quantities involved in the process. Weighing represents one way to measure products and appears to be the most efficient for some of them, such as metal, salt or even textiles. But even if it is weights that concern us here, we also have to keep in mind the existence of measures of length and volume. Metrological concepts can be applied to currencies as well: the need to define a norm, to create units and potentially fractions and multiples, as will be demonstrated below.

The practice of depositing weighing instruments in graves in the Iberian Peninsula spread particularly between the fifth and third centuries BC, essentially along Iberia's Mediterranean seaboard (Poigt 2015a: 136) (Figure 1). The same phenomenon can be observed in other geographic areas and periods, like the central European Bronze Age (Pare 1999: 510). It seems unlikely that the deposition of tools in graves is a consequence of a change in weighing practice: the appearance of weights in tombs is not associated with a change of weighing instruments or the metrological system, even if data available for the latter have to be used with care. We probably have to attribute their appearance in the funerary record to changes in how this activity was represented in funerary ritual.

Indeed, the typology of the Iberian weights, made of copper alloy or lead, has been well known since the beginning of the twentieth century, primarily through the works of I. Ballester (1930). Mostly, we are dealing with perforated cylindroids, with few variations. They can be of cylindrical or discoid shape, sometimes without perforation.[1] In rare cases, one of the faces is inscribed. These marks could be linked to a metrological system in some instances (e.g. Syrian *shekel*, Athenian *drachma* or double-*drachma*). In an article from 2003/04, I. Grau Mira and J. Moratalla Jávega suggested a Phoenician origin for the morphology of Iberian weights, using as an example two pyramidal perforated weights from Kerkouane (Tunisia), contemporary with those from the Iberian area (Grau Mira and Moratalla Jávega 2003/2004: 42).[2] However, along the western seaboard of the Iberian Peninsula we find cylindroid weights with a central perforation from the Bronze Age onwards, as shown by the work of R. Vilaça (2003; 2011). Weights of this type are present in a large part of Iberia (Figure 1). However, the distribution of the weighing instruments in the Iberian Peninsula shows empty zones, which leads us to believe that there are still many artefacts to identify.

Among the 268 weights identified for Spain and Portugal in the Bronze and Iron Ages (at the time of writing this paper), the heaviest weighs 493.3g (La Bastida de les Alcuses, Moixent, Valencia) and the average mass equals 47.1g. But more research is certainly necessary to verify that heavier weights of different types and/or different materials have not been missed. Evidence for 'heavy weighing' could completely change the scenario derived from the archaeological data currently available and might alter our perception of how trade was conducted during this period.

From comparison to measurement

To clearly understand the problems concerning weighing practice and its possible application to the definition of value in a premonetary economy, it is important to explain some points of the cognitive context underpinning its development. Firstly, the appearance of weighing is the answer to a need, which is not universal. As stated above, the Iberian Peninsula is at the centre of complex trade networks, which influence this practice. And secondly, we will give a brief overview of our current knowledge about the phenomenon of premonetary currency in the study area.

Why weighing? How to weigh?

The practice of weighing can involve a wide range of measuring devices. The need to measure can result from many factors and relate to different properties, involving mass, length, or capacity. However, we have to distinguish two different approaches: the direct comparison of data and the calculation of an absolute value with respect to a reference scale.

1 Referring to the typology introduced in the abstract of my PhD project (Poigt 2015b).

2 These weights are not pictured in the original publication.

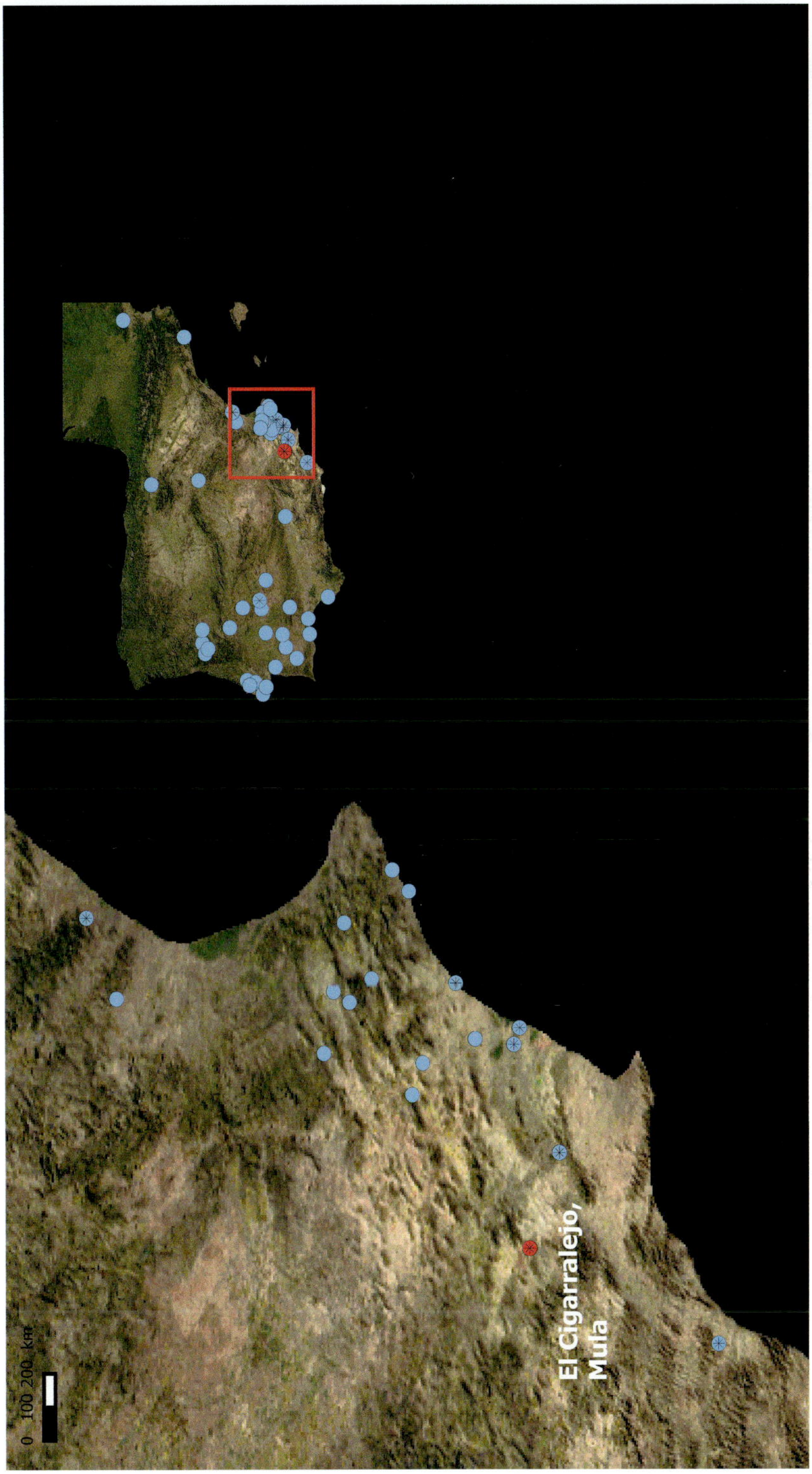

Figure 1. Distribution of weighing instruments in the Iberian Peninsula.

This is to say that when it comes to weighing, it is in the first instance a comparison and, from this point of view, it is quite intuitive and universal. It consists in comparing the mass of one product with another, to determine the heaviest one and the lightest one. Where weighing involves actual 'measurement', it instead addresses the need to attribute a numeric value to analogical data not recordable intuitively. This type of measure depends necessarily on a pre-established system and thus on the existence of a metrology and a norm. The creation of a weighing norm requires the definition of a standard, a quantity of product *lambda* becoming the reference of the system. Subsequently, all the measurements are compared to this standard. To facilitate the calculation, set multiples and fractions are generally organised around this unit of reference. Like all norms, it has to be imposed by an authority. This fact is important because, in consequence, a 'normative' weighing has its limits, which are conditioned by the influence of the authority which implements it.

We can broadly distinguish two types of weighing. One is what we will refer to as 'heavy weighing', which permits the measuring of great quantities of material and which necessitates large scales for being effective. Concerning the Iberian period, at the moment there is no archaeological evidence for such a practice. The weights are light, always below 500g (the great majority is below 200g), and the average diameter of the scale pans that have been identified approximates ten centimetres. We can thus refer to the corresponding practice as 'precision weighing'. Even if it remains difficult to define a clear boundary between these two types of weighing practice, the difference greatly influences possible usage.

The distinction between 'heavy' and 'precision' weighing, and the existence or non-existence of a reference standard, are fundamental issues in the study of ancient metrologies. They entirely determine the weighing metrology applied, which cannot be understood without including these criteria in the reasoning. Indeed, the manufacture of a weight, in line with the nature of its function, necessarily depends on a combination of the following factors: establishment of the norm, cultural traditions and intended uses.

The practice of weighing implies the mastering of several abstract concepts. First, mass has to be defined as an invariable value in time and space. This means that an object always possesses the same mass and this remains true everywhere on the surface of the earth.[3] This is not to say that later prehistoric people could not have observed and understood these concepts through practical experience. Even today, the modern definitions of 'weight' and

[3] The mass (calculated in grams for the metric system) is an invariable value. This unit differs from the weight, which depends on the gravity, calculated in newtons.

'mass', only conceptualised since the seventeenth century AD, are generally not completely distinguished from each other. Furthermore, the adoption of a standard, even the simplest, requires an understanding of basic arithmetic concepts like addition and subtraction, or, in the case of complex metrological systems, of multiples and fractions. Knowledge of this type of abstract concept was probably not widespread during the Bronze and Iron Ages, but would have been a privilege of well-educated and high-status individuals. This means that a part of the population probably could not understand the more complex weighing operations, an even harder task where a written medium was lacking.

As pointed out above, any metrology depends on a standard validated by an authority. By the same token, a metrological system will not have any value outside the sphere of influence of the authority that guarantees it, which can range from the nuclear family to the international scale. The system will be of no consequence for the exchange of goods and the capacity for trade outside of this sphere of influence. No such systems existed at an international level before the development of the metric system. Even in France in 1795, before the adoption of the metre and its derivatives, there were several hundred different metrological systems (Palaiseau 1816).

Apart from the above, another necessary condition for making scale weights is the capacity to model a material in order to give it the required mass and form. Since the Palaeolithic, humans have modified natural materials to create forms adapted to their needs. However, to obtain a specific mass, numerous steps of control are required during the manufacturing process. This can be relatively easy when using stone as a material, but becomes really difficult with materials like lead, copper or metal alloys, which necessitate a calculation of the required quantity of raw material and involve a risk of losing metal during the casting process. The process becomes harder still when the weights take complex forms, like the octahedral weights from the western part of the Iberian Peninsula, dated to the Late Bronze Age (Vilaça 2003: 262–5; 2011: 141–2, 152–4).

To summarise, the manufacture of weights requires many conditions to be met: an authority guaranteeing the norm, the mastering of abstract mathematical concepts by the users of the weighing tools and the mastering of sophisticated techniques for shaping the weights. We can also argue that this array of competencies has to be organised by the relevant authority in order to impose the norm and maintain the coherence of the system.

Uses and exchange process

One of the most important points concerning the practice of weighing during the Metal Ages, at least regarding western Europe, is to determine the framework of its use. As we saw, in essence the archaeological evidence refers to precision weighing. Thus, when it comes to the use of this practice in trade, it is only reliable for weighing small quantities, possibly precious materials, but the weighing instruments found are not well suited for trade in bulk commodities. It is important to stress that the lack of evidence for heavy weighing does not mean such a practice did not exist. This lack might be attributable to deficient research and a poor identification of the respective weighing instruments, but precision weighing definitely exists, and we have to ask in which context it would have been used.

There are many possible contexts in which precision weighing might be practised: trade in small quantities, currency exchange, metallurgy, pharmaceutics or cooking, to name but a few. The difficulty lies in identifying evidence that permits us to define or distinguish uses. This information could, in theory, be provided by the archaeological context, but in fact, evidence showing a link between weighing instruments and the context of their use is still rare. In funerary contexts, where weights and scales are buried as grave goods, they can be associated with other tools, but they do not refer to one particular activity. We find associations with metallurgical equipment, potential evidence for trade or even textile production, which leads us to think that weighing represents an independent activity, not limited to the control of a single category of products (Poigt 2015a: 137).

Concerning money, as stated above, the earliest weights manufactured in the Iberian Peninsula date from the Late Bronze Age, many centuries before the appearance of the first local coinage. Furthermore, the main areas of weight finds do not match the distribution of the Punic and Greek colonies where the first coined money was issued. Thus, we cannot link weighing practice to the control of coined money, whether it be for the weights from grave 200 at El Cigarralejo or for the rest of the Iberian Peninsula.

What is the place of exchanges in this context? The circulation of goods between the Iberian Peninsula and its neighbours is well attested. However, the relevant networks probably also provided conduits for the movement of ideas, knowledge and people. These contacts are ancient, with long-distance trade since the Bronze Age demonstrated for instance by the Iberian origin of copper used in Scandinavia (Ling *et al.* 2014: 125).

Even if they do not use the same system of measurement or even numeral system, the archaeological evidence shows the capacity of the Iberian peoples to maintain relationships, commercial or not, with near and distant neighbours. At the same time, they were able to handle complex and abstract mathematical concepts and apply them to their weighing practice. On the other hand, there is no evidence for the use of such weights in trade.

Premonetary currency systems

One of the biggest differences between pre-money and struck money, directly linked to our subject, is the former holding only its own intrinsic value. Thus, pre-money does not require a nominal value as guaranteed by a political authority stamped on it and, logically, a formal transformation does not change the intrinsic value. The main consequence of this principle is the need for a way to evaluate the raw material composing it. Two steps are then necessary, the estimation of the quality of the material and the calculation of its quantity. It is this second aspect which interests us particularly. Indeed, the measuring of quantity by weight is often mentioned (Callegarin and García-Bellido 2012: 123; García-Bellido 2011: 133), even if the archaeological evidence is not obvious.

The presence of pre-money based on a metal standard (principally gold and silver) is well attested for the Iberian Peninsula, with — in some cases — the identification of metrological standards (Callegarin and García-Bellido 2012: 126; García-Bellido 2011: 131). These observations are essentially based on the evidence from hoards, either containing complete objects, destined to be broken up or not, or scrap metal of *hacksilber* or *hackgold* type. One observation that might support an interpretation of these as a form of pre-money is the progressive substitution of these artefacts by coined money in the hoards, with a phase of coexistence of the two categories. However, a link between the units into which the metal is broken up and the weight system is not so obvious. Indeed, the area of the greatest concentration of weight finds (around Murcia, Valencia and Alicante) has not produced many hoards and an exhaustive metrological study is still lacking.

Furthermore, under circumstances where the relevant metrological standards and the precision of weighing are unknown, this type of work faces an inevitable obstacle: if we are looking for some logical sequence in a data set, we always find one. It does not mean that such hoards reflect a weight standard. However, in most cases, the distinction between units of metal weighed to an approximate standard and pieces of metal cut more or less to the same size faces considerable difficulties.

Concerning the potential use of other types of material as premonetary currency, we have little information to go by. Manufactured goods may represent abstract value in commercial transactions. We know for example that textiles could be used as a form of payment during Antiquity, as described in Linear B tablets for Mycenaean Greece (Luján 2011: 28–9) and we can suspect that precious materials might have played the same role, such as salt, amber or precious stones. However, salt and textiles do not normally survive in the archaeological record and there is no evidence for the use of other materials, at least as far as the Iberian Peninsula is concerned.

Material context

Iberian Peninsula

In order to clearly understand in which context weighing practices evolved and the impact of external influences on them, it is important to provide a quick historical overview of the Iberian Peninsula from the sixth century to the first century BC.

The Iberian area in the east of the peninsula represents a geographical zone where people shared the same language and material culture between the sixth and the first centuries BC (from the end of the fifth century BC where language is concerned) (Figure 1). Writing, in a Phoenician-derived alphabet, has survived in the form of epigraphic inscriptions on pottery, coins or other materials, such as lead sheets (Gorgues 2014: 157). This area maintained relationships with several Mediterranean peoples: first the Phoenicians, then the Greeks and finally the Romans, until the Punic Wars brought about the creation of the two Roman provinces of Hispania in the second century BC, marking the beginning of the progressive Romanisation of the entire peninsula. Since the early sixth century BC and increasingly during the fifth century BC, trade in Greek pottery developed along the Mediterranean seaboard, particularly around Albacete, Alicante and Murcia (Pare 1997: 264), our main area of interest. C. Pare explains this quick development by the previous involvement of the local population in trade with the Phoenicians (Pare 1997: 263).

Thus, the Iberians had been used to interacting and dealing with foreign people for many decades when our set of weights was buried in grave 200 at El Cigarralejo. However, this exposure to foreign trade probably did not transform the local economy for several centuries. Furthermore, M. P. García-Bellido emphasises the tendency of metrological systems to withstand innovations and preserve archaic features (García-Bellido 1999: 363), which makes us think that the Iberian metrological system might have continued unaltered for a long time after the introduction of Mediterranean weighing standards.

The first local coinage, the Iberian *drachma*, appears in the context of the second Punic War, but it is only used in the area under Greek colonial influence

(Gorgues 2010: 69). Before that, we observe the circulation of silver coins issued by Greek colonies like Emporion, which coin *oboles* and *hemioboles* from the fifth century BC onwards, and Rhode, coining *drachmas* since the end of the fourth century BC (García-Bellido and Blázquez 2001b: 129–35, 318–19; Gorgues 2010: 69). The metrology is based on a *drachma* weighing 4.7g, which results from a mix between Phocaic and Punic metrologies. The Punic coins, made of silver or bronze, are introduced somewhat later in the Iberian Peninsula, around the late fourth or early third centuries BC, from the colony of Ebusus (García-Bellido and Blázquez 2001a: 114–15).

A. Gorgues has also commented on the relationship between metrology and coinage and reminds us of the impossibility for a metal or any other material to have a conventional value without agreeing on a system to measure its quantity, either by volume or by weight (Gorgues 2010: 72). However, contrary to him, we think the presence of weighing scales does not necessarily imply the use of a metrological system. We can postulate that the balance permits 'relative weighing', this is to say comparing the mass of two products without using weights for measuring. But, as stated by Gorgues, the way from weight measurement to the establishment of an agreed weighing system applied to commercial transactions is long (Gorgues 2010: 73).

If the Iberians were probably trading with several foreign peoples, the Greeks were the only ones maintaining permanent settlements in the Iberian area: Emporion, Agde, Rhode (Gorgues 2010: 76). There are various and numerous indicators of the importance of Greek influence on Iberian culture, most notably writing (on lead tablets), imported goods and iconographic influence.

The various interactions of Iberians with other peoples, each with its own distinct metrological system (if not several), make the study of weights and measures much more complex. Obviously, any attempt to deduce metrological standards from the archaeological record needs to compare the available finds to all systems potentially used in the area, with all their fractions and multiples.

History of research

To better understand the matter of Iberian metrology and the current hypothesis concerning it, it is necessary to consider the history of research. Indeed, the latter very much conditioned the current view of the metrological systems in use in the Iberian Peninsula.

For our study area and period of interest, the first scholar to identify weights was I. Ballester at the beginning of the 1930s, taking an interest in the copper alloy or lead artefacts with a discoid or troncoconical shape and central perforation. These pieces are generally found in Iberian settlements from the provinces of Valencia, Murcia and Alicante, and Ballester was the first to observe the repetition of masses on a regular weighing scale, which led him to identify them as weights. He proposed their matching to a metrological system based on a unit of 4g (Ballester 1930). His study was based particularly on the set of weights from Covalta (construcción 27, departamento b), which were reanalysed by P. Beltrán in 1948, adding specimens from La Bastida de les Alcuses (Moixent, Valencia), Cabeço de Mariola (Alfafara-Bocairent, Alicante), La Serreta (Alcoi-Concentaina-Penáguila, Alicante) and one weight from El Xarpolar (Vall d'Alcalà, Alicante). Beltran was the first researcher to attribute a foreign origin to the Iberian weights. According to him, the Iberian metrological system uses the same divisions as the Mediterranean systems, an idea which would become a sort of dogma during the following decades. He also identified a 'covaltine' *mina* (501.43g), corresponding to 60 *shekels* of 8.48g, close to the light Babylonian *mina* (504–505g) (Beltrán Villagrasa 1948: 136–7).

In 1964, E. Cuadrado published the 13 weights from grave 17 at Cabecico del Tesoro (Verdolay, Murcia) and also the set of ten weights from grave 200 at El Cigarralejo (the latter forming the subject of the present case study), adding them to the previous corpus. He kept the idea of an importation of the metrological system into the Iberian Peninsula, but attributed its origin to the Greeks, because of their influence. So the Iberian metrological system proposed by Cuadrado is composed of a Greek *mina*, divisible into 100 *drachmas*. The best candidate for him was the Solonian *mina*, equal to 436.6g, corresponding with a *drachma* of 4.36g (Cuadrado 1964: 344).

Working with the same corpus, D. Fletcher Valls and C. Mata Parreño organised their analysis according to a chronological framework and left out any artefacts with a doubtful origin. Nevertheless, they kept the standard and the system proposed by Cuadrado (Fletcher Valls and Mata Parreño 1981). Fletcher Valls wrote another paper on the subject in 1995 with L. Silgo Gauche, incorporating a study of the marks observed on some weights. Although they have a diffusionist understanding of the weighing metrology, they applied a mathematical approach, ordering the mass of the weights into groups of 13 values, labelled *a* to *m* (Fletcher Valls and Silgo Gauche 1995: 273).

In 2003/2004, I. Grau Mira and J. Moratalla Jávega based a new article on the weights from the geographical area around Valencia, Alicante and Murcia, adding weights from 14 new sites to the corpus. Combining a search for eastern Mediterranean influence and the detailed observation of the artefacts, they came to the conclusion that various metrological systems were used in the

Iberian Peninsula (based on standards of 7.2g and 8.6g for the fourth and third centuries BC, and another around 7g for the second and first centuries BC), some existing at the same time (Grau Mira and Moratalla Jávega 2003/2004: 50). In particular, they saw evidence for the existence of adjustable weights, which functioned by filling the central perforation with an insert of a different metal (iron or lead in most cases) or the attachment of a ring or a wire. They explained this adjustment as a way to make the weights usable simultaneously within two different metrological systems (Grau Mira and Moratalla Jávega 2003/2004: 43–4).

Adopting another method, we recently proposed a different system than those presented above. Starting with the set of ten weights found in grave 200 at El Cigarralejo, we tried to reconstruct the system used to build it, based only on the arithmetic links between weights (Poigt 2015a).

The set from grave 200

The set of ten weights from grave 200 at El Cigarralejo, published originally by Cuadrado (1964), is particularly interesting with regard to Iberian metrology. Its context of discovery, a tomb, and its arithmetical construction permit us to formulate many hypotheses concerning it. Furthermore, its comparison with weighing instruments from neighbouring sites gives an idea of the standards shared among the Iberians.

The tomb in question is a cremation grave, maybe of two individuals, containing the weighing instruments alongside weapons, harness elements, spindles, ornaments, pottery and other artefacts. With more than 200 grave goods, it is the 'richest' tomb of the 494 graves excavated in the necropolis.

Photogrammetry

Three-dimensional photogrammetry was used to accurately record the objects under study. This technique gives 3D properties to an object derived from 2D images, using specific algorithms. In most cases, particularly for aerial photogrammetry, the models obtained are not full 3D objects but only convex surfaces (Bourke 2012: 71). Our objective here is to create complete meshes, i.e. closed models that permit full rotation as well as the calculation of their volume. Combining mass, volume and 3D reconstruction, we should be able to reconstruct the original mass of deteriorated or adjusted weights, opening up opportunities for new metrological perspectives on the evolution, rejection or adoption of weighing systems.

For this study, we used the *Agisoft Photoscan®* software, permitting fast and precise treatment of the images. The usual method consists in taking pictures by moving the camera around the object. In our case, to save time and enhance precision, the camera was fixed and the artefact was rotated using a turntable. A problem that may arise with this method when stitching together the different images is caused by the object's movement in relation to the lighting source, which remains stationary. In order to reduce the impact of the stationary lighting source, it is possible to place the turntable in a small lighting tent, which diffuses the light and reduces uneven shadows.

Concerning the scan itself, pictures were taken at four different angles, corresponding approximately to 40°, 70°, 110° and 140° from a vertical camera position. In practice, the object was turned over between taking images at the two first angles and taking pictures at the latter two. At each angle, between 24 and 36 images were taken, depending on the artefact (smooth or rough surface, circular or irregular shape etc.) (Figure 2).

After this step, the rest of the process does not require access to any archaeological material, which is an important advantage of the method. The time required for recording an object *in situ* rarely exceeds ten minutes. However, masking is an essential requirement for the further procedure. It consists simply in applying a rectangular mask around the artefact on every picture in order to isolate it from any background features. Using the software, the 3D model is then built in four steps: alignment of the images, construction of the point cloud, construction of the mesh and construction of the texture. It should be noted that this last step is not essential for determining the volume and only affects visual appearance. In most cases, the entire process could be done without modification of the data, but in some cases, particularly with the perforated artefacts, cleaning of the point cloud is essential, that is to say, deleting any intrusive points (due e.g. to shadows in the area of the perforation). The final step consists in applying a scale to the digital model through the use of suitable reference points. For this, we used points from a measuring scale visible in the pictures.

Photogrammetry is not normally used with the objective of calculating volumes of objects, and it was necessary to test its reliability for this purpose. Thus, we used it on a wooden sphere, because its volume can be calculated by applying the rules of geometry, and we obtained a deviation below 1% between the geometrical calculation and the numerical calculation derived from the 3D model. For the weights from El Cigarralejo we tried a range of different methods and we observed that several factors could alter the calculated volume. These are the uniformity of lighting between images, the shape of the object, the distance between the object and the scale, or the method of mesh creation. The

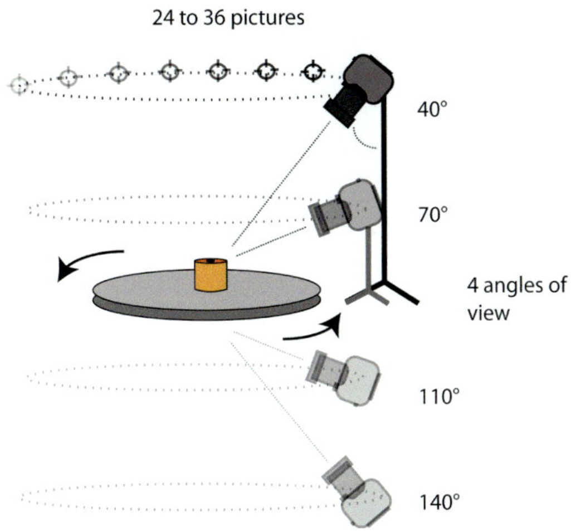

Figure 2. Photogrammetry method: schematic representation.

light has to envelop the shape of the object without overexposing and requires a routine control of the pictures. The perforations, when they are relatively deep, can be the cause of a faulty mesh, because the inside of the perforation does not appear in the pictures. As far as the scale is concerned, it has to be placed as closely as possible to the artefact. However, from our experience, the main distortion for the calculated volume comes from the use of two separate point clouds for constructing the mesh, corresponding to the two faces of the object, and aligning them subsequently. Every time we used this method, we observed deviations in the calculated volume of around 5% compared to models built directly. Changes in the number of images taken, focal length or viewing angles respectively cause variations below 1.5% in most cases.

In our point of view this method holds real potential for metrological studies. Determining the exact degree of precision for this method will necessitate other tests, but based on work carried out so far we can consider it to be around 1–2%. We think these figures are compatible with an intended use in ancient metrology studies, but it is necessary to take them into consideration.

Reexamination

E. Cuadrado conducted his study of this set of weights fifty years ago and it appears necessary for us to take a fresh look at this material.[4] In spite of a few small deviations, the masses recorded today are not very different from

[4] All the archaeological finds from the site are currently kept at the Museo de Arte Ibérico 'El Cigarralejo' (Mula, Murcia, Spain).

Figure 3. 3D models of the weights from grave 200.

the ones measured by Cuadrado in 1964. This fact is reassuring for metrology studies; it allows us to postulate that the masses did not change significantly since the excavation in 1963. New data are available from the weighing of the two artefacts from tomb 18. These copper alloy weights, labelled here Cig-K and Cig-L, weigh 5.56g and 90.74g respectively.

An examination with the naked eye already provides some information about the weights. Firstly, the functioning of the weights as a set is evident. Their dimensions allow them to be neatly stacked (Figure 3). Secondly, the wear observable around the perforation on the lower face supports the hypothesis formulated by Beltrán (1948: 134), and subsequently repeated several times in the literature, that they would have been stored threaded on an axis. A small indentation on the inner surface of the perforation of some weights leads us to think that this system could at some stage have been substituted by keeping them threaded on a simple string (Figure 4).

Cuadrado exposed the morphological heterogeneity of the pieces even though the drawings accompanying his article did not clearly support his observation. This dissimilarity between pieces was corroborated by the present study, as

Figure 4. Detail of wear on one of the weights.

demonstrated by the digital models. All the weights belong to the category of cylindrical weights according to the typology proposed in Poigt (2015b: 178), but if weights E, G, H, I and J are clearly of a truncated conical shape with a slightly concave outer surface, the others (A, B, C, D and F) look more discoidal, if not cylindrical in the case of weight B (Figure 5).

In a previous article, we proposed the identification of an indigenous system on which the set from grave 200 at El Cigarralejo was based (Poigt 2015a). The method employs a very basic calculation: a 'division table' (Table 1). Every intersection in the table represents the result of the division of the row by the column. In this way, for every column's entry, we have its ratio compared to the other data. In our case, we note a particularly interesting feature of weight Cig-F, of 20.48g. It has interesting relations with the other weights. Indeed, it presents whole numbers for the multiples and logical associations for the fractions, which permits us to consider it as the base unit or standard. Without going into too much detail regarding the other results, we see that in relation to weight Cig-F, weights G, H, I and J represent multiples (×2, ×4, ×6 and ×10) with only small deviations. Considering the fractions, we can reconstruct them as 1/10, 1/6, 1/4, 1/3 and 3/4, which is consistent with the idea of a system mixing decimal and duodecimal counts.

The way the set has been constructed further supports this hypothesis. Considering Cig-F as the base unit, the set of ten weights starts with a 1/10 fraction and ends with a multiple of 10. Finally, combining the weights, it is possible to constitute a fraction of 1/2 and an uninterrupted sequence of multiples from 2 to 24 times the base unit. Adopting a theoretical reconstruction with a standard equal to 20.77g, the average deviation equals approximately 1% (Poigt 2015a: 144).

Weights		Cig-A	Cig-B	Cig-C	Cig-D	Cig-E	Cig-F	Cig-G	Cig-H	Cig-I	Cig-J
	Mass (g)	1.98	3.38	5.01	7.4	15.83	**20.48**	41.46	81.65	125	208.45
Cig-A	1.98	1	0.59	0.4	0.27	0.13	0.1	0.05	0.02	0.02	0.01
Cig-B	3.38	1.71	1	0.67	0.46	0.21	0.17	0.08	0.04	0.03	0.02
Cig-C	5.01	2.53	1.48	1	0.68	0.32	0.24	0.12	0.06	0.04	0.02
Cig-D	7.4	3.74	2.19	1.48	1	0.47	0.36	0.18	0.09	0.06	0.04
Cig-E	15.83	7.99	4.68	3.16	2.14	1	0.77	0.38	0.19	0.13	0.08
Cig-F	**20.48**	10.34	6.06	4.09	2.77	1.29	1	0.49	0.25	0.16	0.1
Cig-G	41.46	20.94	12.27	8.28	5.6	2.62	2.02	1	0.51	0.33	0.2
Cig-H	81.65	41.24	24.16	16.3	11.03	5.16	3.99	1.97	1	0.65	0.39
Cig-I	125	63.13	36.98	24.95	16.89	7.9	6.1	3.01	1.53	1	0.6
Cig-J	208.45	105.28	61.67	41.61	28.17	13.17	10.18	5.03	2.55	1.67	1

Table 1. Division table used to spot correspondences between weights.

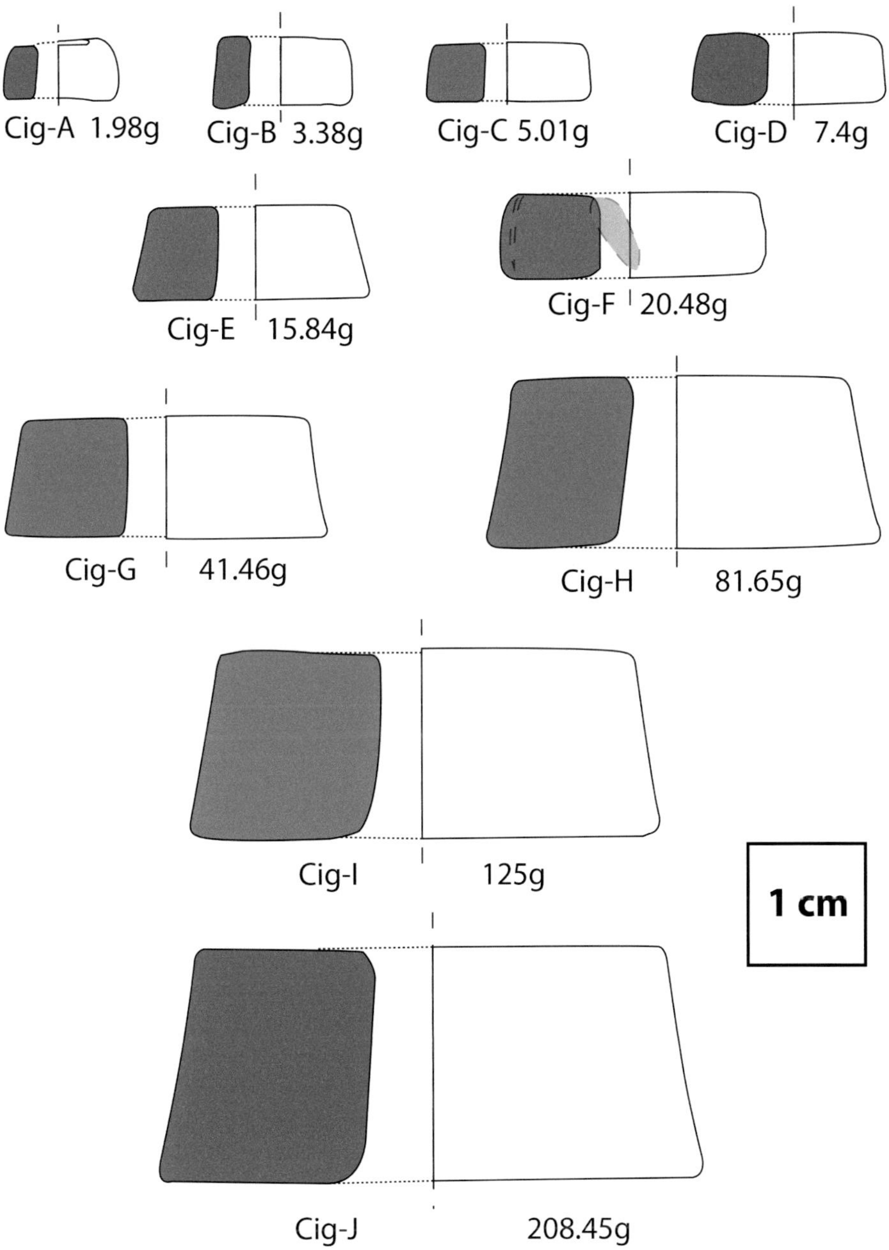

Figure 5. Weight units from grave 200 at Cigarralejo.

The examination of the set does not invalidate the above proposition, but it is interesting to make a few observations. We can further reflect on the morphology of the weights. On the one hand, the metrological coherence of the set is obvious; on the other hand, this is not incompatible with the idea of a rebuilt assemblage. There is no evidence permitting conclusions about the possible reconstruction of the set, except for the morphological aspect of the pieces. The reconstruction of weight F in its state prior to the cutting of the two notches, according to our digital modelling, gives it an approximate mass of 21.0–21.5g. This difference of mass is too small to allow for metrological conclusions. Even if it is harder to achieve, the complex metrological make-up of the set could have been devised when the set was rebuilt (assuming that we are indeed dealing with a rebuilt set). If that is the case, the craftsperson probably made slight modifications to adjust the mass of individual weights (through notching, planing sides and so on).

One of the principal pieces of information from this new examination concerns weights K and L from grave 18. The two tombs are not contemporaneous but separated by approximately one generation, judging by the associated grave goods. The possibility of a succession in time of two different systems cannot be totally ruled out. If the weights from grave 18 do not function very well with a standard of 20.77g, within a logical sequence similar to those from grave 200, conversion between the two systems is quite easy. Indeed, Cig-K (5.56g) approximately equals Cig-C, that is to say a 1/4 fraction, and Cig-L (90.74g) corresponds to 4.5 times the base unit from grave 200 (Cig-F).

We cannot go further in the interpretation of the weights from grave 18, except for saying that they represent a different metrological construction from the ones in grave 200. This observation supports the idea of local systems, functioning within a very small sphere of influence or during a short time. The possible existence at the same site of two weighing systems, almost contemporaneous, urges caution when it comes to large-scale metrological studies based on a statistical approach incorporating all the data from the Iberian area, independent of chronology and geography. Obviously, the data from this necropolis are too sparse to determine if we are dealing with a single system expressed in different sets of multiples, or if there are two different systems functioning simultaneously. For this reason, it is necessary to expand our observations and look at the compatibility of the system from grave 200 with evidence from neighbouring sites.

Comparisons

The Iberian Peninsula is one of the areas in Europe that have provided most balance weights, with almost 300 artefacts identified. Approximately two thirds of this corpus are concentrated in the small region around Alicante, Murcia and Albacete. This area corresponds roughly to the Roman *Contestania,* a name used for the region inhabited by an indigenous population referred to as *Contestani*, to whom some scholars, particularly I. Grau Mira and J. Moratalla Jávega (2003/2004), attribute a specific material culture. We are choosing in this article to avoid the term *Contestania*, only known from later Roman sources, in order not to introduce any chronological confusion. Nevertheless, the fact is that we find a great quantity of balance weights in this geographical zone, both in funerary and settlement contexts (Figure 1).

As outlined above, several previous works have treated these artefacts, including those from El Cigarralejo. It is not the aim of the present contribution to provide an exhaustive list of weights from the Iberian Peninsula, thus we will only compare our results with metrological data furnished by previous studies.

The first observation we can make concerning Iberian weights is that we cannot easily identify the standard from El Cigarralejo within that corpus. The reason behind this is not the absence of objects weighing approximately 20.77g but, on the contrary, a large number of weights whose masses fall close to this figure, without forming a coherent range. Indeed, nine weights fall within c. 5% of the standard from El Cigarralejo (19.73–21.81g), but we do not observe a clear concentration of masses around it (Figure 6). Significantly, the same observation can be made for the double standard of 41.53g. The difficulty comes from the impossibility to differentiate clearly between a weight approaching a theoretical value with a lack of precision and a weight corresponding to another metrological system, but with a multiple that lies close to that first theoretical value (for example, the double of the standard from El Cigarrelejo could be confounded with ten *drachmas* of 4.36g).

Finally, it is maybe the multiple ten which permits the easier comparison, because the imprecision of the measures is smaller than the difference between two distinct weights. There are 15 weights with a mass between 191.04g and 211.58g, and ten of these show a deviation of less than 2% from the tenfold multiple of the standard from El Cigarralejo. These pieces originate from La Serreta, La Bastida de les Alcuses (sections 16, 100 and an isolated find), Covalta (structure 27 and isolated finds), Cabecico del Tesoro and El Puig. We can postulate that the weights approaching 195g correspond to other systems. Indeed, an imprecision of 10g seems unlikely given the precision of the set from grave 200.

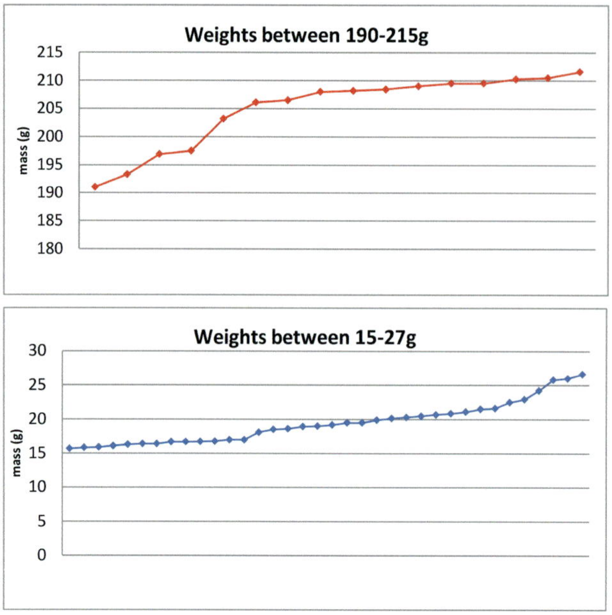

Figure 6. Mass of Iberian weights around the standard of 20.77g and its multiple by ten.

I. Grau Mira and J. Moratalla Jávega (2003/2004) already proposed an identification of several metrological systems, and the one based on the weights from El Cigarralejo could just be another one. But are other sets metrologically similar to it? We can postulate that sets share the metrological system of El Cigarralejo if they use similar multiples and fractions or another logical sequence starting from 20.77g. In a previous study on the subject, we attributed a percentual value to the extent to which other sets matched the metrological system from El Cigarralejo, based on the match of their respective component weights with those known from El Cigarralejo (Poigt 2015a: 145–6). It is probably necessary to break down this average value and distinguish between individual fractions and multiples to shed light on the problematic points. Doing so shows the weak correspondence that generally exists between the system from El Cigarralejo and those from neighbouring sites (Table 2). Nevertheless, excluding isolated weights, we can identify two sets as having important similarities with the one from grave 200. The first is a set of four weights from structure 27 at Covalta (42.2g : 81.8g : 122.25g : 209.5g). The second is the set from section 100 at La Bastida de les Alcuses, also composed of four weights (19.9g : 82.3g : 123.8g : 208g). In these two cases, the absolute average percentage of deviation amounts to 1.5%, an entirely acceptable figure.[5] We also found nearly the same values in

[5] The deviations are respectively equal: 1.6%, -1.5%, -1.9% and 0.9% for Covalta, and -4.2%, -0.9%,

	1/10	1/6	¼	1/3	1/2	3/4	1	2	3	4	5	6	7	8	9	10	24
	2.08	3.46	5.19	6.92	10.38	15.57	20.77	41.53	62.30	83.06	103.83	124.59	145.36	166.12	186.89	207.65	498.36
Cabecico del Tesoro	-1.8%	**15.6%**	1.4%	**24.8%**			-4.5%	-8.9%		-0.2%		-0.5%				-2.0%	
Cabezo Lucero					6.0%												
Cap Negret						-5.4%											
Covalta								1.6%		-1.5%		-1.9%				0.9%	
Covalta HC	-8.5%	6.9%		**18.5%**		2.7%	-1.3%	-4.8%		-5.4%		2.7%				1.4%	
El Cabeçó de Mariola				**13.8%**	**23.3%**	7.7%	-4.3%	-15.3%							-4.5%		
El Cigarralejo 18			7.1%							9.2%							
El Molar 134								7.9%									
El Molar 135								6.1%									
El Monastil			-7.5%	2.3%		-7.5%											
El Oral						-4.4%											
El Puig		-11.0%				7.4%		-1.3%								1.9%	
El Xarpolar								**-14.6%**			3.1%						
La Albufereta			-11.3%			3.4%						-5.6%		3.9%			
La Alcudia						-3.0%	**24.7%**	**-24.2%**									
La Alcudia HC						-4.1%		0.0%	-10.7%		7.4%				0.9%		
La Bastida de les Alcuses 16					**-6.2%**	7.2%	4.0%	-1.0%		1.0%		-0.2%				0.7%	
La Bastida de les Alcuses 100							-4.2%			-0.9%		-0.6%				0.2%	
La Bastida de les Alcuses 118	**18.0%**	-4.6%	**-13.3%**	**21.4%**		7.2%											
La Bastida de les Alcuses HC	**20.4%**	-4.0%	-3.7%	2.9%	-9.9%	**16.2%**	10.0%	-9.0%	9.8%	-4.6%	-1.6%	2.8%			3.4%	-0.6%	-1.0%
La Escuera							0.4%										
La Serreta		-4.6%		13.1%		0.4%	-6.1%	-1.9%				-3.2%	3.1%			-0.3%	
Nécropole de Villaricos									**-14.9%**								
Orleyl				11.2%			10.4%	5.2%		11.5%		6.7%					
Puntal de Salinas				**15.6%**	**-16.2%**					-8.5%							
Tossal de Cala						-11.9%			**13.7%**								

Table 2. Comparison between Iberian weights and the weighing system used for the set from grave 200.

large series of weights without any precise context from Covalta, La Bastida de les Alcuses and La Serreta. In some sets, such as those from Cabecico del Tesoro or La Bastida de les Alcuses, section 16, we see values that align well with the standard from El Cigarralejo, while others cannot be matched.

Conclusions

As we have seen, the use of weighing during the Iberian period is multifaceted. It takes place within a very complex system of thinking, where the metrological and mathematical aspects are incorporated into a social, political and possibly religious environment. For this reason, we should be cautious to approach it from a modern perspective regarding metrology as a trade tool, controlled by institutions and not subjected to personal interpretation.

Consequently, the weighing of goods in order to assign them a premonetary function is possible, but difficult to prove. In effect, the multiplicity of relationships (economic, social, political and so on), as well as the different trade networks and metrological standards, obscure our image of the practice and of its framework of use. This is exacerbated by the identification of exogenous standards as indigenous and the difficulty to establish their order in time and in several cases their geographical origin. For this reason, the research concerning weighing standards in hoarded goods faces the issue of determining which one is credible in regard to its cultural, geographical and chronological context. For the area around Valencia, Murcia and Alicante, where most of the Iberian weights come from, we cannot establish a clear link between the practice of weighing with the identified standards and the premonetary process. However, such a link may be easier to identify for other regions of the Iberian Peninsula, as is demonstrated for the hoard from Driebes, based on the Syrian *shekel* (García-Bellido 2011: 131), or the jewellery from Seville and Padilla, with a potential connection to the weighing system from Cancho Roano (García-Bellido 1999: 377).

In order to answer the remaining questions, a better understanding of the emergence and of the development of weighing instruments in the entire Iberian Peninsula is required. Presently, research demonstrates the existence of various metrological systems, expressed in weights with morphological similarities across the entire territory. At the moment, however, we cannot satisfactorily explain this phenomenon. Answers will likely be coming from the identification of new weights which will fill the existing gaps in time and space. Understanding the origin of the morphology of the Iberian weights and of the

–0.6% and 0.2% for La Bastida de les Alcuses.

indigenous standards will probably open up new lines of research on weighing practices and their implementation.

To conclude, sets of weights with complex arithmetical construction, like the one from grave 200, show that the Iberians mastered abstract concepts and knew how to apply them to the physical world. On the one hand, we observe hoards with a premonetary purpose; on the other hand, we cannot associate their creation directly with the process of weighing. The link with trade is also not clear; because of the limited mass of weights and the limited size of scales, the tools identified are ill-suited to weigh great quantities of material. It is difficult to draw conclusions about the link between trade, premonetary currency and weighing for the Iberian Peninsula. To make progress in this matter, a considerable amount of work is still necessary when it comes to identifying relevant artefacts and interpreting them.

Acknowledgments

I would like to thank Virginia Page del Pozo and Juan García Sandoval, curators at the Museo de Arte Ibérico 'El Cigarralejo' at Mula (Murcia, Spain), for letting me access and study the collection of weighing instruments from the El Cigarralejo necropolis under excellent conditions. I also thank Carissa Di Scala and the editors, especially Dirk Brandherm, who applied their linguistic abilities to the improvement of this paper.

Bibliography

Ballester Tormo, I. 1930. *Los ponderales de tipo covaltino. Comunicaciones al IV Congreso Internacional de Arqueologia.* Valencia, Tipografía Moderna (Cuadernos de Cultura Valenciana 3/4).

Beltrán Villagrasa, P. 1948. El 'ponderarium' de Covalta y la 'Mina covaltina'. In *I Congreso Arqueológico de Levante*: 131–7. Valencia, Diputación Provincial.

Bourke, P. 2012. Automatic 3D reconstruction: an exploration of the state of the art. *GSTF Journal on Computing* 2(3): 35–40.

Callegarin, L. and García-Bellido, M. P. 2012. Métal, objets d'échanges et systèmes pondéraux en péninsule Ibérique et dans le sud-ouest de la Gaule durant l'Antiquité. In P. Pion and B. Formoso (eds), *Monnaie antique et monnaie moderne, monnaies d'ailleurs... Métissages et hybridations*: 117–39. Paris, De Boccard (Colloques de la Maison René-Ginouvès 8).

Cuadrado Díaz, E. 1964. Sobre ponderales ibéricos. In *VIII Congreso Nacional de Arqueología, Sevilla-Malaga, 1963*: 339–52. Zaragoza, Secretaría General de los Congresos Arqueológicos Nacionales.

Fletcher Valls, D. and Mata Parreño, C. 1981. Aportacíon al conocimiento de los ponderales ibéricos. *Saguntum* 16: 165–76.

Fletcher Valls, D. and Silgo Gauche, L. 1995. De nuevo sobre ponderales ibéricos. *Verdolay* 7: 271–5.

García-Bellido, M. P. 1999. Sistemas metrológicos, monedas y desarrollo económico. In *IV Symposio sobre Celtíbericos: economía, Daroca 1997*: 363–85. Zaragoza, Institución Fernando el Católico.

García-Bellido, M. P. and Blázquez, C. 2001a. *Diccionario de cecas y pueblos hispánicos I: introducción*. Madrid, Consejo Superior de Investigaciones Científicas.

García-Bellido, M. P. and Blázquez, C. 2001b. *Diccionario de cecas y pueblos hispánicos 2: catálogo de cecas y pueblos que acuñan moneda*. Madrid, Consejo Superior de Investigaciones Científicas.

García-Bellido, M. P. 2011. Hackgold and hacksilber in protomonetary Iberia. In M. P. García-Bellido, L. Callegarin and A. Jiménez Diéz (eds), *Barter, money and coinage in the Ancient Mediterranean (10th–1st centuries BC)*: 121–35. Madrid, Consejo Superior de Investigaciones Científicas (Anejo de Archivo Español de Arqueología 58).

Gorgues, A. 2010. *Economie et société dans le nord-est du domaine ibérique, IIIe–Ier s. av. J.-C.* Madrid, Consejo Superior de Investigaciones Científicas (Anejo de Archivo Español de Arqueología 52).

Gorgues, A. 2014. L'honneur et le pouvoir. Les élites de l'Âge du Fer dans le nord-est de la péninsule Ibérique. In L. Coste, S. Minvielle and F. Mougel (eds), *Le concept d'élite en Europe de l'Antiquité à nos jours*: 157–68. Pessac, Maison des sciences de l'homme d'Aquitaine.

Grau Mira, I. and Moratalla Jávega, J. 2003/2004. La regulación del peso en la Contestania ibérica: contribución al estudio formal y metrológico de las pesas de balanza. *Anales de Prehistoria y Arqueología* 19: 25–54.

Ling, J., Stos-Gale, Z., Grandin, L., Billström, K., Hjärthner-Holdar, E. and Persson, P.-O. 2014. Moving metals II: provenancing Scandinavian Bronze Age artefacts by lead isotope and elemental analyses. *Journal of Archaeological Science* 41: 106–32.

Luján, R. 2011. Payment and trade terminology on Linear B tablets. In M. P. García-Bellido, L. Callegarin and A. Jiménez Diéz (eds), *Barter, money and coinage in the Ancient Mediterranean (10th–1st centuries BC)*: 25–32. Madrid, Consejo Superior de Investigaciones Científicas (Anejo de Archivo Español de Arqueología 58).

Palaiseau, J. F. G. 1816. *Métrologie universelle ancienne et moderne ou rapport des poids et mesures des empires, royaumes, duchés et principautés des quatre parties du monde*. Bordeaux, Lavigne Jeune.

Poigt, T. 2015a. Le lot de dix poids d'El Cigarralejo (Murcie). Approche de la métrologie ibérique à partir d'un exemple archéologique. *Pallas* 97: 133–58.

Poigt, T. 2015b. Les instruments de pesée en Europe occidentale aux Âges des Métaux: conception, usages et utilisateurs (XIVe-IIIe s. av. n.è.). In M. Nordez, L. Rousseau and M. Cervel (eds), *Recherches sur l'Âge du Bronze, nouvelles approches et perspective. Actes de la journée d'étude de l'association pour la promotion des recherches archéologiques sur l'Âge du Bronze, 28 février 2014, Saint-Germain-en-Laye*: 177–9. Nantes, Association pour la promotion des recherches sur l'Âge du Bronze (Bulletin de l'APRAB, supplement 1).

Pare, C. 1997. La dimension européenne du commerce grec à la fin de la période archaïque et pendant le début de la période classique. In P. Brun and B. Chaume (eds), *Vix et les éphémères principautés celtiques. Les VIe et Ve siècles avant J.-C. en Europe centre-occidentale. Actes du colloque de Châtillon-sur-Seine (27–29 octobre 1993)*: 261–86. Paris, Editions Errance.

Pare, C. 1999. Weights and weighing in Bronze Age central Europe. In V. L. Aravantinos, J. A. Barceló and C. Brockisch-Bräuer (eds), *Eliten in der Bronzezeit: Ergebnisse zweier Kolloquien in Mainz und Athen*: 421–514. Mainz, Römisch-Germanisches Zentralmuseum (RGZM Monographien 43).

Van Driessche, V. 2009. *Etudes de métrologie grecque I: des étalons pré-monétaires au monnayage en bronze.* Louvain-la-Neuve, Association de numismatique 'Professeur Marcel Hoc'.

Vilaça, R. 2003. Acerca da existência de ponderais em contextos do Bronze Final/Ferro Inicial no território português. *O Arqueólogo Português*, Serie IV, 21: 245–88.

Vilaça, R. 2011. Ponderais do Bronze Final-Ferro Inicial do ocidente peninsular: novos dados e questões em aberto, In M. P. García-Bellido, L. Callegarin and A. Jiménez Diéz (eds), *Barter, money and coinage in the Ancient Mediterranean (10th–1st centuries BC)*: 139–67. Madrid, Consejo Superior de Investigaciones Científicas (Anejo de Archivo Español de Arqueología 58).

Of warriors, chiefs and gold. Coinage and exchange in the late pre-Roman Iron Age

David Wigg-Wolf

Abstract

The initial impulse for the production of Celtic coinages came from the experience of Celtic warriors and their leaders as mercenaries in the service of the Hellenistic states in the Mediterranean, and it was in this same context – that of ensuring the loyalty of a following and in elite exchange – that the first coinages were introduced. This paper considers the way in which the coinages then developed over the 300 years of their production, in particular how they were used and whether their introduction brought about social transformation. Furthermore, for the final phase of the coinages the questions arise as to the extent to which the appearance of regional coinages affected the role of coins as an expression of the membership of a widespread network of elites, and the effect of the appearance of smaller denominations and the spread of the use of coins beyond the elites and their immediate entourages.

Keywords: Celts, elite, iconography, coinage

Résumé

De guerriers, de chefs et d'or. Monnayage et échange a l'Âge du Fer préromain

L'impulsion initiale pour la production des monnaies celtiques provient de l'expérience des guerriers celtiques et de leurs chefs qui œuvraient comme mercenaires auprès des cités hellénistiques en Méditerranée, et c'est dans ce même contexte – celui d'assurer la fidélité d'un suivant et au sein des échanges entre les élites – que les premières monnaies furent introduites. Cet article traite de la façon dont les monnaies se sont développées au cours des 300 années de leur production, et en particulier comment elles ont été utilisées et si leur introduction a entrainé des changements au sein de la société. En outre, pour la phase finale des monnayages, des questions se posent quant à la mesure dans laquelle l'apparition de productions régionales a affecté le rôle des monnaies comme expression de l'appartenance à un vaste réseau d'élite et de l'effet de l'apparition de plus petites dénominations. La question de la propagation de l'utilisation de monnaies au-delà des élites et leurs entourages immédiats est également envisagée.

Mots-clés: Celtes, élites, iconographie, monnayage

Zusammenfassung

Von Kriegern, Häuptlingen und Gold. Münzprägung und Tausch in der späten vorrömischen Eisenzeit

Bei der Entstehung der ersten keltischen Münzprägung spielte die Erfahrung keltischer Krieger als Söldner in den Heeren der hellenistischen Staaten im Mittelmeerraum eine wichtige Rolle. Es war in diesem Kontext der Bindung einer Gefolgschaft an einen Anführer bzw. Auftraggeber und im Austausch zwischen Mitgliedern der Eliten, dass die ersten keltischen Prägungen entstanden. Im vorliegenden Beitrag wird untersucht, wie sich die Prägungen über ihren 300-jährigen Produktionszeitraum entwickelten, und vor allem wie die Münzen verwendet wurden. Auch wird diskutiert ob ihre Einführung zu sozialen Transformationen führte. Für die Spätphase keltischer Münzprägungen ist zudem zu fragen, welche Auswirkungen das Aufkommen regionaler Emissionen auf die Funktion von Münzen als Ausdruck der Mitgliedschaft in einem weitreichenden Elitenetzwerk hatte, sowie welche Folgen das Aufkommen kleinerer Nominale und die Ausweitung des Gebrauchs von Münzen über die Eliten und ihre unmittelbare Gefolgschaft hinaus nach sich zogen.

Schlüsselwörter: Kelten, Eliten, Ikonographie, Münzprägung

Introduction

The peoples of north-west and southern central Europe who entered the ancient historical record as *Keltoi* or *Celti* produced a series of quite characteristic coinages. Inspired initially by contacts with the Mediterranean world, these coinages soon developed their own distinctive artistic style and iconography, much in the tradition of Late La Tène art, and it is not without justification that the study of Celtic coins has come to form a very distinct sub-discipline within ancient numismatics. The Celtic coinages subsequently underwent intensive changes during the three centuries or so that they were produced, including developments in the materials employed and the manner in which coins were used. It is particularly the latter that is the subject of this paper, which will primarily address three interrelated questions: who was responsible for the production of the coinages; how were they used; and to what extent did their introduction bring about social transformation?

Close contacts had existed between the Celts and the Mediterranean world long before the former adopted the use and production of coins. Evidence of such contacts are the priceless objects imported from the south that were placed in the elite burials of the Iron Age Late Hallstatt culture, such as bronze vessels and fine ceramics; the burial beneath the barrow at Hochdorf even included a bronze *kline*. Mediterranean influence is also clearly visible in the architecture of some Hallstatt settlements, for example in the mud brick wall of the Heuneburg on the Upper Danube in southern Germany, or in the apsidal halls on Mont Lassois in Burgundy. These imports from the Mediterranean world and their imitations were an important element of the media of self-representation, and thus of the structures of power within and between the Iron Age elites to the north of the Alps (Fougère 2016; Kimmig 1992; Krausse 2006).

In a discussion of the rise of individualism as articulated in the appearance of distinctive attire in prehistoric cultures, A. Hernando (2016) points out that such elements of attire were 'the hallmarks of individuality and power'; at the same time,

> while these men's apparel was highly distinctive if compared with the garments worn by most people within their social group, it was nevertheless quite similar to the outfits and clothes displayed by other men of a similar high status throughout Europe. In other words: at the same time that they were singularising themselves as individuals within their respective groups, they were identifying themselves with men of other groups who were experiencing the same process (Hernando 2016: 60).

Much the same applies to the import and imitation of luxury Mediterranean goods and architecture in the Late Iron Age Hallstatt world. On the one hand, their possession emphasised the outstanding social standing of the owners; on the other, they identified them as members of a widespread network of elites whose power and connections enabled them to import such objects or have them manufactured. This network and the collectiveness it represented was a further aspect of the demonstration of their power.

However, the nature of the contacts with the Mediterranean world changed radically from the fourth century BC. During the course of what are sometimes referred to as the Celtic migrations, large groupings moved to the south and south-east, appearing on the historical stage there as raiding and invading war bands. In 387 BC the *Senones* invaded central Italy, defeating the Romans at the Battle of Allia and plundering Rome itself. Only the Capitol was spared. In 280 BC a Celtic army commanded by Brennus plundered large areas of mainland Greece, before it could be defeated one year later at Delphi. A group of survivors were finally settled in Asia Minor, giving their name to the area, Galatia.

First contacts with coinage

But it was not only as raiders that the formidable warriors left their mark in the south. They also served as mercenaries in the armies of the major powers in the Mediterranean world, of the Greeks, the Carthaginians and the Romans. It was in the course of such service that the warriors will have experienced their first contacts with the use of coinage, and this within a very specific context: as a means of cementing the relationship between a leader and his entourage — in this case between a group of mercenaries and the person who had engaged them. The written sources provide us with a great deal of information about the mechanisms and modalities of how the mercenaries were recruited and payed. For example, Livy (4,26) recounts the negotiations between the last King of Macedon, Perseus, and a group of Celts ('*Galli*' as Livy calls them) who had invaded Illyria. An agreement was reached that ten *staters* each were to be paid to 10,000 horsemen, five *staters* each to 10,000 foot soldiers and 1000 *staters* to their leader, King Clondicus. Nothing came of the agreement (Livy tells us that Perseus was too mean to pay so much money!), but Livy's description makes it clear that it was the leader of the Celtic war band who was the central figure in the negotiations. Such leaders acted as intermediaries between the employer and the warriors, and a clear hierarchy can be recognised within the war band itself. It was the leader who conducted the negotiations and secured payment — in the form of sums of money — for his following, receiving the most substantial sum himself. The ability to secure such employment for the mercenaries, and so to ensure that they received appropriate payment, cemented the position of the leader within his own community. For him coinage thus became a new means of securing his position and power. This mechanism was then to become a central feature of the manner in which coinage was introduced and functioned north of the Alps.

In areas of direct contact at the edge of the Mediterranean, for example in southern Gaul or south-east Hispania, coins will already have been known from the fourth century BC and will have been employed to a limited extent as a medium of exchange in contacts with traders from the Mediterranean world (see, for example, Bats 2011; García-Bellido 2011). But further north, in the Celtic heartlands, where Hellenistic, Italic or Carthaginian coins of the fourth century are known in only very small numbers, it is clear that virtually no coins at all reached the area in the course of exchange or trade. Thus John Sills (2003: 7, map 1), in his exhaustive study of early Celtic gold coinage in Gaul and Britain, records only 12 Macedonian Philippus *staters* of the late fourth century BC in all of Gaul, only two to the north of the Loire. In contrast to the situation near the Mediterranean littoral, in central and north Gaul it was most likely not merchants but mercenaries returning from service in the south who brought back coins from the Mediterranean with them, and their leaders later began to produce coinage themselves (cf. Nick 2006: 99–101).

Two exceptional coins found at Gersheim 'Pfuhlfeld' (Saarpfalz-Kreis) in Saarland in south-west Germany are testimony to the return of such Celtic mercenaries and provide evidence of the special role that coins which had been brought back from the south could play in Iron Age society. The two coins consist of a Carthaginian issue from Sicily/*Zeugitania punica*, struck in the late fourth century BC, and a Campanian issue from *Cales* or *Teanum Sicidunum* that was struck in the mid-third century BC (Wigg-Wolf 2010a). The most likely explanation for these unusual finds is that a warrior had returned home with them as keepsakes and unusual prestige objects demonstrating his status, perhaps from Sicily, where he could have participated in the wars between the Greeks and Carthaginians. Significantly, the only other finds of coins produced in the western Mediterranean in the years before c. 200 BC recorded from Germany on the left bank of the Rhine are of a similar date and origin: two Punic issues, one each from Schwarzenacker and Alzey (Alzey: FMRD IV 1002, 1; Schwarzenacker: FMRD III 1020, 1). These coins were most probably also brought there by mercenaries returning home, and the warrior from Gersfeld will not have been the only person from south-west Germany to have served as a mercenary in the conflicts in the western Mediterranean and to have left his trace in the archaeological record in the form of such coins.

The broader archaeological context of the two coins from Gersfeld reveals a great deal about the persons who participated in such adventures. In the closer vicinity there is a remarkable concentration of find complexes and sites that are indicative of an important early Iron Age power centre (Reinhard 2010: esp. 56 with fig. 45). At the centre of the area of settlement around Reinheim in the lower Blies valley was the 'Homerich', an 8ha plateau situated on a prominent spur above the valley, which has been interpreted as a 'princely seat' (*Fürstensitz*) (Reinhard 2004). There are also a number of richly furnished Early Iron Age burials in the surrounding area, including that of the 'Princess of Reinheim' located near the site of an opulent Roman villa. More remarkable is an enigmatic circular structure that was erected at Reinheim 'Horres' in the second half of the second century BC, consisting of a double circle of posts straddling a circular ditch (Reinhard 2010: 250–317). The Celtic coins found in association with the structure are similarly enigmatic: they have little in common with other Iron Age coin complexes found in the wider region and instead consist primarily of issues from areas in north and central Gaul further to the south-west. Similar issues are also known from other sites nearby, and only from there, for example Homerich-Ober Brücker Trischer, Homerich-Galgenberg, Pfuhlfeld and Rubenheim (Wigg-Wolf 2010b). This concentration of unusual coins suggests that during the Iron Age the area around Reinheim was a paramount centre of power that enjoyed important close links with distant regions. Its wealth and significance is reflected in the 'princely seat', the richly furnished burials and the unusual circular structure at 'Horres'.

The two coins from the Mediterranean will have been brought back from campaigns there by a high-ranking warrior who had set off south with his following and offered his services during the wars between the Greeks, Romans and Carthaginians. They were souvenirs or status symbols that articulated his extensive and powerful connections. Quite possibly the warrior came from Reinheim himself, or else the coins reached the site through a process of elite exchange with the original owner. But at this early date they will not have found employment as objects with a monetary function, for small denomination bronze coins played no role in the use of coinage in north Gaul before the late second century BC. They were more likely prestige objects, markers of status by virtue of their peculiarity.

If the two coins from Gersfeld reflect the circumstances under which the Late Iron Age inhabitants of northern Gaul came into contact with the Mediterranean world and so learned the function and use of coinage, then the contacts were very different to those that had led to the construction of the mud brick fortification at the Heuneburg or the apsidal halls at Mont Lassois, or to the import of the luxury goods placed in the richly furnished burials. In the fourth and third centuries it was no longer a matter of long-distance contacts such as had existed during the Halstatt period; instead warriors from the north were active in large numbers around the Mediterranean (Griffith 1935), where they were paid with coins and so came to gain experience of their use and function.

The example of the powerful centre at Reinheim confirms just how central the martial elites were in such contacts with the Mediterranean world, contacts that ultimately led to the adoption of coinage by the Celts. And these martial elites were also an important factor in the further development of Celtic coinages.

Own production

The earliest coins to be produced in the Celtic regions of north-western Europe were imitations of Hellenistic gold coins: in central and north Gaul above all of the *staters* of Philip of Macedon (with the head of Apollo on the obverse and the *biga*, a two-horsed chariot, on the reverse), on the Upper Danube of Alexander III (with the head of Athena and with Nike). The first of these imitations were produced soon after their prototypes at the end of the fourth and the beginning of the third centuries BC (Polenz 1982; Sills 2003: 123, fig. 26 dates the earliest Philippus imitations in Gaul to 275–250 BC) and could hardly be distinguished from the originals (Figures 1–2).

During the third and early second centuries BC mainly large denominations were produced, gold *staters* and their fractions. They are relatively rare and were struck in only small numbers (although their rarity as finds will be partly due to the fact that during the Iron Age many will have been melted down in order to produce later issues). Such small quantities of high value coins were not intended as a medium of exchange in a monetised economy involving frequent low-value transactions. They did not serve as money in the same way as coinage does today. In the vocabulary of Karl Polanyi and colleagues, they

Figure 1. Gold *stater*, Philip I (Numismatik Lanz München 154, 106).

Figure 2. Imitation of a gold *stater* of Philip I (private collection).

were not 'all-purpose money' or 'general purpose money', which could fulfil up to five basic functions: as a medium of exchange, a medium of payment, a measure of value, a unit of calculation and in order to store wealth (e.g. Polanyi 1957: 264; see also Wigg-Wolf 2011). Rather, these earliest Celtic coinages were 'special purpose money' (Polanyi 1957, 266) that only served one or two of the basic functions, in our case as a medium of exchange and a store of value. These were primarily the needs of the martial elites, either for exchange between elite groups in the form of tribute, diplomatic payments, dowries etc., or in order to secure the loyalty to a leader of a following of warriors, just as the Celtic warriors in their forays to the south had experienced coinage as a means of securing their loyalty to their employers. John Sills even proposes that the payment of soldiers was the primary purpose of the production of Celtic gold coinages: 'The episodic nature of many, if not most, of the early series, the high value of individual coins and the fact that several major issues appear to be contemporary or near-contemporary with each other suggest that they were probably struck as military pay' (Sills 2003: 224). He also sees an important distinction between the function of various denominations, suggesting 'that (*sc.* Gallo-Belgic) Ca was struck to make high-value payments rather than, say, for local trade', while 'comparatively low value issues may have been produced for commercial reasons' and gold 'retained a largely military function' (Sills 2003: 337). This topic will be addressed further below.

A series of gold hoards, most of which date to the second half of the second century BC, demonstrate how these early gold coinages were used in exchange (Figure 3). The hoards include a whole series of die-linked coins (Nick 2005; 2006: 88–104). While this in itself may not be particularly surprising, what is unusual is just how intensive the network of die links is, the distances over which the die links exist, and above all that they not only comprise links between individual pieces, but often links between whole groups of coins. It is clear that the coins were exchanged in large packages, and not with any great frequency. If they had been used in frequent exchanges involving small numbers of coins, as would be the case if they were used in intensive circulation, for example in commerce as 'general purpose money', then we should expect the die-linked groups of coins to have quickly been split up and the individual coins separated.

Many of the hoards also include other valuable objects, above all torcs, neckrings and armrings (Fitzpatrick 2005; Nick 2005). Such objects had long been used as markers of social status and in elite exchange networks (Nick 2006, 96–8), suggesting that the coins were being employed in an existing context of power and exchange, and that networks such as those which the coins reveal were long-standing.

Thus the innovative potential of coinage in this early phase lay less in coins as a medium of exchange and trade within the context of a monetised economy, and more in its role as a medium of the demonstration and consolidation of power for the elites within individual groups, as well as a medium of communication between various elite groups. For Nick (2006: 100) it is primarily the first of these two roles that characterised the early gold coinage, as a medium of social differentiation. This means that rather than being the catalyst for new forms, the coins were employed within existing contexts of exchange that involved torcs and other objects of value.

Later developments

The second half of the second century BC then saw an important development in the form and function of coinage in Gaul. Although the earliest imitations could hardly be distinguished from the originals (Figure 2) and enjoyed often very widespread distribution, soon coinages of a more regional nature with their own imagery developed, imagery that had little to do with the original Hellenistic prototypes (Figures 4–5). In addition, from the mid-second century BC smaller denominations appeared alongside the high-value gold issues, first of all in silver and cast tin-bronze (potin), later in struck bronze. The emergence of smaller denominations coincided with the emergence of the proto-urban *oppida*, where the low-value coins can appear in huge numbers. Already at the turn of the second to the first century BC potin coinages accounted for as much as three quarters of the coins at north Gallic *oppida* such as the Titelberg or Martberg,

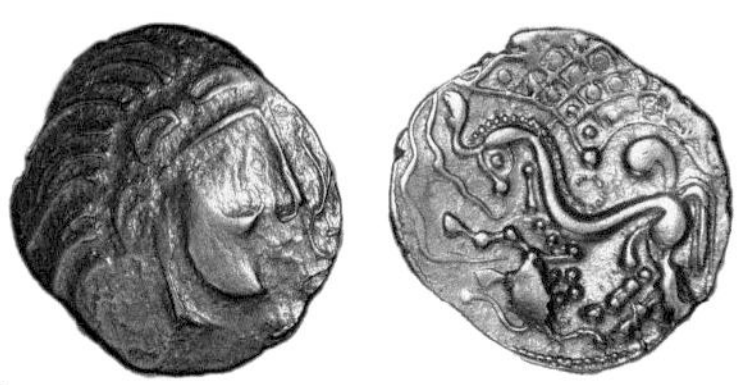

Figure 4. Gold *stater* of the Parisii (LT 7777: private collection).

Figure 5. Gold *stater* of the Treveri (Scheers 30 classe V; find spot: Martberg).

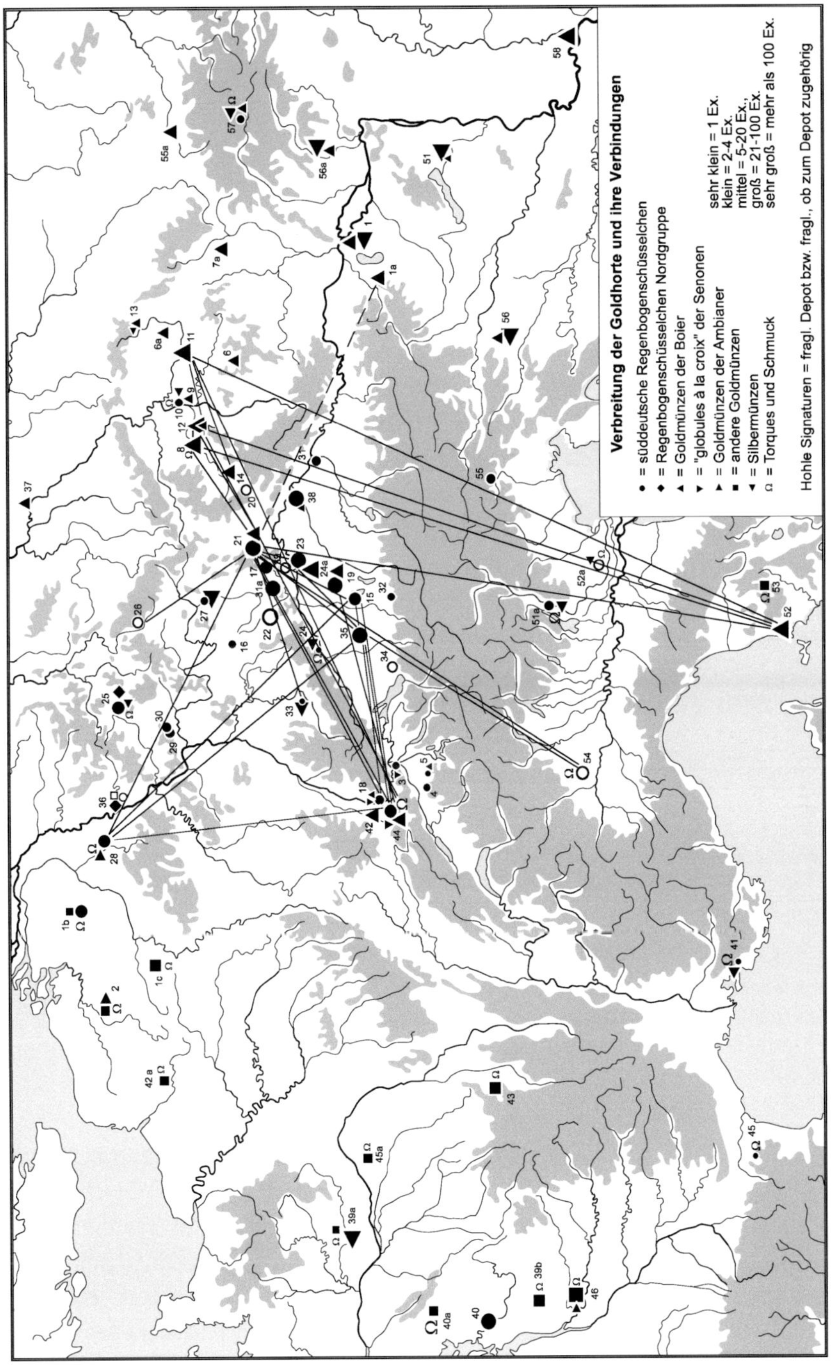

Figure 3. Distribution of the gold hoards of the second and early first centuries BC, and the die links between them (Nick 2005, Abb. 1).

Titelberg

	AV	AR	Pot	AE
LTD1	1	15	137	7
	0.6%	*9.4%*	*85.6%*	*4.4%*
LTD2a	7	217	275	23
	1.3%	*41.6%*	*52.7%*	*4.4%*
LTD2b	5	22	4	1788
	0.3%	*1.2%*	*0.2%*	*98.3%*

Martberg settlement

	AV	AR	Pot	AE
LTD1	1	29	80	1
	0.9%	*26.1%*	*72.1%*	*0.9%*
LTD2a	4	95	124	4
	1.7%	*41.8%*	*54.6%*	*1.7%*
LTD2b	-	1	1	98
		1.0%	*1.0%*	*98.0%*

Martberg sanctuary

	AV	AR	Pot	AE
LTD1	-	7	33	2
		16.7%	*78.6%*	*4.8%*
LTD2a	15	148	173	5
	4.4%	*43.4%*	*50.7%*	*1.5%*
LTD2b	3	3	1	340
	0.9%	*0.9%*	*0.3%*	*98.0%*

Table 1. The proportions of coins of various metals at the Titelberg *oppidum* (Reding 1972) and the Martberg settlement and sanctuary (FMRD IV 4,1 and 4,2) in the periods LTD1 (c. 150–95 BC), LTD2a (c. 95–55 BC) and LTD2b (c. 55–25 BC).

and struck bronzes were almost the only coins produced in the region after Caesar's Gallic War (Table 1).

The nature of this final phase of Celtic coinages was very different to the exclusively high-value coinage of the first century and a half.

These low-value coins could now fulfil a broader spectrum of functions than the large gold units, including trade and exchange involving smaller amounts. Gradually something that had some of the characteristics of a market economy began to emerge along the lines of Polanyi's 'general purpose money', albeit at a very basic level. This development will have gone hand-in-hand with the growth of the *oppida*, which were based partly on the specialisation of activities rather than self-sufficiency and autarchy. With low-value coins individuals could now obtain the necessities of everyday life more easily, with the result that they also had more time, and thus work capacity, for their relevant specialisation. This in turn will have led to a strengthening of the *oppida* as economic centres.

But even if coins were now available to and useful for a wider social spectrum and their economic use was now more extended, nevertheless the coinage itself still remained an instrument of the self-representation and exercise of power for the aristocratic elites. This is best illustrated by the legends which are found on coins in Gaul from the late second century. On the whole they refer to persons (Colbert de Beaulieu *et al.* 1998). For the most part we do not know who the individuals concerned are, since we can seldom connect the legends with known historical figures; but generally they will have been *nobiles*, members of the aristocratic elite. The most famous of all is surely Vercingetorix, the leader of the Gallic resistance against Julius Caesar in 52 BC, who placed his name on coins (Figure 6).

Only in a few cases are tribes rather than persons named, and then only after Caesar's conquest of Gaul; for example the legend REMO(S) is to be found on coins struck by the Remi (Scheers 146–7) (Figure 7). Nick (2006: 233, 237) suggests that these rare examples reflect a deliberate policy on the part of Rome to establish stable administrative units to replace the unstable competition between *nobiles* and factions that otherwise characterised tribal groupings.

Figure 6. Gold *stater* of Vercingetorix (LT 3778; Bibliothèque nationale de France).

However, such examples are rare, and for the most part the coinage, even in this final phase, appears to have remained in the sphere of the interest of individuals (whereby an individual could, of course, act as the representative of a tribe).

Figure 7. Bronze coin of the Remi with the legend REMOS (Scheers 146) (nomos 1, 25).

Apart from such references to individuals in the legends found on the coins, the iconography of the last Celtic coinages in northern Gaul also tells us a great deal about the ways in which coinage could be used for self-representation, and thus by individuals and elites in order to cement their claims to power. After the Gallic War and the conquest of Gaul by the Romans, coinages started to appear in large numbers which incorporate classical 'Roman' elements in their iconography, or else directly imitate Roman coin types. For example, on the bronze coins with the legends ANDOBRV and GARMANOS that are attributed to the Atrebates (Scheers 46) little remains of the abstract elements of the Celtic issues of the first half of the first century BC (Figure 8; cf. Figures 4–5).

Figure 8. Bronze coin of the Atrebates with the legend ANDOBRV (Scheers 46 classe I) (J. Elsen 92, 53).

A further example is provided by the bronze and silver issues of the Treveri (Loscheider 2005). Several are direct imitations of coin types struck by the rival parties of the civil war between Caesar and Pompey (Figures 9–10).

Treveran cavalry were actively involved in the campaigns in Spain and north Africa and will have

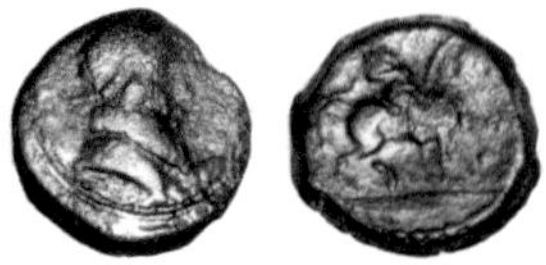

Figure 9. Bronze coin of the Treveri with the legend ARDA (Scheers 30a classe II) (Inst. f. Arch. Wiss. Abt. II, Goethe Universität, Frankfurt).

Figure 10: *Denarius* of the Roman Republic (RRC 447/1a), struck 49 BC (American Numismatic Society 1944.100.3273).

encountered the prototypes there. Here, this direct experience of the Roman coinage in a military context will have played an important part in the adoption of elements of the iconography of the Roman coinage – just as it was Celtic mercenaries who three hundred years earlier had played a central role in the adoption of coinage north of the Alps. In some cases the types themselves give the impression that they could have been the products of a Roman mint, and for some issues that have an extremely 'Roman' appearance it has even been suggested that the dies for the coins were actually provided by the Romans (Creighton 2005: 106; Nash 1987: 129). Loscheider (1995) identified one particularly remarkable case: the obverse of the Treveran silver type Scheers 30a classe I bears a striking similarity to a silver issue of the Numidian King Juba I. Loscheider suggests that the die for the Treveran coin was hubbed (i.e. moulded) directly from a Numidian coin. If this was the case, then a Treveran must have had the die made from a coin that he had brought back with him from the civil wars. However, there is an alternative explanation: that a die originally intended for a coin of Juba was provided by the Romans and re-cut with the new legend before being used by the Treveri. The Romans were by no means unaware of the power of coinage as a medium of self-representation, as is impressively evidenced by the great variety and choice of types on the Late Republican *denarius* issues. They clearly also saw the opportunities that coinage provided for pro-Roman Gallic *nobiles*, indeed even providing selected members of the elites with coin dies.

An Early Roman burial at Chassenard (Dép. Allier) in central Gaul provides further striking evidence for this role that coinage could play in both the self-representation of the Gallic elites and in their relationship with Rome. The grave goods include two pairs of coin dies for gold or silver issues of the emperor Tiberius. As von Kaenel (2002) has so convincingly argued, the Roman coin dies apparently enjoyed a high symbolic value for the deceased or the community that buried him. They document his status and close relationship with Rome and the Roman Emperor.

Interestingly, in contrast to other Early Roman imperial coin dies, the two pairs of dies from Chassenard are not made of bronze, but of iron. Their shape is also unusual. Von Kaenel (2002)suggests that they may have been produced purely as prestige goods and were never intended for actual use.

Figure 11: Bronze coin of the Lexovii with the legend PVBLICOS LIXOVIO SIMISSOS / CISIABOS CATTOS VERCOBRETO (LT 7159) (Or Gestion Numismatique. Réf. n° 10559).

In one case alignment with Rome was even indicated by recourse to the name of a Roman denomination in the legend: certain issues of the Lexovii were designated as SIMISSOS (= Semis) (Figure 11). The type is also significant for another reason. The complete obverse and reverse legends read PVBLICOS LIXOVIO SIMISSOS and CISIABOS CATTOS VERCOBRETO, making the coin not only a rare example of a direct reference by name to a Gallic tribe but also the only occasion when a Vergobret, a Gaulish magistrate, is mentioned on a coin. This use of Roman elements was an important aspect of the language of power following the Roman conquest of Gaul. In this way the Celtic elites demonstrated their loyalty to Rome and so secured their own position within their tribal grouping, a position that depended to a great extent on Rome's favour. In this context it is important to remember that the Gallic War was not a simple matter of a black-and-white conflict between Rome and the Gauls. For many tribes and tribal groupings an alliance with Rome presented a unique opportunity of gaining the upper hand in conflicts with other groupings. To a certain extent the Gallic War was in fact a 'Gallic civil war' that involved conflict not only between, but also within tribes, such as the struggle between pro- and anti-Roman factions within the Treveri in 54/53 BC (Caes. Gall. 5,3,36. 53, 55, 58).

Discussion

From the above it is clear that in the Late Iron Age world of Gaul, coinage was much more than just an economic medium, more than just a measure of value that could be useful in exchange or to store wealth. Coins were also — and in the earliest stages of Celtic coinage in fact primarily — a medium of the exercise of power and the formation of identity on the part of the elites. This is perhaps in no way surprising, given that Roman coins also fulfilled this role, even in the Roman economy, which enjoyed a much greater degree of monetisation and where the economic function of coins was significantly more developed. Nor should we forget that in today's Europe, Euro coins and banknotes propagate the manifold aspects and layers of European and national identity in a quite subtle manner. It was only in the last phase of the coinage, after the Gallic War, that we can speak of genuine monetisation in which coinage acquired a more universal use outside the sphere of elite exchange and was employed for a wider spectrum of transactions. It had now become something more like general purpose money, but even then only to a limited extent and in the context of the *oppida* and other important centres.

These latest, post-Conquest coinages of Gaul were very different creatures from their predecessors of the third century BC. As we have seen, the earliest issues were an important element not only of elite self-representation and power structures, but also of elite exchange. They were exchanged over significant distances, as the gold hoards discussed above demonstrate. In this way they formed a connecting element in exchange and relationships between individual groups and elites, just as in the Hallstatt culture imports from the Mediterranean world played an important part in the network of power structures of Early Iron Age societies. On the one hand, the outstanding social position of leaders within their groupings was emphasised by the possession and production of coins, and their wealth was an articulation of their claim to power within their own grouping. On the other hand, since the elites of different groupings had recourse to the same language of power, e.g. gold coinage, they identified themselves as members of a widespread network of ruling elites, thus further emphasising their status. This is particularly apparent in the gold hoards discussed above, which are telling evidence of the important role of coins in elite exchange, as well as demonstrating the great distances over which contacts between the elite groups existed.

Furthermore, the combination of coins together with other long-standing prestige goods such as torcs in the hoards suggest that, at least initially, they were being used within existing contexts and forms of exchange and transaction, rather than being the catalyst for new forms at this early stage. However, we must nevertheless assume that the availability of units of exchange that were more practical and easily portable than, for example, torcs will not have been without its effects on the range and types of such transactions.

Two questions arise from the subsequent development of the coinage from the mid-second century, when coinages took on a more regional character and smaller denominations were struck in larger numbers. First, to what extent did the appearance of regional coinages affect the role of coins as an expression of the membership of a widespread network of elites? And second, what was the effect of the appearance of smaller denominations and the spread of the use of coins beyond the elites and their immediate entourages?

With regard to the first point, the regional coinages of the first century did not enjoy the widespread distribution of many of the earliest issues. For example, in contrast to the *Vogelkopf* (bird's head) rainbow cup *staters* that are a regular component of the gold hoards discussed above, the Treveran *staters* of the second quarter of the first century BC are found only in small numbers outside the territory of the Treveri (Figure 12). This was a coinage for a regional or local context, not for widespread exchange with distant groups. The regionalism is also visible in the iconography of the coins. During the course of the second century BC direct imitations of Mediterranean types were gradually replaced by regional iconographic traditions, and many of them can be attributed to Celtic tribal units that are known from the historical record, such as the Treveri or the Parisii (Figures 4–5). Instead of the connective element of the early phase that is visible in the gold hoards, regional identities now became apparent. Individual groups singled themselves out from others through their own coinage. A similar development is to be observed, if somewhat later, for the potin (cast tin-bronze) emissions. The earliest potins in north and east Gaul (e.g. the '*à sanglier*' [Féliu 2008: fig. 26] and group A of the '*grosse tête*' potins [Nick 2000: Karte 16]) were supra-regional coinages and enjoyed an extremely wide distribution. However, from the second third of the first century BC they were increasingly superseded by regional types, such as the Treveran potins (Loscheider 1998: 102–7).

This in turn is of significance for the second point, the appearance of smaller denominations, for this growing regionalism coincided with the appearance of growing numbers of extensive low-denomination coinages. This meant that the iconography of the coinages addressed a very new audience. To be sure, the massive silver coinages of the mid-first century are to be associated with Caesar's Gallic War and thus with the payment of mercenaries, a context reminiscent of that in which Celtic warriors had first encountered coinage. However, the massive post-Caesarian bronze issues circulated only locally. As we have seen above, they generally bear legends referring to individuals, presumably *nobiles* who initiated the production of the coinages. The communication these coinages and their iconography represent was communication between a chieftain and a following, or a tribal leader and a tribe; it was no longer communication that articulated connections between elites, between the leaders of separate tribal groupings. This in turn implies that coins were now being used in a very different sphere of exchange within the discourse of power, as is also evidenced by the predominantly local distribution of the majority of these coinages.

The very Roman iconography also speaks of a new alignment of power structures. Instead of basing power on links with other elite groups, it is a reference to Rome that becomes the justification of power. At a number of levels, what in the second century BC gives the appearance — at least in the coinage — of being a closely linked network, in the first century BC had become increasingly disarticulated.

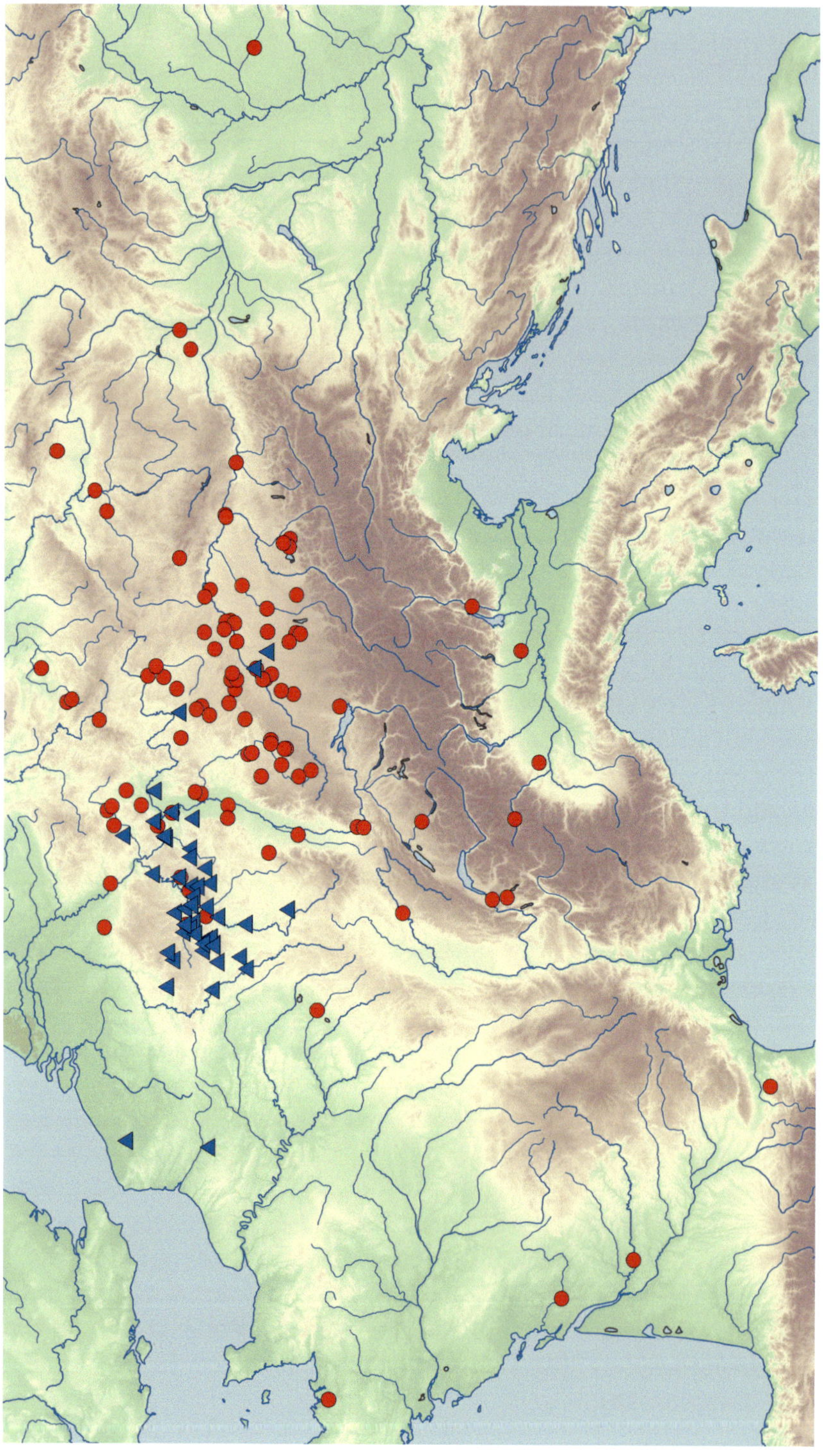

Figure 12: Distribution of the *Vogelkopf* (bird's head) rainbow cup *staters* (red circles: after Nick 2006: Karte 7) and the Treveran *staters* Scheers 30 classe V (blue triangles: after Loscheider 1998: 136).

But although the networks and the character of exchange and communication involving coins changed, one thing remained. In all phases of the Celtic coinage, it served the interests and needs of the elites; initially the coins were an element in the articulation of power relationships within a network of elites, later an expression of individuals' status within their own communities, often emphasised with reference to an external power, Rome.

Abbreviations

RRC	Crawford, M. 1973. *Roman Republican coinage*. Cambridge, Cambridge University Press.
FMRD	Akademie der Wissenschaften Mainz (eds). 1960 ff. *Fundmünzen der Römischen Zeit in Deutschland*. Berlin/Mainz, Gebrüder Mann/Zabern.
LT	de La Tour, H. 1892. *Atlas des monnaies gauloises*. Paris, Plon.
Scheers	Scheers, S. 1977. *La Gaule Belgique. Traité de numismatique celtique 2*. Paris, Les Belles Lettres.

Bibliography

Bats, M. 2011. Métal, objets précieux et monnaie dans les échanges en Gaule méridionale protohistorique (VIIe–IIe s. a. C). In M. P. García-Bellido, L. Callegarin and A. Jiménéz Díez (eds), *Barter, money and coinage in the Ancient Mediterranean (10th–1st centuries BC)*: 97–109. Madrid, Consejo Superior de Investigaciones Científicas.

Colbert de Beaulieu, J.-P. and Fischer, B. 1998. Les légendes monétaires. Recueil des inscriptions gauloises 4. *Gallia*, supplément 45.

Creighton, J. 2005. Links between the classical imagery in post-Caesarean Belgica and the rest of the Roman world. In J. Metzler and D. Wigg-Wolf (eds), *Die Kelten und Rom: Neue numismatische Forschungen (Fond de Gras/Titelberg, Luxemburg, 30.4.–3.5.1998)*: 87–107. Mainz, Zabern.

Féliu, C. 2008. *Leuques et Médiomatriques à La Tène moyenne et finale: organisation sociale et territoriale de l'habitat dans deux cités du nord-est de la Gaule du IIIe au Ier siècle avant notre ère*. PhD dissertation, Université Marc Bloch, Strasbourg II. https://tel.archives-ouvertes.fr/tel-00613830.

Fitzpatrick, A. P. 2005. Gifts for the golden gods: Iron Age hoards of torques and coins. In C. C. Haselgrove and D. Wigg-Wolf (eds), *Iron Age coinage and ritual practices*: 157–82. Mainz, Zabern.

Fougère, F. 2016. *La tombe de Vix: un trésor celte entre histoire et légende*. Lyon, Fage éditions.

García-Bellido, M. P. 2011. Hackgold and hacksilber in protomonetary Iberia. In M. P. García-Bellido, L. Callegarin and A. Jiménéz Díez (eds), *Barter, money and coinage in the Ancient Mediterranean (10th–1st centuries BC)*: 121–38. Madrid, Consejo Superior de Investigaciones Científicas.

Griffith, G. T. 1935. *The mercenaries of the Hellenistic world*. Cambridge, Cambridge University Press.

Hernando, A. 2016. The impact of social differentiation on identity: lights and shadows of the individualization process. In M. Fernández-Götz and D. Krausse (eds), *Eurasia at the dawn of history: urbanization and social change*, 52–64. Cambridge, Cambridge University Press.

Kimmig, W. 1992. Etruskischer und griechischer Import im Spiegel westhallstättischer Fürstengräber. In L. Aigner-Foresti (ed.), *Etrusker nördlich von Etrurien. Etruskische Präsenz in Norditalien und nördlich der Alpen sowie ihre Einflüsse auf die einheimischen Kulturen. Akten des Symposions von Wien, Schloss Neuwaldegg, 2.-5. Oktober 1989*: 281–328. Vienna, Österreichische Akademie der Wissenschaften.

Krausse, D. 2006. Prunkgräber der nordwestalpinen Späthallstattkultur: Neue Fragestellungen und Untersuchungen zu ihrer sozialhistorischen Deutung. In C. von Carnap-Bornheim, D. Krausse and A. Wesse (eds), *Herrschaft, Tod, Bestattung: zu den vor- und frühgeschichtlichen Prunkgräbern als archäologisch-historische Quelle: Internationale Fachkonferenz Kiel 16.-19. Oktober 2003*: 61–80. Bonn, Rudolf Habelt.

Loscheider, R. 1995. Ein Beitrag Numidiens zur keltischen Numismatik des Trevererlandes: Arda d'argent au buste de la victoire laurée. *Hémecht* 47: 579–90.

Loscheider, R. 1998. Untersuchungen zum spätlatènezeitlichen Münzwesen des Trevererlandes. *Archaeologia Mosellana* 3: 69–225.

Loscheider, R. 2005. Militär und Romanisierung: Zum Münzwesen der Treverer nach dem Gallischen Krieg. In J. Metzler and D. Wigg-Wolf (eds), *Die Kelten und Rom: Neue numismatische Forschungen (Fond de Gras/Titelberg, Luxemburg, 30.4.-3.5.1998)*: 109–27. Mainz, Zabern.

Nash, D. 1987. *Coinage in the Celtic world*. London, Seaby.

Nick, M. 2000. *Die keltischen Münzen von Typ 'Sequanerpoti'. Eine Studie zu Typologie, Chronologie und geographischer Zuweisung eines ostgallischen Münztyps*. Rahden, Leidorf.

Nick, M. 2005. Am Ende des Regenbogens... Ein Interpretationsversuch von Hortfunden mit keltischen Goldmünzen. In C. C. Haselgrove and D. Wigg-Wolf (eds), *Iron Age coinage and ritual practices*: 115–55. Mainz, Zabern.

Nick, M. 2006. *Gabe, Opfer, Zahlungsmittel: Strukturen keltischen Münzgebrauchs im westlichen Mitteleuropa*. Rahden, Leidorf.

Polanyi, K. 1957. The economy as instituted process. In K. Polanyi, C.M. Arensberg and H.W. Pearson (eds), *Trade and market in the early empires: economics in history and theory*, 243–69. Glencoe (Ill.), Free Press.

Polenz, H. 1982. Münzen in latènezeitlichen Gräbern Mitteleuropas aus der Zeit zwischen 300 und 50 vor Christi Geburt. *Bayerische Vorgeschichtsblätter* 45: 27–222.

Reding, L. 1972. *Les monnaies gauloises du Tetelbierg*. Luxembourg, Ministère des Arts et des Sciences.

Reinhard, W. 2004. 'Fürstensitz' von Reinheim. *Archäologie in Deutschland* 2004/4: 50.

Reinhard, W. 2010. *Kelten, Römer und Germanen im Bliesgau*. Reinheim, Stiftung Europäischer Kulturpark (Denkmalpflege im Saarland 3/3).

Sills, J. 2003. *Gaulish and early British gold coinage*. London, Spink.

von Kaenel, H.-M. 2002. Ungewöhnliche Grabbeigaben — Überlegungen zu den Münzstempeln in einem Grab der frühen Kaiserzeit aus Chassenard (Allier). *Bericht der Römisch-Germanischen Kommission* 83: 179–90.

Wigg-Wolf, D. 2010a. Zwei seltene Münzen aus Gersheim. In W. Reinhard, *Kelten, Römer und Germanen im Bliesgau*: 50. Reinheim, Stiftung Europäischer Kulturpark (Denkmalpflege im Saarland 3/3).

Wigg-Wolf, D. 2010b Fundmünzen aus Reinheim 'Horres' und Umgebung. In W. Reinhard, *Kelten, Römer und Germanen im Bliesgau*: 291–303. Reinheim, Stiftung Europäischer Kulturpark (Denkmalpflege im Saarland 3/3).

Wigg-Wolf, D. 2011. The function of Celtic coinages in northern Gaul. In M. P. García-Bellido, L. Callegarin and A. Jiménéz Díez (eds), *Barter, money and coinage in the Ancient Mediterranean (10th-1st centuries BC)*: 301–41. Madrid, Consejo Superior de Investigaciones Científicas.

New wealth from the Old World: glass, jet and mirrors in the late fifteenth to early sixteenth century indigenous Caribbean

Joanna Ostapkowicz

Abstract

One of the most momentous cross-cultural collisions occurred in the Caribbean in 1492, heralding a period of rapid change in both 'New' and 'Old' Worlds. During the early years of the colonial period, when new relationships were being established, material objects became active agents in the interactions between the indigenous Taíno and the Spanish. The Taíno gifted the Spanish with objects that had significance in their own world, in an attempt to enmesh the Spanish into Taíno socio-political and economic networks. In turn, Spanish objects entered into Taíno value systems. Glass and jet beads, mirrors and brass ornaments were integrated into prestigious objects, such as the two surviving Taíno cotton sculptures that form the focus of this paper: a belt in the collections of the Weltmuseum Wien and a composite sculpture in the Museo Nazionale Preistorico Etnografico 'Luigi Pigorini', Rome. These pieces offer a glimpse into how Old World exotics were reinterpreted and integrated into indigenous value systems during a period of cultural transition and change.

Keywords: Caribbean, early colonial period (AD 1492–1550), Taíno/Lucayans, European 'exotics', indigenous value systems

Résumé

Nouvelles richesses du Ancien Monde : verre, jais et miroirs à la fin du XV et au début du XVI siècle dans les caraïbes indigènes

Une des plus importantes collisions interculturelles s'est produite en 1492 dans les caraïbes, annonçant une période de rapide changement au sein du Nouveau et de l'Ancien Monde. Pendant les premières années de la période coloniale, quand les nouvelles relations s'établissaient, les biens matériels devinrent des agents actifs au sein des relations entre les indigènes Taïno et les Espagnols. Les Taïnos ont donné aux Espagnols des objets qui avaient une signification dans leur monde dans le but d'emmener les Espagnols dans les systèmes socio-politique et économique Taïno. A leur tour, les objets espagnols entrèrent au sein des systèmes socio-politiques et économique Taïno. Les perles en jais et en verre, les miroirs et les ornements en laiton furent intégrés comme des objets prestigieux à l'image des deux sculptures de coton Taïno qui sont l'objet de cet article: une ceinture issue des collections du Musée du Monde de Vienne et une sculpture composite dans le Musée National de Préhistoire et d'Ethnographie 'Luigi Pigorini', Rome. Ces pièces donnent un aperçu de la façon dont les produits exotiques de l'Ancien Monde ont été réinterprétés et intégrés dans les systèmes de valeur indigènes pendant une période de transition culturelle et de changement.

Mots-clés: Caraïbe, début de la période coloniale (AD 1492–1550), Taïnos/Lucayens, produits exotiques européens, systèmes de valeur indigène

Zusammenfassung

Neue Reichtümer aus der Alten Welt: Glas, Gagat und Spiegel am Ende des 15. und Beginn des 16. Jahrhunderts in der indigenen Karibik

Zu einer der folgenträchtigsten Kollisionen zwischen verschiedenen Kulturen kam es 1492 in der Karibik, womit eine Zeit rapiden Wandels sowohl in der „Neuen" als auch in der „Alten" Welt eingeleitet wurde. In den Anfangsjahren der Kolonialzeit, als neue Beziehungen Gestalt annahmen, wurden materielle Gegenstände zu aktiven Medien im gegenseitigen Umgang zwischen indigenen Taíno und Spaniern. Die Taíno beschenkten die Spanier mit Gegenständen, die in ihrer eigenen Welt als Bedeutungsträger agierten; damit versuchten sie, die Spanier in ihre eigenen soziopolitischen und wirtschaftlichen Netzwerke zu verstricken. Im Gegenzug hielten spanische Gegenstände Einzug in die Wertsysteme der Taíno. Perlen aus Glas und Gagat, Spiegel und Messingschmuck wurden in Prestigeobjekte eingearbeitet, wie zum Beispiel in die beiden erhaltenen Taíno Baumwollskulpturen, die im Mittelpunkt dieses Beitrags stehen: ein Gürtel in den Sammlungen des Weltmuseums Wien und eine Kompositskulptur im Museo Nazionale Preistorico Etnografico 'Luigi Pigorini', Rom. Diese Gegenstände gewähren einen Einblick in die Praxis der Reinterpretation und Integration altweltlicher Exotika in indigene Wertsysteme während einer Zeit kulturellen Übergangs und Wandels.

Schlüsselwörter: Karibik, frühe Kolonialzeit (1492–1550 n. Chr.), Taíno/ Lucayan, europäische Exotika, inidigene Wertsysteme

Introduction

1492 marked a critical turning point in history, when two worlds collided and a truly global economy began. During the early years of this new trans-Atlantic world, when languages failed to connect people, material culture was an immediate means of communication and negotiation, initially carried out via mutually beneficial transactions. The 'Taíno' (the problematic umbrella term that has come to represent the indigenous people of the Caribbean Greater Antilles, but glosses over their cultural and linguistic diversity; Curet 2014) were enthusiastic in their acquisition of introduced Spanish goods such as brass, glass beads and mirrors. Crucially, these 'exotics' had resonance with their own valuables, such as the lustrous surfaces of gold and *guanín* (a gold-copper alloy), the iridescent qualities of shell and bird feather ornaments, the rich tones of hardwoods and the deep greens of jadeites. The allure of such materials has been termed the 'aesthetic of brilliance' (Oliver 2000; Saunders 1998; 1999; 2003), binding circum-Caribbean cultures in a network of exchanges that spanned the vast region and stretched into the surrounding mainland. Vibrancy, brilliance and iridescence whether in materials, artefacts or natural phenomena

— were qualities understood to have cosmological force, tapping into the numinous. Valuables central to Taíno elite status, such as *guiazas*, or masks, ceremonial chairs known as *duhos* and elaborate cotton belts, were specifically gifted to the Spanish by *caciques*, or chiefs, in efforts to draw the foreigners into indigenous socio-political and economic networks, and in so doing build long-term reciprocal relationships. In turn, the objects the Spanish exchanged entered into Taíno systems of value. Glass beads, mirrors and brass ornaments were integrated into high-value objects, such as the two surviving Taíno cotton pieces that form the focus of this paper: a composite zoo/anthropomorphic sculpture in the Museo Nazionale Preistorico Etnografico 'L. Pigorini' in Rome (Figure 1), and a belt in the collections of the Weltmuseum Wien (Figure 2), both attributed on stylistic grounds to Hispaniola (Haiti/Dominican Republic; for ease of reference, the two pieces will be referred to in the remainder of the text as the 'Pigorini *cemi*' and 'Vienna belt').

Figure 1. Three views of the Pigorini *cemí*, showing the two faces of this janus-like figurine: the human side featuring a rhinoceros horn mask, and the animal face — possibly that of a bat — covered lavishly with green glass beads. This composite sculpture consists of an elaborate, figural top (*cemí*) positioned over an adult-sized belt, wrapped around a wood base (a later display mount). Its history in Europe can be traced back to the 1680 inventory of Fernando Cospi's collection in Bologna. Cotton, shell and glass beads, mirrors, gold, vegetable fibre, feathers(?), resin, pigment, wood base; AD 1492–1524 (Bayesian modelled), Hispaniola. H: 31.5cm; Diam: 20.5cm (max). Photograph: Ostapkowicz; courtesy of the Polo Museale del Lazio - Museo Nazionale Preistorico Etnografico "L.Pigorini", su concessione del Mibact, acc no. 4190.

These objects provide insight into the value systems of the indigenous Caribbean during the early years of contact, and this paper serves as an introduction to ongoing work on their manufacture, context and meaning.[1]

The early colonial period, when interactions between the Spanish and Taíno were at their most sustained and intense, is generally thought to have ended c. 1520 on Hispaniola, with Taíno demographic and cultural collapse due to forced labour, disease and religious conversion (e.g. Deagan 1987b: 343). However, there are suggestions that some cultural traditions persisted: in 1517, many *indios* were escaping into the mountains and other regions outside Spanish control (Guitar 1998: 249) and, left 'unsupervised', were reverting back to traditional ways, to 'do those things that their parents and ancestors had done' (Guitar 1998: 226–7). By 1534 the Spanish were reporting the return of some *indios* to 'idolatry, vices, sins and other abominable customs' (Guitar 1998: 132). Archival documentation suggests that indigenous rebellions, with *cimarron* (escaped African slaves) support, continued into the 1540s (Guitar 1998: 391), that some cultural practices, such as *areítos* (ceremonies involving dance and songs), were still being practised at this time, and that cacical authority was still recognised by the Spanish as late as 1547 (though not on the scale of influence seen during the first two decades of the colonial encounter; Guitar 1998: 115, 207). However, the use of elite accoutrements, such as belts and elaborate *cemís* (a representation of a spirit, deity or ancestor), which required skilled, intensive labour and an intact cultural context, could not be maintained for long. As Guitar (1998: 423) acknowledges, 'after 1492, the privileged groups of Classic Taíno artistic specialists who designed and produced prestige goods for *caciques* [...] disappeared' and only domestic artistry survived (see also Deagan 2004). Given the above, and the uncertainties pertaining to this turbulent period of indigenous history, a date of 1550 seems a reasonable chronological marker for the demise of Taíno 'traditional' elite material culture (Ostapkowicz 2013). However, this in no way implies an end point to colonial interactions, nor to the ongoing merging of cultural traditions (cf. Guitar *et al.* 2006; Hayes and Cipolla 2015).

[1] As the study of these pieces is as yet incomplete, one caveat is necessary: there is still some uncertainty over the security of association between the European materials on the Vienna belt, given that they are not fully integrated into the belt's weave (Ostapkowicz 2013). In contrast, while the Pigorini *cemí* features European beads woven tightly into its structure, some have questioned whether the entire piece is an early sixteenth century pastiche made for a princely *Kunstkammer* rather than an indigenous creation (Scalini 2001: 129–32, 142). While there are clear interventions — the cotton structure being nailed to an early wooden display mount — there are many other features that argue for both the Pigorini and Vienna pieces being the work of indigenous hands, conforming to Taíno aesthetics and demonstrating stylistic parallels with depictions of such artefacts in other media (i.e. ceramics). Given this, while suggestions raised in this paper are in some instances speculative and must await confirmation through further work, they are based on a firm foundation of comparative studies and contextual ethnographic documentation.

Figure 2. Cotton belt with indigenous shell beads and European jet, brass and mirror additions, featuring a central zoomorphic *cemí* with upturned hands, AD 1475–1635 (95.4% probability; three radiocarbon dates combined). Full length, with straps, 116.5 cm (beaded strap only, 85.5cm), height 70mm. Photograph: Ostapkowicz; courtesy of the Weltmuseum Wien, inv. no. 10.443.

The two artefacts described in this paper are the only surviving Taíno elite objects from this relatively short period of initial interaction currently known. As such they are a critical starting point for assessing how 'valuables' such as European exotics resonated with the value systems of the peoples of the New World.

Capturing foreign wealth

From their very first encounters, the Spanish and the Taíno were bound together by gift giving, exchange and barter (Keehnen 2011; 2012; Mol 2007; Oliver 2000; 2009). Each had ample experience in far-flung trade — the Spanish within Europe, North Africa and, albeit less directly, Asia (indeed, the aims of the Columbian enterprise were to establish direct trade with Japan and China; Kagan 1991: 56; Kamen 2005) and the Taíno (as well as other Caribbean peoples) throughout the length of the Caribbean chain (Siegel 2011), into the South American mainland (Hofman *et al.* 2007; 2011) and possibly the Isthmo-Colombian region (Rodriguez 2011). Neither, therefore, was new to the allure of the exotic (Helms 1988). Worth was quickly established by both parties, initially fuelled by the desirability of the new, but as interaction increased, there was a growing understanding of what the 'Other' valued most: gold was clearly the focus of Spanish interest while for the Taíno (who also valued gold), it was other highly coveted luminous materials (whether glass or brass). These valuables — or rather their qualities — were long appreciated on both sides of the Atlantic and each side interpreted the transactions in terms of their own value systems, setting the terms of trade accordingly (cf. Keehnen 2012). The Taíno were not, as often implied, ignorant of worth (a highly biased view that privileges Western aesthetics and value systems above all others); they simply had their own concepts of what was important, desirable and valuable. And it is this context that is of interest here.

On 12 October 1492, Columbus's first day on San Salvador, Bahamas, the admiral's log noted a multitude of transactions: 'they brought us parrots, spun cotton [...] javelins, and many other things; and they traded them to us for other things that we gave them, such as small glass beads and bells' (Lardicci 1999: 48). Columbus used his trade commodities from the start as gifts: 'in order that they might feel great amity towards us [I] gave to some among them some red caps and some glass beads, which they hung round their necks, and many other things [...]. At this they were greatly pleased and became so entirely our friends that it was a wonder to see' (Parry and Keith 1984: 29). To the Lucayans (inhabitants of the Bahamas, and culturally linked to the Taíno), this magnanimity was expected given Columbus's role as leader — or *cacique* — whose high status required generosity and reciprocity. In this way, Spanish exotics quickly entered into indigenous trade networks: only three days after their initial exchanges on San Salvador, Columbus encountered a man travelling in a canoe between the Bahamian islands of Rum Key and Long Island, carrying with him a basket containing a string of small glass beads and two Spanish coins (Dunn and Kelley 1989: 85). News of the foreigners — and their trade goods — was preceding them via the long-established indigenous networks that bound these island communities together.

But it was not until his arrival in Hispaniola in December 1492 that Columbus entered into the realm of politicised gift exchanges with the local *caciques*. Indigenous wealth in the form of belts, stone bead necklaces and gold were presented to Columbus in a series of formalised offerings. As recorded by the early *cronistas* (Spanish chroniclers), belts were among the first gifts offered by Taíno elite to Columbus. On 18 December 1492, for example, a Hispaniolan *cacique* presented Columbus with his first native belt, prompting Columbus to reciprocate with a variety of gifts, including red shoes, amber beads and a flask of flower water (Parry and Keith 1984: 40–1). Four days later, on 22 December, Columbus was sent a belt featuring a mask inlaid with gold by *cacique* Guacanagari's emissaries. It is this example that the historian Bartolome de Las Casas delights in describing, clearly having handled the original:

> the ambassador was sent with a belt that, instead of a purse, had a mask, which had two large ears, a tongue and nose of hammered gold; this belt was made with something like fine stones, very small and pearl-like, made of white fish bones [shells], interspersed with some coloured ones, like a kind of needlework; [it was] worked in such a way, with the cotton thread so

> tightly sewn and with such beautiful skill, that both the front and back of the belt appeared beautifully made [...] all in white, that it was a pleasure to see, as if it was woven on a frame and in the way that the weavers make the edges of chasubles in Castile; and [it] was so hard and so strong that without doubt I believe an arquebus could not shoot through it, or only with difficulty; it was four fingers in width, in the manner of those used by the kings and great lords of Castile, embroidered or made of gold thread (de las Casas 1951: 272).

It is noteworthy that belts were the first official presents to the Admiral in recognition of his status, as they were among a select group of objects that distinguished members of the Taíno elite. Their production was labour-intensive – from the manufacture of the shell beads to the weaving of the cotton – reflecting the wealth and affluence of the *cacique* in being able to accrue these valuable materials and in securing the labour of skilled artisans to transform them into wearable works of 'art' (Ostapkowicz 2013).

The Vienna belt

One such belt is held in the collections of Weltmuseum Wien (Figure 2). It was originally part of the Schatzkammer, the imperial treasury of Vienna established in 1556, though it is not known when the belt first entered the collection (Ostapkowicz 2013: 295–6). Framed by a band of geometric designs and executed in nearly 11,000 drilled conch (*Strombus gigas*) and jewel box (*Chama sarda*) beads, it features a central maskette depicting the hands and face of a *cemí*. The sheer quantity of shell beads underscores the labour that went into this belt, when one considers that each tiny bead (c. 5mm diameter) was made using stone tools – from cutting, grinding down and drilling to the final polishing. One seventeenth-century account of bead manufacture by the neighbouring Carib/Kalinago notes that they 'could not make one [bead] to perfection and pierce it with the tools that they use in less than three days' (de la Borde in Roth 1924: 119). Replication studies suggest that a skilled specialist may have made as many as five beads in a day, with 300 over a period of two months (Carlson 1993: 70); at this rate, 11,000 beads would represent six months' labour for ten specialists. This does not take into account the labour involved in making the cotton framework – from picking, processing and spinning to weaving. If this one belt entailed such work, then Guacanagari's gift of 12 belts to Columbus on his return voyage in 1493 not only highlighted the affluence of the *cacique*, but his desire in forging links with the Spanish (Ostapkowicz 2013).

Amidst the wealth of indigenous shell beads featured on the Vienna belt are a number of European imports: two flat mirrors for eyes, a pair of jet beads at the top of the head secured with brass pins, as well as one small facetted jet bead in the right earflare. These have been placed precisely where traditional inlays of gold or shell would normally be featured, echoing the qualities of these bright, reflective surfaces and maintaining the Taíno aesthetic while extending it to include foreign materials. However, these items appear to be surface additions rather than directly woven into the framework of the belt, suggesting that they were added some time after the belt was woven, possibly when it was repaired or modified to accommodate the new foreign valuables (for more detailed discussion, see Ostapkowicz 2013). As the symbol of cacical authority, belts offered an appropriate medium for capturing the reflective allure of new materials in the service of indigenous symbolism and meaning.

The Pigorini cemí

If the Vienna belt selectively features a few choice foreign valuables, integrating them subtly and in accordance with traditional Taíno aesthetics, then the Pigorini *cemí* is a tour-de-force (Figure 1). Often presented as a single object, it is actually made of two entirely separate pieces: a full-sized adult belt (Biscione 1997: 158), made entirely of indigenous shell beads, and a separate Janus-figure *cemí* that could have been worn as an elaborate headpiece. One side of the *cemí* features a prognathic face, variously identified as a bat (Biscione 1997: 162) or a human skull (Roe 1997: 165); the other shows a human face. The Pigorini belt and *cemí* share the same geometric designs, materials and manufacture techniques, suggesting that they were made as a set. They also exhibit many similarities with the Vienna belt, and these three objects have long been linked, potentially suggesting the same source, or even the same maker, as well as a shared history in European collections prior to being separated (Biscione 1997; Feest 1991; Roe 1997; Schweeger-Hefel 1952; Vega 1987).

Nearly 1700 glass beads have been incorporated into the design of the Pigorini *cemí*: approximately 1200 small green beads are used on the face and back of the head, roughly 450 deep blue corner-faceted beads are featured at the shoulders and originally 10 small turquoise/white Nueva Cadiz beads, of which only one remains, would have adorned the head. When these European beads are added to the sheer volume of indigenous beads, the piece exudes sixteenth century Taíno wealth. Over 20,000 shell beads are woven into the surface, suggesting a year's full time work for ten specialists. In addition, six cut mirrors feature in the eyes and ear flares. But the most exceptional aspect of this astonishing sculpture is the use of rhinoceros horn for the human mask (Biscione 1997: 162) — whether of Asian or African origin is the subject of future investigation. Yet the mask again conforms to Taíno aesthetics. The Pigorini *cemí* is thus a lavish display of Old World exotics harnessed within the confines of an indigenous prism, in the service of the *cemí* it represents and the *cacique* who had the power to wield it.

'Dividuals': defining the web of connections

In the following discussion, the Vienna belt and Pigorini *cemí* are deconstructed to their component parts in an effort to understand how their different materials were perceived, appreciated and valued, and particularly how the European materials may have echoed or complemented indigenous valuables. The aim is not to treat them so much as isolated objects but as nodes in a web of interaction between the Taíno and the Spanish. They are, in a sense, the material equivalents of Strathern's dividuals (1988), in which persons are not discrete entities, but rather are extended in space and time through their interactions and connections with others, and indeed are defined by them. In order to engage with these aspects, and using these two objects as the foci, six early colonial period materials are explored through *cronista* references to their use, combined with archaeological evidence:

1) Spanish *cuentas/abalorios* (glass beads) and indigenous shell and stone beads (the latter known by the Taíno term *cibas* or *sibas*);

2) jet (Spanish: *azabache*) and lignite/fossil woods, a less well-known indigenous valuable that nevertheless likely had a deep history in the circum-Caribbean region;

3–5) metals, both indigenous and Spanish: *caona*, the Taíno term for gold; *guanín,* the indigenous name for a gold-copper-silver-alloy; *turey,* a term used by the Taíno to refer to the sky but which also came to identify brass (copper-zinc) imports;

6) *espejos,* a Spanish term denoting mirrors, which were highly prized by the Taíno, both in their indigenous form (gold/*guanín*) and in their new manifestation: European glass mirrors.

These materials were undoubtedly graded both within and between each category; nevertheless the parallels between them provide a point of departure for discussion. One aspect to their value was their colour and brilliance: green, black and warm gold, together with their shining, reflective surfaces coalesced in objects that were not only aesthetic and desirable, but spiritually charged. Individually and collectively these categories of objects provide a clearer picture of indigenous value systems, and of the role of exchange in the process of social change in the indigenous Caribbean (cf. Appadurai 1986; Gosden 2004).

The approach taken here focuses on the role of the Vienna belt and Pigorini *cemí* as active intermediaries in social relationships (Appadurai 1986; Gell 1998) and investigates how their materiality may have shaped identity and social action

(Gosden 2004). Their divisible nature (cf. Strathern 1988) reflects the socio-political and economic interconnections being forged in early colonial Caribbean history, a perspective refreshingly 'scripted' by the Taíno, as opposed to the reliance on historical documents that provide an overwhelmingly Eurocentric view of this period. These objects also reflect social ontologies, the webs of connection between materials and people (Gosden 2008), specifically through an active focus on both indigenous and introduced valuables. In integrating foreign goods into the structure, the creator/s of the Pigorni *cemí* interwove the Spanish into the history of not only the piece, but into every future use, display and interaction with it: the foreigners were thus assimilated into the community's perceptions and understanding of this object. In this capacity, the European 'Other' became intimately entangled with Taíno representations of their own ideology, and ultimately themselves (cf. Gosden 2004), influencing people's understandings of this shifting, transitional period and their place within it (cf. Gell 1998).

Cuentas for *cibas* and the allure of emerald colours

Both shell and stone beads (*cibas*) were prized by the Taíno as personal ornaments and as exchange valuables. Early *cronista* accounts document their use: from strands worn at the neck, arms and/or wrists, to the hundreds, if not thousands, woven into elite belts, caps and *naguas*, or women's skirts (Alegria 1995; Bernaldez in Jane 1967: 162). The large quantities of beads required for the Pigorini *cemí* and Vienna belt meant that shell was the dominant medium, given that stone beads were far more laborious to make. Necklaces of stone *cibas* strung with gold or *guanín* were the prerogative of *caciques* and were understood to have a mythical source, originally gifted by the ancestress Guabonito to the culture hero Guahayona at the sacred mountain Cauta, where the first people emerged (Colón 1992: 155; see Oliver 2000: 205–13). Martyr D'Anghera, recounting this myth in the early sixteenth century, notes that 'the kings [*caciques*] hold these necklaces sacred even today' (in Arrom 1999: 48). Stone *cibas*, which had the appearance of marble (Colón 1992: 155), were thus fitting gifts between high-ranking individuals, such as the 'eight hundred small, figured white, green and red stone beads together with one hundred figured gold beads' presented by the *cacique* Guacanagari to Columbus upon his return to Hispaniola in 1493 (Colón 1992: 120). Particularly significant examples were incorporated into high-status artefacts, such as the stone *ciba* inlaid into the chest cavity of a wooden Jamaican *duho* (Ostapkowicz 2015: 98, fig. 5). Yet others were gifted or traded across the archipelago: such sites as Hope Estate, St Martin and La Hueca, Vieques, Puerto Rico feature exotic stone beads and pendants that suggest long-distance networks stretching to South America (Chanlatte-Baik 2013: 179; Haviser 1999: 202). In this sense, imported beads were in circulation in the Caribbean well before 1492.

Quantities of shell beads have been recovered from Caribbean archaeological sites, including the manufacturing site at Governor's Beach (GT-2), Grand Turk, where 1600 complete and 7000 incomplete beads were recovered together with 13,000 pieces of production waste (Carlson 1995). As burial offerings, beads could also be taken out of circulation completely, as seen for example in the 1100 conch (*Strombus gigas*) shell beads found on the pelvis of a female skeleton in a burial at Anse à la Gourde, Guadeloupe (Hofman and Hoogland 2004: 51), suggesting a *nagua*. It is likely that beads were graded on a scale of increasing value, based on the material, investment of labour, acquisition history (e.g. via long-distance exchange) and other aspects of their biography (e.g. the renown of previous owners).

The Pigorini *cemí* and Vienna belt both feature small shell beads of 3–5mm diameter and 0.6–2.5mm thickness (Figure 3), comparable in size to those found at such sites as GT-2, suggesting a fairly standardised system of manufacture within the region. This distinctive shape — a small, perforated disk with slightly bulging sides — is also seen in the gold microbeads (2mm diameter) from the site of Chorro de Maita, Cuba (Martinón-Torres 2012: fig. 8), suggesting a preference for this specific shape, regardless of raw material. Thus, when European glass beads — particularly the small, wire-wound beads, with their doughnut shape and bulging sides — were introduced in 1492, they fit neatly within the established canons of indigenous beadwork. Other early glass beads, such as Nueva Cadiz, were more similar to the stone *cibas*, with their longer, cylindrical shapes, and so also had an indigenous precedent. Within this context, glass beads had an immediate impact: not only were they exotic yet familiar in form, but their unfading colours and reflective properties had deep resonance, as will be seen below.

The indigenous reception of beads during the earliest exchanges cemented their popularity as a trade commodity in the Caribbean. To Spanish eyes, the exchanges appeared most favourable. Columbus himself noted that '[they] would barter with some pieces of gold hanging from the nose [...] which they would willingly give [...] for glass beads' (in García-Arevalo 1990: 271). Glass — and particularly glass beads — were sought out in trade, as documented by Foresti da Bergamo: '[the Indians] exchange gold for glass, because nothing is more valuable among them than glass' (Symcox 2002: 30). The Taíno also viewed this as a favourable transaction in terms of their own value systems: as noted in the myth, *cibas* originated from distant lands (and were certainly circulated over long distances in trade), and so the exoticness of Spanish beads was fitting, and, coupled with their brilliant appearance, highly desirable. Las Casas notes their swift incorporation into local ornaments: 'The beads, having the further merit of novelty and rarity, were added to the conch disks and to the

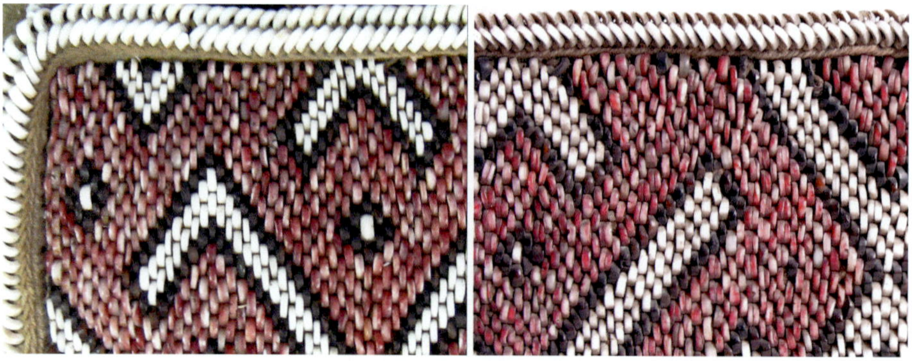

Figure 3. Stylistic and material similarities in the layout and use of indigenous shell beads on the Pigorini *cemí* (left) and Vienna belt (right). Note the raised, double-layered ridge of white shell beads in both and the black framework around the white geometric designs (two deep in the Pigorini, vs. three deep in the Vienna belt). Photograph: Ostapkowicz; courtesy of the Polo Museale del Lazio - Museo Nazionale Preistorico Etnografico "L.Pigorini", su concessione del Mibact, acc no. 4190; courtesy of the Weltmuseum Wien, inv. no. 10.443.

cibas, colored stones, [the latter] held in high regard, a gift worthy of a *cacique*' (Biscione 1997: 163, italics added).

Surviving shipping records indicate that between 1511 and 1526 roughly 179,000 beads were exported to the Spanish colonies, as compared to 10 million in 1583–1613. The comparatively small quantities available in the first decades of contact suggests that glass beads were not as common as often assumed, and their absence from such important indigenous colonial period sites as En Bas Saline in Haiti[2] appears to confirm this: the site was occupied by the Taíno to about 1515 (Deagan 1987b; 2004: 613). Only a few examples have been recovered from early colonial indigenous sites, such as the three compound (blue/green/white) Nueva Cadiz and two cobalt blue faceted beads from El Cabo, Dominican Republic, occupied until 1504 (Samson 2010: 284), or a tubular cobalt bead from Playa Grande, DR, a site abandoned in 1505 (Keehnan 2012: 150). Deagan (2004: 621) suggests that the paucity of such artefacts might reflect a Taíno 'indifference to and rejection of Spanish cultural elements and values'; conversely, the rarity of these beads in the archaeological record may reflect both their relative scarcity and their value during the early colonial period, and hence their curation.

Abalorios — a Spanish term for small beads 'of little value' (Deagan 1987: 157) — feature abundantly on the Pigorini *cemí* (Figure 4). Columbus himself gifted

[2] Guacanagari's village, close to La Navidad, the first Spanish colonial outpost, established 1492, and 2km away from Puerto Real, established 1503.

Figure 4. The 'bat' face of the Pigorini *cemí*, featuring 1200 green glass beads, and cut mirrors for the eyes. Photograph: Ostapkowicz; courtesy of the Polo Museale del Lazio - Museo Nazionale Preistorico Etnografico "L.Pigorini", su concessione del Mibact, acc no. 4190.

the Táino with green and yellow *abalorios* during his first voyage, and over 100,000 beads in these specific hues were sent to the Caribbean during the early voyages between 1511 and 1526, though they are not listed in subsequent inventories (Deagan 1987: 110, 157). Thus, they are understood to be reliable chronological markers for the first quarter (M. Smith in Hoffman 1987: 242) or, more conservatively, the first half of the sixteenth century (Deagan 1987: 169). Of course, their 'currency' (use/circulation) could have extended past this. Six complete and three fragmentary green *abalorios* have been recovered from the site of Long Bay, San Salvador, Bahamas, along with several other European goods, including a *blanca* coin dating between 1471 and 1474 (Hoffman 1987: 241). These wirewound beads (c. 3.5mm in maximum diameter) are distinguished by their emerald green colour, and have an unusually high lead oxide content (65–75%). This is higher than any other category of early European lead glass and suggests a specific region and tradition of manufacture (Brill 1987: 251), although no source has yet been identified. Another set of small green beads were recovered from a cave in Quebradillas, Puerto Rico in the 1980s, held within an intricately carved wooden bowl (Figure 5). Analysis of one of these beads showed strong parallels to the San Salvador *abalorios* in terms of size, colour and lead content (Brill 2012: 544–8). Puerto Rico was 'discovered' in 1493, but the Spanish only settled the island 15 years later, in 1508. It is not clear whether the Quebradillas beads were in circulation on the island prior to Spanish settlement – potentially traded from Hispaniola via indigenous channels – or whether they were acquired subsequently, directly from the newly settled foreigners, though their material parallels to the Bahamian examples suggest a potentially early date.

The more than 1200 green *abalorios* on the face and back of the head of the Pigorini *cemí* not only support a pre-1550 manufacture of the *cemí* (Roe 1997: 164; Vega 1987: 28) and highlight the investment of beads in a single artefact, but also raise the question of specific colour preferences within indigenous value systems. The colour green had a deep resonance among the Taíno, from the iridescent splendour of green parrot feathers to the highly prized 'greenstone' artefacts circulating via exchange routes spanning the circum-Caribbean (Boomert 1987; Rodriguez Ramos 2011). The vibrant emerald glass

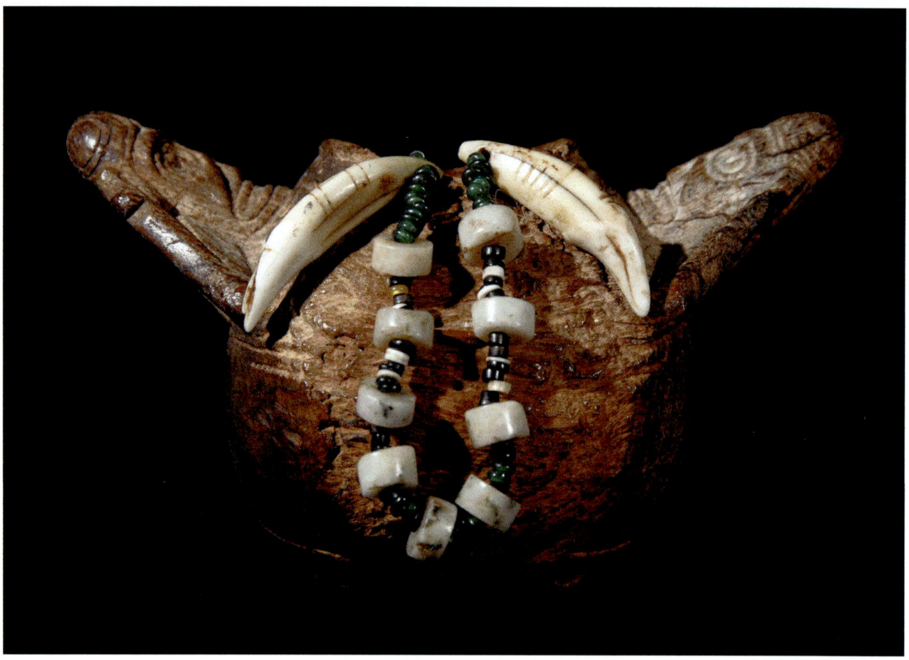

Figure 5. Wooden vessel recovered from a cave in Quebradillas, Puerto Rico, containing 30 deep green, three blue and two yellow glass beads, together with two dog canines. Vessel: *Guaiacum* sp., AD 1297–1406, L: 12.2cm; W: 80mm; H: 70mm (max). Photograph: Ostapkowicz; courtesy of the Museo de Historia, Antropología y Arte, Universidad de Puerto Rico, Recinto de Río Piedras, 1.2008.0671-2.

beads must have echoed this quality.[3] Further, they came in a diminutive size (c. 3.5mm diameter) that would have been almost impossible to replicate in greenstone: jadeites, for example, are extremely difficult to work, and objects made from these materials were frequently on a larger scale as a result. Small, drilled greenstone *cibas* (<10mm in diameter) are rarely encountered in the archaeological record (Figure 6) and, given the work needed to shape and drill them, must have been of significant value. They would have been the purview of *caciques* and were likely the focal points of pendants or other body ornaments. One account of Columbus's first visit to Jamaica in 1494 notes that amidst the spectacle of regalia worn by the welcoming Taíno envoys sent out in three canoes to the ship, a *cacique* wore stones of 'high value' and on his head a 'garland of small stones, green and red, arranged in order, and intermingled with some larger white stones, producing a pleasing effect'; he also wore a matching belt 'of the same workmanship as the garland' (Bernaldez in Jane 1967: 162). But given the level of difficulty in producing small greenstone *cibas* and the need for large quantities of beads for belts and headdresses, it is possible that the 'green stones' were in fact green shell beads, specifically selected for their desirable, natural colour.

Given the cachet of such prized green materials, glass beads of emerald hues, gifted or traded from the start of Columbus's initial voyages (and part of the cargo on subsequent voyages of the first half of the sixteenth century; Deagan 1987: 156–7), must have had an immediate resonance within indigenous value systems. Undoubtedly, their use — whether strung on a necklace or integrated into a composite artefact — followed swiftly on from initial exchange. *Caciques* with access to large quantities of beads would have had them integrated into objects befitting their status. A belt belonging to Caonabó with a 'green face and two leaves of gold' may be a case in point. This belt was inventoried by the Spanish on 9 July 1495 (Torres 1868), shortly after they captured Caonabó and imprisoned him at La Isabela. This was over two years after Caonabó's purported sacking of the first Spanish settlement, La Navidad, and his (unsubstantiated) threats on Fort Santo Tomás which lead to the Spanish march on the Vega Real in

[3] Certainly, this was the case in the wider circum-Caribbean: during the Spanish expeditions into Mexico, green glass beads were also distributed in great quantity (Smith and Good 1982: 3) and in their specific choice of green, the Spanish had stumbled upon a colour resonant with one of the prime valuables in the region. Montezuma himself ordered that his governors welcome Spanish interests in bartering indigenous gold for green beads, because they were similar to *chalchihuites* (jadeites), which are valued 'as highly as emeralds' (Smith and Good 1982: 4). In just one example, the expedition led by Juan de Grijalva reached Rio de Tabasco in 1518, where it was greeted by canoes full of warriors: '...and we showed them strings of green beads and small mirrors and blue cut glass beads, and soon as they saw them they assumed a more friendly manner, for they thought they were *chalcihuites* [...] which they value greatly' (Smith and Good 1982: 4).

Figure 6. A small, broken jadeite (?) bead, recovered from the site of Morel, Guadeloupe. Diameter: 9mm; thickness: 4mm; hole diameter: c. 4mm. Photograph: Ostapkowicz; courtesy of the Direction des Affaires culturelles, Guadeloupe, 5801.

an effort to pacify the situation (Colón 1992: 127; Wilson 1990: 83) – events that made him a notorious enemy of the Spanish. Whether the green face of Caonabó's belt was made from a single piece of carved greenstone, quantities of greenstone (or shell) beads – as worn by the Jamaican *cacique* – or, potentially, newly imported green glass beads is not clear from the records, but given Caonabó's status as one of the principal *caciques* of Hispaniola, it is likely that he had access to glass beads. Although an enemy of the Spanish, he may not have rejected their imports. Indeed, the inventory, on 19 February 1496, intriguingly links him to a stone cross and two *latón* (brass) pieces (Torres 1868), which were only acquired via the Spanish – and the legend of his capture recounts how his interest in *turey* (in this instance, foreign metals) led to the Spanish offering him a 'gift' of metal handcuffs, which were quickly snapped shut as he tried them on (Wilson 1990: 84–7). Given the green glass beads incorporated into the bat face of the Pigorini *cemí*, it is an intriguing possibility that the centrepiece of Caonabó's belt may have been similarly constructed.

It is clear from the above that Spanish *cuentas* were but an addition to a long-established category of ornament within the Caribbean: shell beads and *cibas*. These new imports, in a range of vibrant and unfading colours, were easily appropriated in the existing framework. Fortuitously, some of them, such as the small green *abalorios*, also echoed the colours and qualities of 'greenstone' ornaments – some of the most spiritually and socio-politically important indigenous valuables, and often themselves exotic. It is small wonder that *cuentas* were so successfully adopted in the circum-Caribbean, and what the Spanish thought were favourable exchange terms (beads for gold), the Taíno likely also viewed as equally satisfactory, given the qualities of these new-yet-familiar valuables and the distance they had travelled.

Dark materials: jet and rhinoceros horn

Glass beads were not the only imports valued by the Taíno: the dark matt finish of jet also held allure. Black beads, ornaments and ceremonial items have a deep history within the circum-Caribbean region; dark, fossilised terrestrial plant material (e.g. lignite) was used prior to European contact, though this is largely an unstudied medium of artistic expression. Carvings in these materials tend to be on a small scale, ranging from c. 3 to 15cm. One example is the composite snuff tube in the form of a bird and monkey recovered from Charlotte Parish, St Vincent, prior to 1870 (Figure 7) (see also Arroyo *et al.* 1971: 233 for two similarly complex carvings found along the Arauca river, Venezuela). At least six small (<3cm), dark brown/black pendants with stylistically similar anthropo/zoomorphic imagery have previously been identified as wood, but may actually be carved of lignite, a soft stone related to coal and similar to jet (Ostapkowicz 2016; in press). Three are from the sites of Morel and L'Allée Dumanoir, Guadeloupe (Etrich *et al.* 2002: 26; Petitjean Roget 1995) and three from Sorcé, Vieques, Puerto Rico (Chanlatte Baik and Narganes Storde 1984: fig. 24c); those with good contextual information all appear to fall within the Early Ceramic Age period (c. 400 BC – AD 600) and come from deposits rich in exotics (e.g. amethyst beads; Chanlatte Baik and Narganes Storde 1984; Etrich *et al.* 2002). Another small carving recovered from St Vincent features a ventral surface in the form of a frog and has long been assumed to be made from manjack or pitch (analyses are under way).

The wide-ranging use of these black materials in the circum-Caribbean, their association with other valuables and their use in ceremonial contexts (e.g. snuff tubes for the ingestion of hallucinogens) suggest significance beyond the merely decorative. Black — like the colour green — may have had complex and deeply rooted meanings (cf. Helms 1986). The use of black by the Taíno was frequently commented on by the *cronistas*: Taíno wood sculpture — particularly elite, ceremonial artefacts — was to Spanish eyes 'black as jet' (Las Casas 1967b: 174; Helms 1986; Martyr D'Anghera 1970: 125). Black was also used in body painting, to enhance features on carvings (such as the black pigment outlining the mouth, nostrils and eyes of the Pigorini *cemí*'s rhinoceros horn mask) and as a dye for cotton and basketry weaving (Las Casas 1967a: 75; Cuneo in Symcox 2002: 58). Indeed, it is possible that the black beads that frame the red and white designs on the Vienna belt had been specifically dyed that colour to enhance the patterns (Figure 8; Ostapkowicz 2013: note 55).

Within this indigenous context, imported Spanish jet may have fortuitously echoed established local values for black materials, like the greenstones/green *abalorios* explored above. The three surviving jet beads on the Vienna belt may

Figure 7. A composite snuff tube from St Vincent, depicting a bird above a monkey. Accession records note that it was '[f]ound (prior to 1870) in a cane piece [plantation] in Charlotte parish to the N.E. of the Id. of St Vincent, W. Indies'. Height: 86mm; width: 53mm; diameter: 67mm. Photograph: Ostapkowicz; courtesy and copyright of the Pitt Rivers Museum, University of Oxford, 1900.44.1

have originally been part of religious Spanish ornaments: two six-sided beads placed at the top of the central *cemí*'s head may have served as *veneras* (literarily, items of 'veneration'; symbols of saints, religious orders etc.) and a single small, faceted jet bead placed in the right earflare may have come from a rosary (Figure 9; cf. Deagan 1987a: 72–4, 182–3). Though jet is not documented as an exchange commodity during the early colonial period, the use of jet for *veneras*, amulets and rosaries by the Spanish is known from at least the thirteenth century, and personal jet ornaments likely featured from the first voyages, as amulets, religious objects and rosaries (Deagan 1987a: 73). Unlike glass beads, which the Spanish viewed purely as a trade item and brought with them in bulk, jet was understood to have strong protective and magical qualities, and as such may not have been so easily parted with in what were primarily viewed as economic transactions (though diplomatic negotiations may have been different, see below). Indeed, at its height in the sixteenth century, the church had the monopoly on jet production via guilds in Compostela, Spain (Deagan 2002: 73); jet carving was in the service of, and sanctioned by, the church. Where records exist, they document that only small quantities of jet were imported into the colonies prior to 1526, in contrast to the late sixteenth and early seventeenth

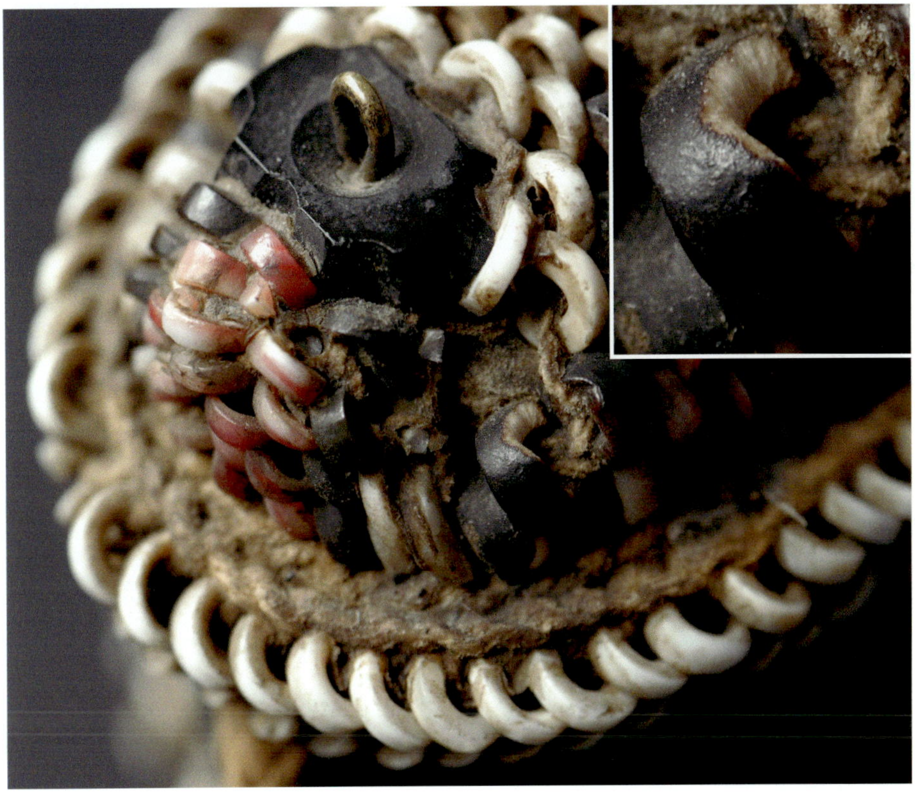

Figure 8. A damaged black bead (inset right), in the context of where it is located on the Vienna belt. It features a black surface, but white interior, suggesting a possible surface dye or colourant. Photograph: Ostapkowicz; courtesy of the Weltmuseum Wien, inv. no. 10.443.

century (Deagan 1987a: tab. 6.1). But even the cumulative quantities of jet imports over the first century of the colonial enterprise were insignificant in comparison to the glass bead imports for the years 1511–1526 alone (Table 1). Jet was therefore an extremely rare material in the early colonial period, making the incorporation of three jet beads into the Vienna belt exceptional.

What is not known is whether the Spanish belief that jet had protective and magical qualities held any significance for the Taíno. It is intriguing in this respect that the jet beads at the top of the *cemí*'s head are in the style of Dominican crosses (cf. Deagan 2002: 73), with St. Dominic being frequently represented in Catholic iconography by a star on his forehead or above his head. Assuming that the jet was incorporated into the belt within an indigenous context (see footnote 1), then might the placement of these particular jet beads on top of the *cemí*'s head reflect Taíno awareness of their meaning to the Spanish, and an integration of some elements of Christianity into their own belief systems

Figure 9. The two styles of jet beads featured on the Vienna belt. Left: one of two large, six-sided beads (length: 12.5mm; width: 7.3mm), secured with a brass pin (possibly from a belt buckle) placed at the top of the *cemí*'s head. Right: a single small faceted bead (max. diameter: 4mm) inserted into the *cemí*'s right earflare. Photograph: Ostapkowicz; courtesy of the Weltmuseum Wien, inv. no. 10.443.

Date	Jet	Quantity
1511–1526	200 finger rings of jet	200
1583–1613	7365 jet rings; 38,000 cut stones of jet; 12 strings of jet; 578 strings of jet rings; 928 necklaces of jet; 7,000 pieces of jet for necklaces; 600 necklaces of jet medallions; 648 earrings of jet and glass; 44,000 small jet beads; 24 small jet chains	99,515
Date	**Glass beads**	**Quantity**
1511–1526	102,000 green and yellow beads; 60,000 necklace beads; 17,000 bunches of beads; 9 strings of necklace beads; 18 strings of glass bangle bracelets	179,027

Table 1. Jet (*azabache*) imported to the Spanish Colonies, 1511–1526 (compiled from Deagan 1987: tab. 6.1. Note the disparity between jet and glass imports for 1511–1526).

and iconography? Could this belt be part of a 'fluid world of spiritual exchange' (Tuer 2003: 78)? Although speculative, there are a number of aspects of the early colonial period that could support this scenario. As well as the presence of missionaries in the colonies from 1493 (with the first Native baptism taking place in 1496), the Spanish *encomienda* system, established in 1503, was an overt policy to acculturate indigenous populations by teaching them Christian doctrine in exchange for their labour. Indeed, the early *cronistas* documented that the Taino selectively adopted Christian elements, including certain saints, whose lives, replete with miracles and explicit material symbolism, may have sat comfortably alongside equally legendary and powerful *cemis* (Oliver 2009: 221–44). That the belt may embody the transition between traditional Taíno iconography and an emerging religious syncretism opens new avenues of exploring its meaning and this critical period in the New World.

Another dark material is — quite remarkably — rhinoceros horn, carved as the human face of the Pigorini *cemí* (Figure 10; Biscione 1997: 162). Its incorporation into the sculpture raises many questions: how did rhinoceros horn, an extremely valuable commodity in sixteenth century Europe and Asia, enter into the Caribbean, when even basic supplies (clothing, food and wine, livestock) for the fledgling colonies were hard to come by? If indeed the horn is original to the piece (rather than a later addition by a European artisan), it may have entered the Caribbean from Europe, or alternatively via the slaving routes that post-1502 brought occasional African materials via the colonies, ultimately destined as luxury goods for the European ports.[4] Contrary to those who — understandably given the material — would see the Pigorini *cemí* as heavily influenced by west African rather than Taíno conventions (Roe 1997: 165), to the degree that it is an 'adumbration of the cultural and spiritual significance of African forms in the shaping of American art' (Sullivan 2006: 40), the facial features are entirely compatible with Taíno aesthetics (Biscione 1997: 162–3; Vega 1987: 26), and certainly wood and shell masks — or *guaízas* as the Taíno called them — were important elite accoutrements, so this resonates with Caribbean traditions in more ways than one. At the same time, it expands these traditions in the use of a unique and exceptional material. Ongoing research aims to resolve these questions, addressing the significance and provenance of this material.

[4] The rhinoceros horn may not be the only potentially African exotic featured on the Pigorini *cemí*: it has also been suggested that the shells used for the *cemí*'s teeth are west African *Prunum monilis* (Feest 1991: 581, based on the original identification by Strouhal in Schweeger-Hefel 1952: 210, 214–5), although it is unclear on what basis this attribution was made. Comparable small white shells also occur in the Caribbean (such as *Volvarina lacteal, Hyalina lucinda*), hence it will be necessary to revisit this issue.

Figure 10. Left profile of the Pigorini *cemí*'s human face, carved of rhinoceros horn, with shell eye inlay and facial lines enhanced with black pigment. Photograph: Ostapkowicz; courtesy of the Polo Museale del Lazio - Museo Nazionale Preistorico Etnografico "L.Pigorini", su concessione del Mibact, acc no. 4190.

Brilliant surfaces, heavenly entities: *caona* (gold), *guanín* (gold-copper-silver alloy) and European brass (*turey*)

Two indigenous metals were highly valued in the Caribbean prior to European contact: *caona* (alluvial, unrefined gold), typically used as inlay for ritual artefacts or attachments to cacical cotton belts or caps, and *guanín* (a gold-copper-silver alloy), used as a high-status trade item and body ornament (Martinón-Torres *et al.* 2012: 442; Oliver 2000).[5] High-temperature metallurgy (smelting and alloying) was unknown in the Caribbean; the manufacture of gold ornaments involved cold-hammering nuggets into small, flat sheets, enhanced occasionally through repoussé. *Guanín* was imported into the Caribbean from South America via the Lesser Antilles, and possibly via more direct links (Oliver 2000: 199–200; Valcárcel Royas and Martinón-Torres 2013: 506, 516, 518).

[5] Indigenous silver was also known — first described by Columbus after seeing a nose-ring ornament while in northern Cuba — but no artefacts have been recovered to date, and it was likely not as important as gold or *guanín* (Oliver 2000: 198).

Gold was a recognised valuable across the Caribbean, referred to by various indigenous names — from *nozay* in the Bahamas and Cuba, to *tuob* in the north-east to *caona* in the west, the Taíno heartland (Lardicci 1999: 116; Valcárcel Royas and Martinón-Torres 2013: 505). The practice of collecting gold involved ritual purification, including physical deprivation such as fasting and sexual abstinence (Oviedo 1959). This imparts a social significance to the material extending far beyond its surface aesthetic. Such ritual preparation was a requirement for other potent substances, such as *cohoba,* a hallucinogenic drug that was only ingested once participants had purged themselves (Las Casas 1967b: 174). Gold was to become the eyes of a *cemí*, the ornament of a *cacique* and the desired treasure of the Europeans — yet it also transcended these charged loci as a substance of both culturally inherent value and numinous power.

Gold soon became the focus of mediations between the Taíno and the Spanish: it was both a means of engaging with and appeasing the strangers, as well as accessing their trade valuables (Martinón-Torres *et al.* 2012: 507; Oliver 2007: 47). Spanish inventories, compiled after the Taíno uprisings of 1494/1495 and detailing objects brought in tribute (and possibly as ransom, Ostapkowicz 2013) provide insight into the diversity of items lavishly inlaid with gold — particularly those that mediated between the natural and supernatural worlds (vomiting spatulas, *cemís*, *guaízas* etc.; Torres 1868). These inlays did not last long once in Spanish hands: the amount of gold present was carefully described and weighed, suggesting that shortly after their collection, they were prised away (e.g. nine gold leaf inlays from two masks collected on 19 February 1496 weighed 4 1/8 ounces, five *tomines* and six grains; Torres 1868: 9). There are only a handful of wood and cotton artefacts now in museum collections that still retain their gold inlays, most famously the Hispaniolan high-back *duho* in the British Museum (Figure 11).

Given their highly charged potency, and their ancestral links to the mythical cultural hero and primordial *cacique* Guayayona, gold and *guanín* were a chiefly prerogative and a divine symbol of chiefly power (Oliver 2000: 205). *Caona* was literarily the root of chiefly names: Caonabó ('He who is like gold') and the honorific title of Bohechio (*Tureygua Hobin* — 'King as dazzling and heavenly as *guanín*') echo the qualities of the materials (Oliver 2000: 205; Whitehead 1999: 881). It is clear that chiefs had control over its distribution, including organising the payment of gold tribute to the Spanish. They wore it as nose rings, or had it inlaid into high-status items (Caonabó's belt featured two gold inlays and his vomiting spatula had 29 pieces of gold; Torres 1868: 9). The sixteenth century Italian historian Scillacio notes that among Guacanagari's gifts to Columbus upon the latter's return in 1493 were twelve belts 'of marvellous workmanship [...] several of them were notable for nuggets of gold worked very artistically into the [cotton]' (Symcox 2002: 43).

Gold was prized for all these properties, but it was not as esteemed as the gold-copper alloy *guanín* (Martinón-Torres *et al.* 2007: 202). *Guanín* had a distinct, reddish hue and, reportedly, a unique scent that the Taíno prized highly (Oliver 2000: 198). This, combined with its mythic associations and distant South American origins, made it the preeminent valuable (Oliver 2000; Valcárcel Royas and Martinón-Torres 2013: 506). Las Casas notes that *guanín* was used as bride price (Oliver 2000: 198–9), and in the early days of colonial expansion on Hispaniola it was used as a type of currency (Valcárcel Royas and Martinón-Torres 2013: 508). The Spanish were quick to manipulate the local desire for *guanín* to their advantage, importing it directly from South America to leverage favourable exchange rates for higher-karat gold: at one stage, the going rate for one piece of *guanín* was 200 pieces of gold (Bray 1997: 49; Martinón-Torres *et al.* 2012: 446). Sued-Badillo notes that archival documents in the Casa de Contratación in Sevilla document the presence of *guanín* ornaments in the form of eagles and frogs (suggesting South American sources) held in storehouses in Santo Domingo, DR, specifically for exchange with the local natives for gold dust and nuggets (in Bray 1997: 50). Its sale was prohibited by royal degree in 1501, so that it could be used specifically in bartering with the Taíno, as it yielded such favourable rates (Valcárcel Royas and Martinón-Torres 2013: 508). *Guanín* is listed in Spanish inventories, such as that compiled by Cristóbal de Santa Clara, of material brought in by the Taíno, potentially as tribute, between 1505 and 1508 (Mira Caballos 2000: 81–104). By 1527, however, it was being melted down by the Spanish, presumably to extract the gold due to the declining amount of the metal being produced on the islands (Valcárcel Royas and Martinón-Torres 2013: 509).

Guanín is rarely encountered in sites of the Caribbean's pre-contact and early colonial period: of the over 60 examples of precious metals found across both the Greater and Lesser Antilles only 15 are *guanín* (Valcárcel Royas and Martinón-Torres 2013: 509–14; Vega in Oliver 2000: 200). The earliest known example, found at the Puerto Rican site of Maisabel, dates to c. AD 70–374 (Oliver 2000: 197), though it is possible that *guanín* may have been among the other items of South American material culture imported into the islands as early as 400 BC (Valcárcel Royas and Martinón-Torres 2013: 517). The majority of pieces, however, broadly date between AD 1200 and 1500 (Martinón-Torres 2012: 440). Thin sheets tended to be the preferred medium, some with embossed designs, though rare anthropo- and zoomorphic figures have also been recovered, suggesting a Colombian origin (Martinón-Torres 2012: 514).

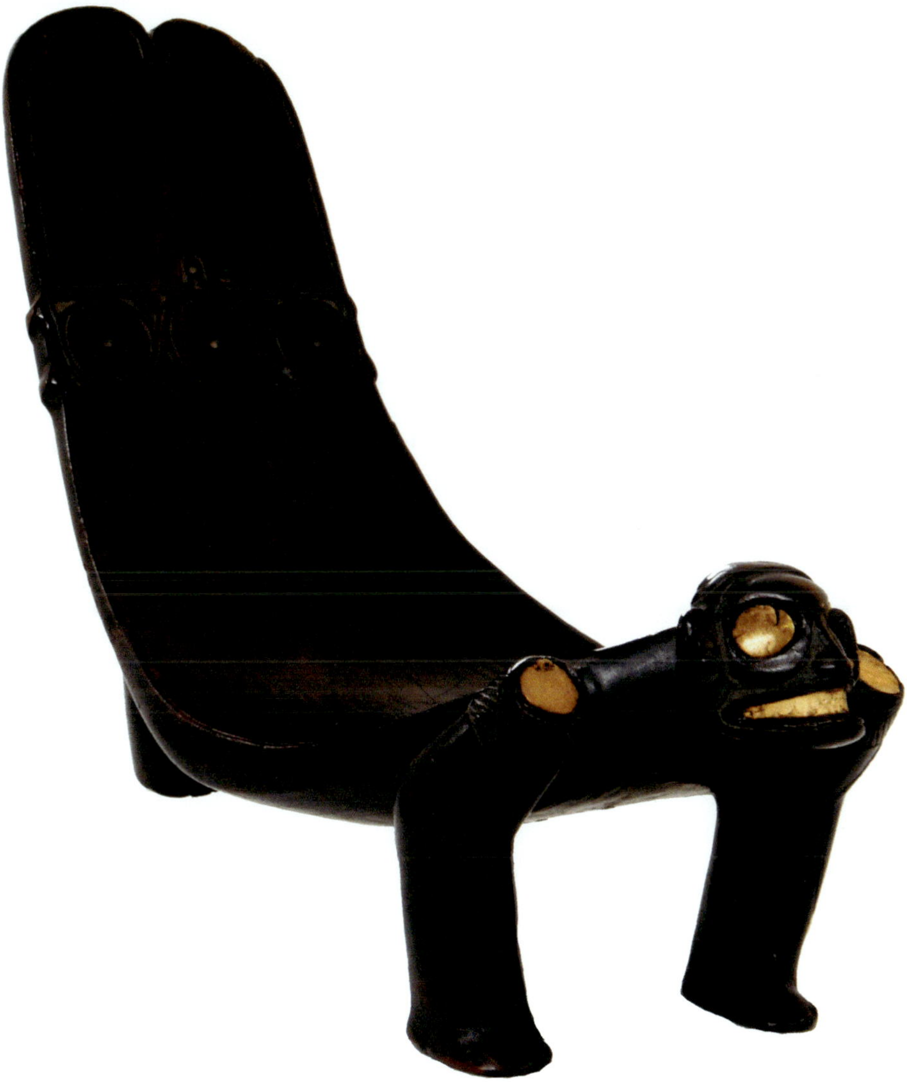

Figure 11. Hispaniolan *duho* (ceremonial seat) featuring gold inlay at the mouth, eyes, ear and shoulders. In Caribbean sculptures, body orifices and joints were frequently embellished with inlays, emphasising their importance. Photograph: Ostapkowicz; by kind permission of the British Museum, Am1949, 22.118.

To this repertoire of indigenous metal valuables were added the most highly prized European imports: copper and zinc alloys (brass) – what the Spanish called *latón*; to the Taíno, it was *turey* – literally 'of the bright sky', a heavenly entity. Las Casas notes: 'Anything made of *latón* was esteemed more than any other [metal]. They call it *turey*, as a thing from the sky, because their name for sky was *turey* [or *tureyro, tureygua*]; they smelled it as if by doing so they could sense it came from the heavens' (Oliver 2000: 198). The first mention of the exchange of European metals is via Columbus, who, after being lavished with gifts by Guacanagari, reciprocated by presenting the *cacique* with 'a large hand-basin made of yellow copper, and several tin rings' (late fifteenth/early sixteenth century Italian historian Scillacio, cited in Symcox 2002: 43). During this exchange, Scillacio continues:

> it was not permitted for all the Spaniards indiscriminately to take gifts from the Indians, but only those who could give back gifts in return: little gifts like pins, glass objects, bronze bells like the ones which are tied to the tinkling talons of hawks (indeed, Ethiopians and Arabs have been very taken with these kinds of gifts, and we often read in histories of their being exchanged in commerce). So it happened that, in exchange for very cheap gifts, the Spaniards received more than thirty *besses*[6] of gold that day. The Indians laughed at how cheaply they got bronze, and our people laughed at exchanging yellow copper for gold, since the Indians would part with an immense quantity of gold for each bronze pendant. This should surprise no one, since *rarity dictates price* (in Symcox 2002: 43–4, italics added).

Scillacio's insight – unlike those of many other historians who documented the indigenous groups as ignorant of value – ascribes as much agency to the Taíno as it does to the Spanish: each got what they desired most – that which was, in their eyes, the most rare and hence, valuable. Scales of value are invariably subjective and culturally prescribed.

This indigenous desire for European metals was not something anticipated during the earliest voyages, but to accommodate trade, even brass aglets from clothing (used to stop lace ends from fraying) were traded. Over 30 examples are known from archaeological contexts, particularly from Chorro de Maita, Cuba, where they are associated with elite burials and would have been worn as ornaments in life (Martinón-Torres *et al.* 2007: 199, 203). In the Vienna belt, two brass pins are used to secure the jet beads on the head of the *cemí*. These may have come from belt buckles, perhaps of the 'ring and pin' buckle style that was common in the first half of the sixteenth century on Spanish colonial

[6] A *bes* was a measure of eight ounces, and 30 *besses* would imply 240 ounces of gold.

sites (see Figure 9; Deagan 1987: 180–1). The jet beads held by the pins appear to cover areas of previous damage, where the belt originally may have held another material, perhaps gold (as the Spanish clearly documented in other belts). Given that the Taíno were known to refurbish important curated objects (Ostapkowicz *et al.* 2012; 2013), it is possible that the jet and brass pins replaced gold or some other material. If so, the original context (the belt) and its use as an elite accoutrement remained unaffected, it was simply modified to facilitate the display of new forms of wealth and status.

Interest in foreign metals stemmed in part from how easily they fit into indigenous understandings of value, not simply their newness or exoticness, but how they integrated into a pre-existing scale of worth, subscribing as they did to the 'aesthetic of brilliance', linking to distant lands and people, and touching upon the numinous. Gold, the most coveted of European materials, while still highly valued by the Taíno, did not have the same resonance as *guanín*, and especially *turey*.

Reflective worlds: *espejos* (mirrors)

Indigenous Caribbean 'mirrors' (*espejos* in Spanish) of highly polished gold or *guanín* sheets (see Martinón-Torres *et al.* 2007: 202) are known from the Spanish inventories (Torres 1865), with 24 listed in that of 1495/1496 (Table 2), clearly distinguished from the gold sheets (*hojuelas*), pieces of gold leaf (*hoja de oro*) and/or gold (*pintas*) also collected from the Taíno at this time. They are described as *espejos de oro* or '*espejos, las lumbres de hoja de oro*', with clear reference to gold or a gold-like material — the term *lumbres* referring to a reflective surface, and so analogous with mirrors. *Lumbres* also refers in some contexts to the embers of a dying fire (Fernández-Crespo 2015, pers. comm.), perhaps evoking the warm glow of the material in a double meaning. The reference to reflective surfaces indicates that the material must have been polished to a high degree. In some instances *espejos* are noted as being backed by cotton, suggesting that they were worn, possibly as neck or head ornaments. There are numerous early references to the presence of gold sheets on cotton body ornaments, including belts and caps, but these are described using other terms, such as *hoja de oro*.

The use of the word *espejos* is significant here: these objects are not simply described in Spanish as disks of gold or flat gold sheets, but are instead identified as mirrors. Though the term may have been used to distinguish large ornaments of flattened gold, it may also reflect nascent Spanish understandings of the Taíno worldview and value systems. As discussed above, gold was associated with cacical power while *guanín* and *turey* were considered gifts of the sky (Saunders 2011: 96) and hence embodied spiritual power (Oliver 2000). Across

Date	Description
10 March 1495	*'dos espejos, las lumbres de hoja de oro [...] que trujo un hermano de Cahonabo'* [sic]; i.e. 'two mirrors, [with] reflective surface[s] of gold leaf [...] that a brother of Caonabó brought'
18 December 1495	*'tres espejos de oro'*, i.e. 'three gold mirrors'
2 February 1496	*'é diez y seis espejos de oro'*, i.e. '16 gold mirrors'
19 February 1496	*'tres espejos de algodon, las lumbres de hoja de oro'*, i.e. 'tree mirrors of cotton, the reflective surface(s) of gold leaf'

Table 2. Gold *espejos* ('mirrors') listed in the 1495/1496 inventory.

the Americas, mirrors were viewed as conduits to a supernatural realm and as such were spiritually active entities that maintained the world, capturing cosmic energy in solid form (Saunders 1998; 2011: 95). By trapping light in their reflective surfaces, they possessed healing, energising and fertilising qualities (Saunders 2005; 115). These surfaces did not need to provide a clear reflection, as the use of the term mirror might imply; rather, recognisable but distorted images provided views into the otherworld (Saunders 1998: 18). For the Tukano of Colombia, for example, a thin shell (*gahsíru*) separates the physical and spiritual worlds, a gateway that can only be breached through hallucinogen-induced altered states of consciousness (Saunders 1998: 7). Shells, with their links to water (standing pools which provide natural mirrors), may have been conceptually linked (Saunders 1998: 15), and these naturally brilliant, reflective surfaces paralleled the qualities of those of other (super-)natural materials such as gold and *guanín*. Shells and gold were used by the Taíno as inlays for the eyes of *cemís*, emphasising the links between vision, reflective surfaces and the numinous. European mirrors (which themselves had only recently become capable of faithfully reflecting an image) were simply an extension of this understanding. Perhaps it is in this sense that the layering of reflective materials in the eyes of the Pigorini *cemí* bat face can be understood: the gold underlying the mirrors may well underscore the connection between the two in Taíno thought and how both were understood as mirrors/*espejos* of other worlds (Figure 12, left).

When gold mirrors were worn, the sunlight reflected in them was dramatically intensified, setting the metal alight. At night, firelight would catch in their surfaces, accentuated by the movements of the wearer. These ornaments were part of the pomp and circumstance of major events, focusing spectator attention on those who had privileged access to them, marking their every movement. Among circum-Caribbean groups, wearing such gold ornaments in quantity was particularly important for chiefs during raiding parties or battles 'in order to be known to their own men and also by their enemies' as Oviedo noted (in Saunders 2011: 109). Perhaps this offers another perspective on the Jamaican *cacique*'s regalia during the momentous meeting with Columbus in 1494, particularly his large *guanín* pectoral: during the tense moments of initial encounter, the Jamaican *cacique* donned his finest *espejos* in order to intimidate his potential adversary or impress a possible ally. European mirrors may have come to fill this role, held within the cotton belts, caps and ornaments worn by *caciques*, as seen in the Pigorini *cemí* and Vienna belt.

Mirrors were introduced as items of exchange from the time of Columbus's first voyage, when the Admiral himself presented the *cacique* Guacanagari with 'many things from Spain, such as glass beads [...] and mirrors' (Biscione 1997: 163). Mirrors are exceptionally rare in the archaeological record from sixteenth century sites in the Americas, suggesting that not only was their export relatively limited, but that they were carefully curated items (Jeffrey M. Mitchem 2012, pers. comm.). The Pigorini *cemí* incorporates six relatively large circular disks featured in the eyes of the bat mask and in the earflares of both faces. In the eyes of the bat, the backing of the mirrors has been scraped back, revealing a secondary eye and pupil, highlighted in hammered gold sheet and dark resin. This parallels the shape of the human eyes on the opposing rhinoceros horn mask, suggesting a link between both animal and human masks and possibly a transformative element between the two (as often seen in Taíno art). The Vienna belt also features cut circular mirrors as the eyes of its central *cemí* maskette (Figure 12, right). This prominent placement of mirrors in both pieces — substituting gold and shell inlays in the eyes and ears of the *cemís* — suggests that mirrors may have been viewed as portals through which to be seen and heard by the numinous (as well as the means to see and hear them), much as the original indigenous substances may have been viewed. Further, their presence in these elite objects quite literarily reflected upon the wearer's ability to harness the tried and tested foundations of power in the form of *cemís* through new sources and materials.

Discussion and conclusions: the role of exchange in processes of social transformation

Until recently, little was known about how European valuables were adopted, adapted and incorporated into indigenous contexts in the Caribbean: the

Figure 12. Glass mirrors in the eyes and earflares of the Pigorini *cemí* (left) and the eyes of the Vienna belt (right). The edges of the disks remain quite rough and are clearly made to the exact dimensions of each aperture. The concoidal damage to the mirrors in both pieces was likely sustained during the cutting process and suggests that cuts were made along the upper side of the mirror, likely to avoid the thin veneer of lead or mercury at the back. Photograph: Ostapkowicz; courtesy of the Polo Museale del Lazio - Museo Nazionale Preistorico Etnografico "L.Pigorini", su concessione del Mibact, acc no. 4190.

favoured, ahistorical view perpetuated the myth of traditional, unadulterated and unchanging indigenous society (cf. Wolf 1982). The peoples first encountered in the New World – the Lucayans, the Taíno and Carib described in sensational accounts and depicted in illustrations thanks to newly established printing presses – remained frozen in perpetual nakedness (Figure 13), be it 'noble chieftain' or 'savage cannibal', lacking any but the most stereotypical accoutrements: feather headdress, war club or a bow and arrow. Although early accounts describe how indigenous people actively bartered for European trade goods such as glass beads, mirrors or metals, the suggestion that they incorporated these into their own material culture, or adapted them for their own purposes, rarely enters the equation (but see Keehnen 2012; Valcárcel Rojas and Martinón Torres 2013).[7] The assumption of a swift demise in the face of European encroachment and newly introduced diseases, and a complete social and cultural collapse in the face of enforced assimilation practices, perpetuated the impression of a people unable to adapt to change. This long-held myth has

[7] For example, both the Vienna belt and Pigorini *cemí* were not identified as Caribbean artefacts until the 1950s (Schweeger-Hefel 1952) and it was not until the 1990s, particularly as a result of the exhibits and events marking the Columbus quincentenary, that researchers began to engage with the materiality of the Pigorini *cemí* and its interconnections to both European and potentially African sources (Biscione 1997; Feest 1991; Roe 1997).

Figure 13. The first European depiction of 'New World' inhabitants, one of whom offers a gold nugget to Columbus. The illustration accompanied Columbus' letter announcing his discoveries. From Columbus, *De Insulis nuper in mari Indico repertis*, Basel, 1494 (fol. IV), woodcut. Courtesy of the John Carter Brown Library at Brown University.

in many ways hindered work on early contact period indigenous (as opposed to Spanish colonial) archaeology in the Caribbean until recent years (for an overview see Deagan 2004: 601–5), though excellent archival studies have provided a more nuanced picture (Anderson Córdova 1990; Guitar 1998) and recent archaeological work on post-contact indigenous sites is set to challenge these assumptions (e.g. Valcárcel Rojas 2012). Now, a broad-scale study of this critical period — Nexus 1492, led by Corinne Hofman, Leiden University (http://nexus1492.eu) — aims to look specifically at this 'historical divide' to better understand indigenous responses and adaptations to the fifteenth to seventeenth century Caribbean.

Artefacts bridging this divide are rare and all the more important for their contribution to the emerging emphasis on indigenous agency at a time of tremendous cultural change and upheaval. The two artefacts anchoring this discussion — the Pigorini *cemí* and Vienna belt — have enabled us to explore Taíno use and perceptions of newly introduced goods such as glass and jet beads, mirrors and brass pins. It is clear that the Taíno were intrigued by Spanish imports and desired their luminous qualities for their own purposes. It is not, as is often perceived, that the Taíno were overwhelmed by the 'sophistication' of European goods; rather, they recognised them as exhibiting qualities paralleling those of their own valuables, and this re-contextualisation speaks to their active involvement in the transformative process of social change.

There may be several levels to Taíno appreciation of the value of European materials. Initially, their exoticness — the distance they had travelled and embodied and their links to the newly arrived foreigners — ensured an audience (cf. Helms 1988). Many were bright, shiny objects that fortuitously recalled indigenous valuables, smoothly aligning with the latter's pre-existing significance (e.g. green glass beads/jadeite ornaments). To gain greater meaning and value, these new materials needed to be integrated into local socio-political and economic systems. Once captured within native networks and incorporated into ornaments or high-status objects — such as seen on the Pigorini *cemí*, for example — the value of these materials transcended the merely 'exotic', absorbed into the service of indigenous meanings and aesthetics. In this sense, meaning and value were accretional and transformative (cf. Gosden and Marshall 1999: 172), ever deepening in New World significance the further integrated the Old World goods became.

Body ornaments were few and select among the Taíno, each carrying information about the wearer's connections and social position, their cultural affiliation, and status. The language of these social signifiers would be carried in a variety of subtle (and not-so-subtle) ways — from the style of woven cotton ornaments to the placement and quantity of shell and stone beads or the size and shape of a gold or *guanín* pendant. One can well imagine the impact of Old World goods on this repertoire of refined, well-understood classifications and meanings: it was the allure of the new, embodied in vibrant, un-fading materials, brought by foreigners from distant lands. Beyond this, it echoed the qualities of materials difficult to acquire, and more difficult to work (jadeites), or captured the elusive, ever-brilliant iridescence of the sun, with its links to the numinous.

The 'aesthetics of brilliance' ruled the world of the Europeans as well — perhaps consumed them is a more appropriate term, given the circumstances and exploitation of indigenous groups post-1492. Quite apart from the use of gold, pearls and precious stones in their own body ornaments, they were far from averse to using gold, mirrors and ornamentation to adorn their own religious icons. The *Virgen de la Estrella*, displayed in the very centre of the massive cathedral of Sevilla, is a case in point: already lavishly 'dressed' in gold leaf when she was created in 1566, the figure was then encased in an ornate Rococo *retablo* in 1770, replete with mirror inlays of various sizes and shapes (Figure 14). This display, in the heart of Catholic Spain and in the very cathedral to which the Taíno were brought during Columbus's triumphant return in 1493 (Las Casas 1951: 332; Parry and Keith 1984: 66), suggests that the use of such ornaments to visually enhance objects of religious veneration was not so different between the Old World and the New.

On the one hand, the Vienna belt and Pigorini *cemí* reflect Taíno traditional aesthetics, valuables and sources of indigenous power; on the other, they ingeniously interweave newly introduced European, and potentially African or Asian, wealth into that powerbase. It is a marriage of worlds, consummately harnessed through an indigenous prism. Here, the 'aesthetics of brilliance' tradition seamlessly substitutes newly introduced mirrors, jet and glass beads for traditional gold, *guanín* and polished shell beads and inlays. It appears to embrace the foreign, yet integrate it within its own milieu, structure and agency. The strategy may have been to tap into this new source of wealth, to link across to foreign lands and peoples and to understand these 'others', ideally integrating them into local social and political systems and thereby gaining insight, power and affluence. As far as we know, this is the first — and last — glimpse of hybrid elite objects made on Taíno terms, before Spanish assimilation policies undermined the cacical authority that was the impetus for such cultural masterpieces.

Figure 14. The *Virgen de la Estrella* (1566) is encased in an ornate Rococo retablo (1770), heavily inlaid with mirrors. Photograph: Ostapkowicz; Sevilla Cathedral.

Acknowledgements

This study of the Pigorini *cemí* and Vienna belt was originally part of the Pre-Hispanic Caribbean Sculptural Arts project, supported by grants from the Leverhulme Trust (2005–6) and the Getty Foundation (2007–10). I am grateful to the museums involved for facilitating access to their collections and enabling detailed photography and various analytical studies (some of which are still ongoing) – particularly the kind assistance of Donatella Saviola, curator of the Americas at the Museo Nazionale Preistorico Etnografico 'L. Pigorini', Rome and Gerard van Bussel, curator of North and Central American collections at the Weltmuseum Wien. I would like to thank colleagues at these institutions, as well as the Museo de Historia, Antropología y Arte, Universidad de Puerto Rico (particularly Directora Flavia Marichal Lugo and the late Iván Méndez, Curator, who was always a wealth of information during my visits to the Museo); the Direction des Affaires Culturelles, Guadeloupe; the British Museum, London; and the Pitt Rivers, Oxford for permissions to use my research images in this article. The John Carter Brown Library, Providence (RI), kindly allowed the use of Figure 11. Teresa Fernández-Crespo and Javier Ordoño assisted with translating some key sections of sixteenth century Spanish text. Daniela Hofmann and Nicholas Wells are thanked for welcoming an Americas perspective in their 'Crystal Formed of Necessity' EAA session in Istanbul (2014), and José Oliver and Rick Schulting for their comments on an earlier version of this paper.

Bibliography

Alegría, R. 1981. *El uso de la incrustación en la escultura de los Indios Antillanos.* Santo Domingo, Centro de Estudios Avanzados de Puerto Rico y El Caribe y Fundación García Arévalo.

Alegría, R. 1995. Apuntes sobre la vestimenta y los adornos de los caciques Taínos de las Antillas y de la paraphernalia asociada a sus funciones mágico-religiosas. In M. Rodríguez and R. Alegría (eds), *Actas del XV Congreso Internacional de Arqueología de Caribe*: 295–309. San Juan, Centro de Estudios Avanzados de Puerto Rico y el Caribe.

Anderson-Córdova, K. 1990. *Hispaniola and Puerto Rico: Indian acculturation and heterogeneity, 1492–1550.* PhD thesis, Department of Anthropology, Yale University.

Appadurai, A. 1986. Introduction: commodities and the politics of value. In A. Appadurai (ed.), *The social life of things: commodities in cultural perspective*: 3–63. Cambridge, Cambridge University Press.

Arrom, J. J. 1999. *An account of the antiquities of the Indians: a new edition, with an introductory study, notes and appendixes by José Juan Arrom.* Translated by Susan C. Griswold. Durham, Duke University Press.

Arroyo, C., Miguel, G., Cruxent, J. M. and Perez Soto de Atencio, S. 1971. *Arte Prehispanico de Venezuela.* Caracas, Fundación Eugenio Mendoza.

Bernaldez, A. 1967. History of the Catholic sovereigns, Don Ferdinand and Dona Isabella. In C. Jane (ed.), *Selected documents illustrating the four voyages of Columbus. Volume 1: the first and second voyages*: 114–67. Millwood, Krause Reprint.

Biscione, M. 1997. Epilogue: the beaded zemi in the Pigorini Museum: history and problems of interpretation. In F. Brecht, E. Brodsky, J. A. Farmer and D. Taylor (eds), *Taíno: pre-Columbian art and culture from the Caribbean*: 158–63. New York, The Monacelli Press.

Boomert, A. 1987. Gifts of the Amazon: 'green stone' pendants and beads as items of ceremonial exchange in Amazonia and the Caribbean. *Antropológica* 67: 33–54.

Bray, W. 1997. Metallurgy and anthropology: two studies from Prehispanic America. *Boletín del Museo del Oro* 42: 37–55.

Brill, R. H. 2012. San Salvador and related glasses (Puerto Rico). In R. H. Brill and C. P. Stapleton (eds), *Chemical analyses of early glasses. Volume 3. The years 2000-2011, reports and essays*: 544–8. Corning, The Corning Glass Museum.

Brill, R H., Tong, S. S. C., Barnes, I. L., Joel, E. C. and Murtagh, M. J. 1987. Laboratory studies of some European artifacts excavated on San Salvador Island. In D. T. Gerace (ed.), *Columbus and his world: proceedings of the First San Salvador Conference*: 247–92. Ft. Lauderdale, The Station.

Carlson, L. A. 1995. Strings of command: manufacture and utilization of shell beads among the Taíno. In M. Rodríguez and R. Alegría (eds), *Actas del XV Congreso Internacional de Arqueología de Caribe*: 97–109. San Juan, Centro de Estudios Avanzados de Puerto Rico y el Caribe.

Chanlatte-Baik, L. A. 2013. Huecoid culture and the Antillean Agroalfarero (Farmer-Potter) period. In W. F. Keegan, C. L. Hofman and R. Rodríguez Ramos (eds), *The Oxford handbook of Caribbean archaeology*: 171–83. Oxford, Oxford University Press.

Chanlatte Baik, L. and Narganes Storde, Y. 1984. *Arqueología de Vieques*. Second edition. Río Piedras, Universidad de Puerto Rico.

Colón, F. 1992. *The life of the Admiral Columbus by his son, Ferdinand*. Translated and annotated by Benjamin Keen. New Brunswick, Rutgers University Press.

Curet, A. 2014. The Taíno: phenomena, concepts and terms. *Ethnohistory* 61(3): 467–95.

Deagan, K. 1987a. *Artifacts of the Spanish colonies of Florida and the Caribbean, 1500-1800. Vol 1: ceramics, glassware and beads*. Washington, Smithsonian Institution Press.

Deagan, K. 1987b. Initial encounters: Arawak responses to European contact at the En Bas Saline site, Haiti. In D. T. Gerace (ed.), *Columbus and his world: proceedings of the First San Salvador Conference*: 341–59. Ft. Lauderdale, The Station.

Deagan, K. 2002. *Artifacts of the Spanish colonies of Florida and the Caribbean, 1500-1800. Volume 2: portable personal possessions*. Washington, Smithsonian Institution Press.

Deagan, K. 2004. Reconsidering Taíno social dynamics after conquest: gender and class in culture contact studies. *American Antiquity* 69(4): 597–626.

Dunn, O. and Kelly, Jr., J. E. 1989. *The Diario of Christopher Columbus's first voyage to America, 1492–1493.* Norman, University of Oklahoma Press.

Etrich, C. 2002. Deviation de Capesterre Belle-Eau, Allée Dumanoir. *Bilan Scientifique* 2002: 23–8.

Feest, C. F. 1991. Beaded belt. In J. A. Levenson (ed.), *Circa 1492: art in the age of exploration*: 580–1. Washington, National Gallery of Art.

García Arévalo, M. A. 1990. Transculturation in contact period and contemporary Hispaniola. In D. H. Thomas (ed.), *Columbian consequences: archaeological and historical perspectives on the Spanish borderlands east. Vol 2*: 269–80. Washington, Smithsonian Institution Press.

Gosden, C. 2004. *Archaeology and colonialism: culture contact from 5000 BC to the present.* Cambridge, Cambridge University Press.

Gosden, C. 2008. Social ontologies. *Philosophical Transactions of the Royal Society* 363: 2003–10.

Gosden, C. and Marshall, Y. 1999. The cultural biography of objects. *World Archaeology* 31(2): 169–78.

Guitar, L. A. 1998. *Cultural genesis: relationships among Indians, Africans and Spaniards in rural Hispaniola, first half of the sixteenth century.* Ph.D. thesis, Vanderbilt University.

Guitar, L., Ferbel, P. and Estevez, J. 2006. *Ocama-Daca Taíno* (Hear me, I am Taíno): Taíno survival on Hispaniola, focusing on the Dominican Republic. In M. Forte (ed), *Indigenous resurgence in the contemporary Caribbean: Amerindian survival and revival*: 41–68. New York: Peter Lang.

Haviser, J. B. 1999. Lithics. In C. L. Hofman and M. L. P. Hoogland (eds), *Archaeological investigations on St Martin (Lesser Antilles)*: 189–213. Leiden, Leiden University.

Hayes, K. and Cipolla, C. 2015. Introduction: re-imagining colonial pasts, influencing colonial futures. In C. Cipolla and Hayes, K. (eds), *Rethinking colonialism: comparative archaeological approaches*, 1–14. Gainsville, University Press of Florida.

Helms, M. 1986. Art styles and interaction spheres in central America and the Caribbean: polished black wood in the Greater Antilles. *Journal of Latin American Lore* 12(1): 25–43.

Helms, M. 1988. *Ulysses' sail: an ethnographic Odyssey of power, knowledge and geographical distance.* Princeton, Princeton University Press.

Hoffman, C. A. 1987. Archaeological investigations at the Long Bay site, San Salvador, Bahamas. In D. T. Gerace (ed.), *Columbus and his world: proceedings of the First San Salvador Conference*: 237–45. Ft. Lauderdale, The Station.

Hofman, C. L. and Hoogland, M. L. P. 2004. Social dynamics and change in the northern Lesser Antilles. In A. Delpuech and C. L. Hofman (eds), *Late Ceramic Age societies in the eastern Caribbean*: 49–57. Oxford, Archaeopress (British Archaeological Reports International Series 1273).

Hofman, C. L., Bright, A. J., Boomert, A. and Knippenberg, S. 2007. Island rhythms: the web of social relationships and interaction networks in the Lesser Antillean archipelago between 400 B.C.–A.D.1492. *Latin American Antiquity* 18(3): 243–68.

Hofman, C. L, Boomert, A., Bright, A. J., Hoogland, M. L. P., Knippenberg, S. and Samson, A. V. M. 2011. Ties with the homelands: archipelagic interaction and enduring role of the south and central American mainlands in the pre-Columbian Lesser Antilles. In A. Curet and M. W. Hauser (eds), *Islands at the crossroads: migration, seafaring, and interaction in the Caribbean*: 73–86. Tuscaloosa, The University of Alabama Press.

Jane, C. 1967. *Select documents illustrating the four Voyages of Columbus*, reprint. New York, Kraus.

Jansen, R. 1999. Shell. In C. L. Hofman and M. L. P. Hoogland (eds), *Archaeological investigations on St Martin (Lesser Antilles)*: 215–28. Leiden, Leiden University.

Kagan, R. L. 1991. The Spain of Ferdinand and Isabella. In A. Levenson (ed.), *Circa 1492: art in the age of exploration*: 55–61. Washington, National Gallery of Art.

Kamen, H. 2005. *Spain 1469–1714: a society of conflict*. Harlow, Pearson.

Keehnen, F. W. M. 2011. Conflicting cosmologies: the exchange of brilliant objects between the Taíno of Hispaniola and the Spanish. In C. L. Hofman and A. van Duijvenbode (eds), *Communities in contact: essays in archaeology, ethnohistory and ethnography of the Amerindian circum-Caribbean*: 253–68. Leiden: Sidestone Press.

Keehnen, F. W. M. 2012. *Trinkets (f)or treasure: the role of European material culture in intercultural contacts in Hispaniola during early colonial times*. Masters thesis, University of Leiden.

Las Casas, B. de 1951. *Historia de las Indias. Volume 1*. Mexico City, Fondo de Cultura Economica (Biblioteca Americana 1).

Las Casas, B. de 1967a. *Apologética historia sumaria. Volume 1*. Mexico, Universidad Nacional Autónoma de México, Instituto de Investigaciones Históricas.

Las Casas, B. de 1967b. *Apologética historia sumaria. Volume 2*. Mexico, Universidad Nacional Autónoma de México, Instituto de Investigaciones Históricas.

Lardicci, F. (ed.). 1999. *A synoptic edition of the log of Columbus's first voyage. Reportorium Columbianum, Vol VI*. Turnhout, Brepols.

Martinón-Torres, M., Valcárcel Rojas, R., Cooper, J. and Rehren, T. 2007. Metals, microanalysis and meaning: a study of metal objects excavated from the indigenous cemetery of El Chorro de Maíta, Cuba. *Journal of Archaeological Science* 34: 194–204.

Martinón-Torres, M., Valcárcel Rojas, R., Sáenz Samper, J. and Guerra, M. 2012. Metallic encounters in Cuba: the technology, exchange and meaning of metals before and after Columbus. *Journal of Archaeological Science* 31: 439–54.

Martyr D'Anghera, P. 1970. *De orbe novo: the eight decades of Peter Martyr D'Anghera*. Translated by Francis August MacNutt. New York, Burt Franklin.

Mira Caballos, E. 2000. *Las Antillas Mayores, 1492–1550 (Ensayos y documentos)*. Vervuert, Iberoamericana.

Mol, A. A. A. 2007. *Costly giving, giving* Guaízas: *towards an organic model of the exchange of social valuables in the Late Ceramic Age Caribbean*. Leiden, Sidestone Press.

Oliver, J. R. 2009. *Caciques and cemí idols: the web spun by Taíno rulers between Hispaniola and Puerto Rico*. Tuscaloosa, Unversity of Alabama Press.

Oliver, J. R. 2000. Gold symbolism among Caribbean chiefdoms. In C. McEwan (ed.), *Precolumbian gold: technology, style and iconography*: 196–219. London: British Museum.

Oliver, J. R. 1999. The 'La Hueca problem' in Puerto Rico and the Caribbean: old problems, new perspectives, possible solutions. In C. L. Hofman and M. L. P. Hoogland (eds), *Archaeological investigations on St Martin (Lesser Antilles)*: 253–97. Leiden, Leiden University.

Ostapkowicz, J. 2013. 'Made...with admirable artistry'. The context, manufacture and meaning of a Taíno belt. *The Antiquaries Journal* 93: 287–317.

Ostapkowicz, J. 2015. The sculptural legacy of the Jamaican Taíno. Part II: 18th–21st century discoveries. *Jamaica Journal* 36(1): 94–106.

Ostapkowicz, J. 2016. Étude sur les figurines en «bois». *Bilan Scientifique: Direction Régionale des Affaires Culturelles Guadeloupe 2014*: 58–61.

Ostapkowicz, J. in press. L'Allée Dumanoir 'bois' pendeloque en form de visage. Paris, Institut national de recherches archéologiques preventives (INRAP/CNRS).

Ostapkowicz, J., Wiedenhoeft, A. C., Ramsey, C. B., Ribechini, E., Wilson, S., Brock, F. and Higham, T. 2011. 'Treasures... of black wood, brilliantly polished': five examples of *Guaiacum* sculpture from the 10th–16th century Caribbean. *Antiquity* 85: 942–59.

Ostapkowicz, J., Ramsey, C.B., Brock, F., Higham, T., Wiedenhoeft, A. C., Ribechini, E., Lucejko, J. J. and Wilson, S. 2012. Chronologies in wood and resin: AMS ^{14}C dating of pre-Hispanic Caribbean wood sculpture. *Journal of Archaeological Science* 39: 2238–51.

Ostapkowicz, J., Ramsey, C. B., Brock, F., Cartwright, C., Stacey, R. and Richards, M. 2013. Birdmen, *cemís* and *duhos*: material studies and AMS ^{14}C dating of pre-Hispanic Caribbean wood sculptures in the British Museum. *Journal of Archaeological Science* 40: 4675–87.

Oviedo y Valdés, G. F. de 1959. *Historia general y natural de las Indias. Biblioteca de Autores Españoles*. Madrid, Ediciones Atlas.

Parry, J. H. and Keith, R. G. 1984. *New Iberian world: a documentary history of the discovery and settlement of Latin America to the early 17th century: the Caribbean. Vol II*. New York, Times Books.

Petitjean-Roget, H. 1995. Note sur deux amulettes de boix trouvées á Morel, Guadeloupe. In M. Rodríguez and R. Alegría (eds), *Actas del XV Congreso Internacional de Arqueología de Caribe*: 417–22. San Juan, Centro de Estudios Avanzados de Puerto Rico y el Caribe.

Rodríguez Ramos, R. 2011. Close encounters of the Caribbean kind. In L. A. Curet and M. W. Hauser (eds), *Islands at the crossroads: migration, seafaring, and interaction in the Caribbean*: 164–92. Tuscaloosa, The University of Alabama Press.

Roe, P. 1997. Epilogue: the beaded zemi in the Pigorini Museum. In F. Brecht, E. Brodsky, J. A. Farmer and D. Taylor (eds), *Taíno: pre-Columbian art and culture from the Caribbean*: 164–9. New York, The Monacelli Press.

Roth, W. E. 1924. An introductory study of the arts, crafts and customs of the Guiana Indians. In F. W. Hodge (ed.), *38th Annual Report of the Bureau of American Ethnology 1916-17*: 27–745. Washington, Smithsonian Institution.

Samson, A. 2010. *Renewing the house: trajectories of social life in the yucayeque (community) of El Cabo, Higüey, Dominican Republic, AD 800 to 1504*. Leiden, Sidestone Press.

Saunders, N. 2011. Shimmering worlds: brilliance, power, and gold in pre-Columbian Panama. In J. W. Hoopes, J. Quilter, N. J. Saunders and R. G. Cooke (eds), *To capture the sun: gold of ancient Panama*: 78–113. Tulsa, Gilcrease Museum and University of Tulsa.

Saunders, N. 1998. Stealers of light, traders in brilliance: Amerindian metaphysics in the mirror of conquest. *RES: Anthropology and Aesthetics* 33: 225–52.

Saunders, N. 1999. Biographies of brilliance: pearls, transformations of matter and being, ca. 1492. *World Archaeology* 31(20): 243–57.

Saunders, N. 2003. 'Catching the light': technologies of power and enchantment in pre-Columbian goldworking. In J. Quilter and J. W. Hoopes (eds), *Gold and power in ancient Costa Rica, Panama, and Colombia*: 15–47. Washington, Dumbarton Oaks.

Saunders, N. 2005. *Peoples of the Caribbean*. San Diego, ABC-Clio.

Schweeger-Hefel, A. 1952. Ein rätselhaftes Stück aus der alten Ambraser Sammlung. *Archiv für Völkerkunde* 6–7: 209–28.

Siegel, P. E. 2011. Competitive polities and territorial expansion in the Caribbean. In L. A. Curet and M. W. Hauser (eds), *Islands at the crossroads: migration, seafaring, and interaction in the Caribbean*: 193–218. Tuscaloosa, The University of Alabama Press.

Smith, M. T. and Good, M. E. 1982. *Early sixteenth century glass beads in the Spanish colonial trade*. Greenwood, Cottonlandia Museum Publications.

Strathern, M. 1988. *The gender of the gift: problems with women and problems with society in Melanesia*. Berkeley and Los Angeles, University of California Press (Studies in Melanesian Anthropology, no. 6).

Sullivan, E. 2006. The black hand: notes on the African presence in the visual arts of Brazil and the Caribbean. In J. J. Rischel and S. Stratton-Pruitt (eds), *The arts in Latin America, 1492-1820*: 39–55. New Haven, Yale University Press.

Symcox, G. 2002. *Repertorium Columbianum. Volume X: Italian reports on America, 1493-1522: letters, dispatches and Papal bulls*. Turnhout, Brepols Publishers.

Torres de Mendoza, D. L. 1868. Relacion del oro y joyas que recibió el Almirante despues que el Receptor Sebastian de Olaño partió de la isla Española para Castilla, desde 10 de Marzo de 1495. In J. F. Pacheco, D. F. de Cárdenas and D. L. Torres de Mendoza (eds), *Colección de documentos inéditos relativos al descubrimiento, conquista y organización de las Antiguas possessiones Españolas de América y Oceanía sacados de los Archivos del Reino, y muy especialmente del de Indias. Tomo X*: 5–9. Madrid, J. Perez.

Tuer, D. 2003. Old bones and beautiful words: the spiritual contestation between Shaman and Jesuit in the Guaraní missions. In A. Greer and J. Bilinkoff (eds), *Colonial Saints: discovering the holy in the Americas, 1500–1800*: 77–97. New York, Routledge.

Valcárcel Rojas, R. 2012. *Interaccíon colonial en un pueblo de indios encomendados: El Chorro de Maíta, Cuba.* PhD thesis, Leiden University.
Valcárcel Rojas, R. and Martinón Torres, M. 2013. Metals in the indigenous societies of the insular Caribbean. In W. F. Keegan, C. L. Hofman and R. Rodríguez Ramos (eds), *The Oxford handbook of Caribbean archaeology*: 504–22. Oxford, Oxford University Press.
Vega, B. 1987. Un cinturón tejido y una careta de madera de Santo Domingo, del períodio de transculturación Taíno-Español. In B. Vega (ed.), *Santos, Shamanes y Zemíes*: 17–29. Santo Domingo, Fundacion Cultural Dominicana.
Whitehead, N. L. 1999. The crises and transformations of invaded societies: the Caribbean (1492–1580). In F. Salomon and S. B. Schwartz (eds), *The Cambridge history of the native peoples of the Americas. Volume 3, South America. Part 1*: 864–903. Cambridge, Cambridge University Press.
Wilson, S. 1990. *Hispaniola: Caribbean chiefdoms in the age of Columbus*. Tuscaloosa, University of Alabama Press.
Wolf, E. R. 1982. *Europe and the people without history*. Berkley, University of California Press.

Gifts of the gods – objects of foreign origin in traditional exchange systems in Palau

Constanze Dupont

Abstract

On the Micronesian islands of Palau in the Pacific, the exchange of gifts, money and food is still a lived tradition and a key part of life from birth to death. Most notably, Palauan bead money (*udoud er belau*) has kept its symbolic importance and is used for certain key occasions, such as celebrations to mark the birth of one's first child, funerals, weddings, appointments of new chiefs or divorces. The value of any given piece is decided by its attribution to one of the many categories and subcategories of money, as well as by its prior history, any previous owners and the occasion on which it came into the family. This contribution traces the mythical and historical origins of Palauan bead money, showing several likely sources from across Asia (Indo-Pacific region, east Java, China). Although no beads were ever produced in Palau itself, in recent years there has been some controversy regarding the separation of traditional and so-called 'new' beads. The latter are often acquired from antiques dealers in the Philippines and challenge existing hierarchies, while also threatening to start a process of inflation. In the final part of this article, I briefly sketch how this discourse maps onto current exchange and status relations in Palau.

Keywords: Palau, exchange systems, beads, currency, trade

Résumé

Cadeaux des dieux – objets exotiques au sein des cycles traditionnels d'échange à Palaos

Sur l'ile micronésienne de Palaos dans le Pacifique, l'échange de cadeaux, de monnaie et de nourriture est toujours une tradition vivante et un élément clés de la vie, de la naissance jusqu'à la mort. C'est en particulier le cas pour la perle monnaie de Palaos (*udoud er belau*) qui a gardé son importance symbolique et est toujours utilisée pour certaines occasions importantes, comme la naissance du premier enfant, les funérailles, les mariages, les nominations des nouveaux chefs ou les divorces. La valeur d'une perle donnée comme cadeau est décidée par son attribution à une des nombreuses catégories et sous-catégories de monnaie ainsi que par son histoire, ses propriétaires précédents et l'occasion pour laquelle elle est entrée dans la famille. Cette contribution retrace les origines mythiques et historiques de la perle monnaie de Palaos, montrant ainsi différentes sources d'origine probables à travers toute l'Asie (région indopacifique, est de Java, Chine). Bien que jamais aucune perle ne fût produite à Palaos même, il y a eu ces dernières années quelques controverses concernant la distinction entre les perles traditionnelles et ce que l'on appelle les « nouvelles » perles. Ces dernières sont souvent acquises auprès de marchands d'antiquités aux Philippines et remettent en question les hiérarchies existantes, tout en menaçant de déclencher un processus d'inflation. Dans la dernière partie de cet article, j'évoquerai brièvement comment ce discours se rapporte aux relations actuelles d'échange et de statut à Palaos.

Mots-clés: Palaos, systèmes d'échange, perles, monnayage, commerce

Zusammenfassung

Geschenke der Götter – Objekte fremder Herkunft in traditionellen Tauschsystemen auf Palau

Auf den mikronesischen Inseln Palaus im Pazifik bildet der Gaben-, Geld- und Nahrungstausch weiterhin eine wichtige Tradition, die das Leben von der Geburt bis zum Tod begleitet. Insbesondere das palauische Perlengeld (*udoud er belau*) hat seine symbolische Bedeutung bewahrt und wird zu wichtigen Anlässen verwendet, etwa die Feiern zur Geburt eines erstgeborenen Kindes, Beerdigungen, Hochzeiten, Einführungen neuer Chiefs oder Scheidungen. Der Wert eines Stückes hängt von der Zuordnung zu einer der zahlreichen Kategorien und Unterkategorien des Perlengeldes ab, ebenso wie von seiner Geschichte, vorherigen Eigentümern und dem Anlass, zu dem es in den Besitz der Familie gelangte. Der vorliegende Beitrag geht den mythischen und historischen Ursprüngen des palauischen Perlengeldes nach und zeigt mehrere wahrscheinliche Quellen in Asien auf (indopazifische Region, Ost-Java, China). Obwohl in Palau diese Art der Perlen nie hergestellt wurde, kam es in der jüngeren Vergangenheit zu Kontroversen über die Unterscheidung zwischen traditionellen und sogenannten „neuen" Perlen. Letztere werden oftmals von Antiquitätenhändlern auf den Philippinen erworben und stellen bestehende Hierarchien in Frage. Zugleich drohen sie einen Inflationsprozess in Gang zu setzten. Im letzten Teil dieses Beitrags wird kurz darauf eingegangen, wie dieser Diskurs sich auf gegenwärtige Tausch- und Statusbeziehungen auf Palau auswirkt.

Schlüsselwörter: Palau, Tauschsysteme, Perlen, Währungen, Handel

Introduction

> Rengil's wife went to the taro field with the wife of the first chief Gourkerdeu and they saw the snake. They did not bring home any taro, which is why Rengil scolded his wife. So she told him about the snake. He polished his adze by the river, went to the field, and when he saw the tail of the creature he struck down. A lot of money came out of it. This is how he became rich and a *rubak* (Krämer 1929a: 140, italics added).

On the Micronesian islands of Palau in the Pacific, the exchange of gifts, money and food is still a lived tradition and a key part of life from birth to death. Through changing lifestyles, economic priorities and consumer thinking, these customs have changed and have by now largely been adapted to the exigencies of modern life. Over the last 300 years, European explorers, whalers, Western traders, Spanish and German colonial administrations and missionaries have left their mark on Micronesian society. Similarly, the aftermath of the Japanese-American war in the Pacific and four decades of American administration have influenced life on the islands. Yet Palauans have shown themselves to be remarkably resistant and have held on to traditional social and family structures. While imported goods were highly sought after, they could be integrated into traditional exchange systems without replacing or supplanting the actual objects of value and exchange. It is particularly these objects of value which have kept their symbolic importance to this day, alongside the US-American dollar.

There are three kinds of objects of value in Palau: *udoud er belau* (Palauan bead money), *toluk* (turtle shell plates) and the US dollar (Figure 1). *Udoud er belau* has remained the object of exchange systems which in this form are unique in the world. Mostly in combination with the US dollar, Palauan money is used for important occasions, such as the celebrations to mark the birth of one's first child, funerals, weddings, appointments of new chiefs or divorces. In everyday life, a woman normally wears a single large piece of Palauan money on a simple black band around her neck (Figure 2). The money generally belongs to her husband's family and is a sign of his relatives' esteem for her. The value of any given piece is not only decided by its attribution to one of the many categories and subcategories of money, but also by its prior history, any previous owners and the occasion on which it came into the family.

In this contribution, I will trace the mythical and historical origins of Palauan bead money, showing several likely sources from across Asia. Although this kind of beads were never manufactured in Palau itself, in recent years there has

Figure 1. Objects of value used on Palau. The Palauan bead-money will be covered by a pepper leaf (*Kebui*) (© C. Dupont).

Figure 2a: Palauan lady wearing a piece of money (© C. Dupont).

been some controversy regarding the separation of traditional and so-called 'new/fake' beads. In the final part of this article, I will briefly sketch how this discourse maps onto current exchange and status relations in Palau.

The mythical and historical origin of Palauan money

The origin of the *udoud er belau* itself is still controversial. In Palau, the history of the development and origin of the beads lies in the sphere of myths and legends, which differ from region to region. They are often connected to gods or chiefs who are said to have brought the money back from now submerged islands. For instance, on Angaur it is told that a bird gave birth to a fish, which in turn gave birth to a girl with supernatural powers. The girl grew unusually tall and gave birth to Palauan bead money. This angered her, and she wiped the money off her finger and disappeared. In contrast, on Kayangel the story involves a boy being dragged off to a foreign island by a fish. On the beach, he picked up rocks which turned into Palauan money (Kubary 1889: 23). The legend told on Melekeok is that a god visited the community and emptied the beads from his testicles (Ritzenthaler 1954: 11).

Figure 2b: Presentation of a young woman at her first child ceremony, displaying Palauan money (© C. Dupont).

Whether from the sky, magical creatures in animal shape, money trees or faraway foreign islands, the origin of money is always located in a non-historical place and not given a specific time, thus underlining the Palauan idea of the otherworldliness of money. Money is alien, from beyond this world or of magical origin, it comes from the eyes of the gods in the sky or from the deep blue sea. It is a gift from the gods and for this reason is highly regarded and plays an important role on the islands of Palau.

First reports of Palauan money are found in the records of Captain Henry Wilson, who spent time in Palau after being shipwrecked in 1783 (Keate 2007). Thanks to Captain Wilson's records, we know that Palauan bead money has been in use for at least several centuries. As will be shown in what follows, today it is regarded as scientifically proven that the beads were not produced in Palau itself.

Some scholars are of the opinion that the beads come from earlier sites in Palau and Yap. Wilhelm Müller-Wismar (1917: 132–3) describes how around the year 1910, glass beads are said to have existed in the Yap islands, but that these were probably later replaced by stone money. Similarly, in her article Inez de Beauclair describes seeing a few pieces of Palauan money during her research on Yap. Thus, the Yapese legend of Giluai narrates how he searched in the sky for a shell bracelet which had been buried with his brother. On his way back to earth, he collected magical fruit out of which he fashioned himself a necklace. When he then set foot back on earth, the fruit had changed into beads. The largest was not round, but had a crescent shape. Many generations later, it passed to Rengenbai, who brought this bead to Palau in order to obtain permission to mine the Yapese stone money there (de Beauclair 1963: 2).

On Yap, there are further legends concerning the origin of Palauan money: the beads fell from the sky, grew over night from the flowers of banana trees or were brought a long time ago by the clan ancestors (Lautz 1999: 31).

One version which gives us a first clue as to the timeframe involved is a story told to the ethnographer Robert Ritzenthaler by his Palauan informant Niratagau and which he renders as follows:

> Two ships came from Portugal together. One of them ran aground at Narwangel (a now sunken island near Kayangel). The other ship was wrecked on Oolong (between Koror and Peleliu). [...] The men needing food and water looked for goods they could use for trade. They broke up the ship's cabin, and cut up the decoration into small pieces, bored holes in the pieces, strung them on cords, and traded them to the Palauans. When they contacted

> the crew of the other ship they told them of their success. This happened about four hundred years ago, before that time the Palauans had no money (Ritzenthaler 1954: 11).

Ritzenthaler himself doubts this version of events, but admits that it is still the most plausible story he has heard regarding the origin of money (Ritzenthaler 1954: 12).

In contrast, Johann Stanislaus Kubary was of the opinion that money reached Palau from Yap since, as mentioned above, it was often found buried in the ground there (Kubary 1889: 25). In addition, Kubary characterises the *udoud* as an 'emanation of Malay culture, since the Malaysian archipelago has entertained trade relations with the Chinese since time immemorial' (Kubary 1889: 28). In his work, Krämer argues that while some pieces came from Yap, their origin was still to be sought in south-east Asia, and that these were undoubtedly Asian (India) or even Mediterranean (Egypt, Murano) products. However, he admitted that there was no complete correspondence that would allow to pin down the exact date and origin. In addition, Krämer was convinced that Chinese seafarers, who entered trade relations with individual Pacific islands early on, introduced these beads (Krämer 1926: 156–7). He hereby refers to a passage in the Colección de documentos ineéditor [sic] (Vol. VS. 19; reproduced in Krämer 1926: 157) which indicates the existence of early trade relations:

> Here we took a native who we brought to the Moluccas, who told us that every year two junks came from China, that there are several ships in which they travel to buy gold and beads, of which there were large quantities, and that further ships visited other islands for the same purpose.

For Ritzenthaler, Krämer's hypothesis that the beads were introduced to Palau by Asian traders is the most common-sense, as he favours Indonesia as their place of origin. He thereby references reports of ancient multi-coloured beads which were also used as money in, amongst others, Borneo, Sumatra and Timor (Ritzenthaler 1954: 12).

Other ethnologists follow Krämer's ideas on the origin and import of Palauan money. Thus, Richard Parmentier (1987: 38) suggested that the presence of opaque and translucent glass beads and bracelet sections could be explained by trade contacts with China, Malaysia, the Philippines or Arab traders. Roland Force also discusses the same possibility of Palauan money being the result of contacts with Chinese, Malaysian, Filipino or Arab traders. He refers to reports of stranded ships and points out the similarity of the beads with archaeological finds from Cebu and Jolo in the Philippines (Force 1959: 42).

In the year 1791, the logs of the *Snow Panther*[1] recorded the following:

> The vessel from day break till sunset was surrounded with canoes, but not a man permitted to come over the gunwale, except the principal men who sat down peaceably on the deck. The appearance of our large China beads roused up the spirit of invention among them, and industry was introduced among them for a while (McCluer 1790/92: 115).

This supports the ethnological hypotheses suggested so far. Without having carried out an exhaustive study himself, Douglas Osborne (1979: 241) suggests that money reached Palau between AD 200 and 900.

Krämer (1929b: 29–30) succinctly summarises ethnological thought on the origins of Palauan money when he states:

> It [bead money] certainly came south from Asia, or at least came via this bridge. In Indonesia, alongside Borneo beads are also known from the graves of Savu, Sumba, Timor, Flores, Alor, Timorlaut. Recall at this point the African aggri beads, which were worth twice their weight in gold. [...] Another argument for India is the Indo-Germanic word *muti* for 'bead', which is rendered *mutija* in Malaysian, *mutya* in Sanskrit. In 1516, a great trade in beads still existed in Cambay; in 400 BC already Indian beads are said to have reached Greece and South Africa, Egypt and so on. To my knowledge, beads of Roman manufacture are only known after the birth of Christ, and only the Alemannian ones — the small, round, yellow and reddish-yellow examples of which recall Palau — are likely to be of European origin. [...] Of the crescent-shaped *bagĕl* I have already said that their shape suggests China, where recently very similar ones have been found. As the Chinese were the ones to bring them to Palau, this find is even more important. The Palauan *bagĕl* are triangular in cross-section and undoubtedly made from bracelets; we will have to wait until we find some original pieces [...]. The question remains open, but for me an Asian origin and trade for these elaborate products seems certain, as not only were the Chinese early traders, but new research shows they were also expansive, conquering Java in the 1200s and 1400s and threatening east Africa. One may thus assume that their knowledge of seafaring goes back much further.

---

1 In August 1790, Captain John McCluer was sent to Palau (Peleliu) on board the *Snow Panther*, accompanied by the *Endeavour* under Leutenant William Drummond. His mission was to inform the Ibedul (paramount chief) of the death of his son, Prince Lee Boo, who had been taken to England by Captain Henry Wilson.

In the following sections, I will review the most likely origins for Palauan money and the likely timeframe of its introduction.

Bead production sites

Three kinds of beads are attested in Palau (Figure 3):

1. Monochrome beads (Indo-Pacific beads)
2. Mosaic or eye beads (East Java glass beads/Jatim polychrome beads)
3. Bracelet segments

Beads had many different functions in the lives of south-east Asian island populations. They were used for adornment, as protective amulets, as badges of political rank, as dowry, as objects of ceremonial exchange, but also as sacrifices to appease supernatural powers. In Indonesia, Malaysia and the northern Philippines, bead ornaments were invested with multifaceted religious and social meanings: they were looked after as an ancestral treasure symbolising the current owner's position in the world. Different patterns and colours signal political, family and mythical relationships of regional importance. What stands out is the immanent value of beads – which were not only turned into ornaments – in south-east Asian cultures: a rare, old example is comparable to a precious gem in other parts of the world, or to a valued antique. The names and histories, former owners and age of each single bead are known. However, in different countries some beads are more valued than others (Dubin 1997: 224–5).

Indo-Pacific beads

In India, glass beads are known as early as 1000 BC from Baghwanpura and Alamgirpur and from around 800 BC from Maki. Larger quantities of beads appear in the trade centre of Taxila from about the sixth century BC. The amounts of beads found there suggest that they were produced locally, although no glass waste was recovered. In the first two centuries AD, Roman gold glass beads and eye beads were imported, but beyond that the Roman Empire appears to have had little influence on Indian production. From the second century AD, glass beads were produced in different places in India using indigenous technologies, whereby the drawn glass method played a dominant role. The glass beads and bead raw materials excavated in Arikamedu,[2] a few kilometres from Pondycherry on India's south-east coast, comprise monochrome items in opaque red, orange, yellow, dark blue, blackish-blue, turquoise and green, alongside semi-translucent blue, green and purple. The beads were made by

[2] Arikamedu is thought to be the earliest bead centre in India (Francis 2002: 27).

Figure 3. Whole necklace of Palauan money (*Iek*) showing different varieties of beads: four orange/yellow bracelet segments, monochrome beads (Indo-Pacific beads) and five green-white eye beads (East Java glass beads).

chopping up glass rods, heating the pieces and rounding their ends (Dubin 1997: 194–5; Francis 2002: 25). Their size varies between 4mm and 4cm. Alongside round beads, cubes with rounded corners, cylindrical, drum-shaped and ring beads were also produced (Adhaytman and Arfin 1996: 60).

In the western part of the Indian subcontinent, the production centre of Brahmapuri existed between 200 BC and AD 200, using similar techniques as at Arikamedu to produce mainly smaller beads, melon-shaped beads and rectangular blue beads with white lines. For centuries, these beads were traded east and west into other countries (Dubin 1997: 194–5). The glass beads produced at Arikamedu and later across large parts of south-east Asia were traded to east Asia (China, Korea), southern Asia, the Middle East and Africa (Ghana, Mali). They were described as 'trade wind beads', as they crossed the sea on ships which exploited the seasonal currents, winds and monsoon rains (Dubin 1997: 194–5). Peter Francis (2002: 19; see also Adhaytman and Arfin 1996: 15) then introduced a new term for these beads that references their distribution, colour, manufacture and material: Indo-Pacific beads, a shorthand for Indo-Pacific monochrome drawn glass beads.

Yet it was not only the beads that travelled, but also the technique. As early as the first century AD, these beads were produced in four other areas, probably by Indian migrants, namely in:

1. Mantai on Sri Lanka (first to tenth centuries)
2. Klong Thom in southern Thailand (second to sixth centuries)
3. Oc Eo in Vietnam (first to seventh centuries)
4. Kuala Selinsing in Malaysia (sixth to tenth centuries)

Oc Eo was a port in the kingdom of Funan providing an important stopover between Malaysia and the Far East and connecting India and China. For several centuries, almost all goods traded between these two countries passed through Funan. However, all four sites listed were important ports at which Roman beads were found and Indo-Pacific glass beads were made (Francis 2002: 31).

At Arikamedu, glass beads appear to have been produced into the twelfth century, at Brahmapuri even into the late sixteenth century (Dubin 1997: 194–5).

From the fifteenth century onwards, the new centres of bead production were located in Venice and in Idar-Oberstein, Germany, and they now began to undercut the Indian markets. In the course of colonialist expansion, India's role in the global bead trade was slowly but surely destroyed. Producers in Venice and Idar-Oberstein copied Indian beads, and the industrial production methods at their disposal allowed them to produce large quantities of the different kinds of beads, identical in size, shape and colour to the Indian blueprints. The traditional production techniques practised in India could no longer compete. In addition, at this time the European bead manufacturing industry experienced a boom caused by the opening up of new markets in the New World, which remained inaccessible to Indian traders. From 1805 onwards, the British government had bound Indians to the purchase of European goods and by the end of the nineteenth century large amounts of beads were imported into the Subcontinent (Dubin 1997: 198–9). Today, Indian beads once again play an important role, as glass bead production has taken off since independence in 1947. Four large manufacturing centres exist, but they no longer produce for overseas trade (Dubin 1997: 199).

The south Asian archipelagos, including Indonesia, the Philippines and Taiwan, lie at the crossroads of the maritime trade routes connecting India, China, western Asia and Europe. Environmental aspects such as currents, winds and monsoon rains ensured that Indonesia, the Philippines and Taiwan were heavily influenced by the cultures of India, China and the south-east Asian mainland (Dubin 1997: 223). Indo-Pacific beads were exported from there in large numbers from the second century BC to the seventeenth century AD. They are for example found in Thailand, Java, Sumatra and Malaysia, as well as eastern and southern Africa, which they probably reached via Arab, Indian and Chinese merchants (Dubin 1997: 184).

In his book on Indo-Pacific beads, Peter Francis Junior (2002: 41) states that

> [t]he Indo-Pacific bead industry produced one of the, if not the, most widespread and ubiquitous trade item of all time, surviving well over 2,000 years.

East Java glass beads

Indonesia, the largest island nation on earth, has been continuously exposed to Chinese and Indian influences since prehistory. The first Indian traders, who acted as middlemen between the Far East and the Mediterranean, arrived in Indonesia around 300 BC, but trade with China had already begun around 400 BC. Powerful Hindu and Buddhist states emerged on Sumatra, Java and Bali between the second and fifteenth centuries AD. Around AD 100, small colonies of Indian traders had been established along the trade routes, and along them Indian philosophy, law and literature, and not least Indian beads, also reached these islands (Dubin 1997: 229–30).

Indian influence was particularly strong on Java and Bali. Some Indonesian beads are identical to those produced in Arikamedu in India, which could mean that both finished beads and knowledge concerning bead production were exchanged. The oldest beads found in Indonesia are monochrome and mostly of yellow, blue or green hues. They were produced by the glass drawing or coiling techniques (Dubin 1997: 23).

It seems that beads played an important role in Indonesia. They are often found in graves dating to around AD 400, for example in Pasemah (Sumatra), Gunung kidul (Java), Besuki (Java) and Gilimanuk (Bali), where they are associated with iron tools, bronze, gold ornaments and pottery (Adhaytman and Arfin 1996: 1). In addition, older beads from Egypt, China, western Asia and Europe are also found. Those from the first three regions are dated to AD 200, illustrating early Indonesian contact with other areas. Indonesian goods travelling in return comprised gold, camphor, scented woods and rhino horn. Identical ancient beads, some polychrome, were found in the neighbouring countries of Sri Lanka, Thailand, Vietnam, China, South Korea, the Philippines, Malaysia and Brunei. The trade in beads did not always involve the finished product; frequently it was the raw materials which were exported. Mosaic ingots, from which beads could then be produced relatively easily, had already been an important trade good in Roman times (Adhaytman and Arfin 1996: 3).

In Palau, alongside Indo-Pacific beads so-called East Java beads are also found, of which two kinds[3] are of particular importance here. The first are mosaic beads, which can have different colours and are decorated with so-called eyes. They can hence also be referred to as eye beads (Francis 2002: 135). Their core mostly consists of a yellow glass fired at low temperatures, but there are also examples with a green or brown interior. The second group are the Pelangi (rainbow) beads made of a green or yellow glass that differs from the material used for the first group. Pelangi beads have a pattern of polychrome, twisted lines, and a huge variety of different colour combinations is possible (Adhaytman and Arfin 1996: 65).

Eye beads vary in size between 1.5 and 4.5cm. They occur in combinations of two, three or four colours, but most combine the two colours greenish-black and white, or blue and white. These beads were produced by heating over a low fire and adding a second layer of glass. Often, they were given their final shape in a mould (Francis 2002: 135).

---

[3] There are five categories of East Java beads: mosaic beads, Penlangi beads, large yellow beads (Big Yellows), beads with a white dot and twisted stripe beads (Francis 2002: 135).

The polychrome Pelangi beads also have a green core, but the material is different from that of the eye beads. The recycling of old beads, which were melted down to make new ones, seems to have been part of bead manufacture in eastern Java. Mosaic strands around the rainbow beads were in all probability made from melted-down Indo-Pacific beads (Adhaytman and Arfin 1996: 67). These beads can combine two colours, blue and white, or four colours, blue, white, red and yellow. In the latter case, the colour blue can also be substituted with dark green or brown. Their size varies between 2 and 3.5cm (Adhaytman and Arfin 1996: 68).

The production of East Java beads probably already began around AD 300 in Indonesia (Adhaytman and Arfin 1996: 65). There are suggestions that the outer glass layer and particularly the hard core were made from melted-down green and yellow Indo-Pacific beads. In Indonesia, finds of eye beads are limited to eastern Java. However, they were also found in graves in the Philippines, on Sumatra and on Borneo, showing that they were also traded (Adhaytman and Arfin 1996: 65–6).

Made in China

New research has shown that by the eleventh century BC, China was part of the bead production centres, which mainly exported to south-east Asia. Between AD 960 and 1280, they distributed goods via overseas trade, resulting in many Chinese Song pottery vessels being found on archaeological sites and in shipwrecks. From the early twelfth into the sixteenth century, the Chinese held a monopoly on the trade with south-east Asia. Amongst others, Chinese beads were in great demand there. Contemporary Chinese sources mention the popularity of these items and the delivery of large numbers of coloured beads to the Indonesian Sulu islands, Palembang and Biliton on Sumatra, Java and Kalimantan on Borneo, to name but a few. A Chinese shipwreck of the Wanli period (AD 1573–1619) found near Palawan in the Philippines also counted trade beads amongst its cargo (Adhaytman and Arfin 1996: 75–6).

Different kinds of beads were produced in China. With regard to Palauan money, the so-called spiral beads are the most interesting. The fact that their size and colour are very similar to Indo-Pacific beads often led to confusion in the past. Early spiral beads were found in ninth and tenth century contexts in the Seungan temple in Kyongju (Korea), in Barus (northern Sumatra) and in Niah (Sarawak, Borneo). In the 1200s, these Chinese beads became the most widely traded variety, replacing Indo-Pacific beads (Francis 2002: 76). Most likely, the Chinese were trying to imitate the beads originally produced in India, as they were a valuable trade item. Bracelets made from the same glass as the spiral beads were also produced in China (Adhaytman and Arfin 1996: 76–7). These bracelets are dated to between AD 1300 and 1500 (Adhaytman and Arfin 1996: 82). It appears that bracelets, too, were first produced in India at an earlier period and as for the beads the technique was then imitated in China (Vierke 2007: 268). Beads and bracelets made in China have a very high lead content, which is not the case for those made in India. This allows experts to distinguish Indo-Pacific and Chinese pieces at a glance, as Chinese spiral beads are not only smaller, but also shinier and heavier than Indo-Pacific ones (Adhaytman and Arfin 1996: 77; Francis 2002: 77). Production in China ended in the seventeenth century.

The end of the Asian bead trade

In 1492, Christopher Columbus discovered America and five years later Vasco da Gama rounded the Cape of Good Hope and sailed on to India. These two historical events had huge repercussions on the Asian bead trade. One of the effects of colonialism was the progressive replacement of Asian beads by European ones. First, European traders followed Asian routes and dominated these markets with their own goods. In spite of initial Asian resistance, in AD 1650 Europe established itself as the new dominant trade power (Van Leur 1955: 159–64).

In this context, four regions are of great importance in terms of the effects on Palau:

1. The Philippines – the westernmost point reached by the Spanish trans-Pacific trade
2. Indonesia – especially Borneo, Sulawesi, Sumatra and Java, forming the eastern edge of the Indian Ocean and the southern shores of the South China Sea
3. China – the great powerhouse in eastern Asia
4. India – the centre of Asian maritime trade (Francis 2002: 169).

In AD 1516, Ferdinand Magellan circumnavigated the southern tip of South America and travelled a further 89 days before finally reaching the eastern side of the Philippines. After the discovery of this route, the Spanish began to transport silver from the mines in Taxaco and Zacateca in Mexico and from Potosi in Bolivia to the Philippines, where they could trade it for Asian goods. A lively trade thus emerged between South America and Asia, dominated by the Spanish (Francis 2002: 169). From the start, the Spanish transported beads to the Philippines. For instance, written sources state that Magellan offered crystal-like beads to the king of Butuan, but it is not clear whether these beads were made of stone or of Venetian glass (Pigafetta 1905: 97).

A memorandum dated to AD 1665 contains a request for various Spanish goods, amongst which were:

> A great quantity of beads, blue, green, and yellow, ten breadth of each sort. Four pound of fine coral of all sorts. Three quintals of glass, (one blue). One thousand bundles of glass beads — green and yellow, Five hundred dozen hawks' bell (Blair and Robertson 1973: 191).

However, this level of information does not tell us which kinds of glass beads were requested. Columbus, too, carried small yellow and green beads, which were traded in the Americas up to AD 1550 (Smith and Good 1982: 3). The beads introduced by Europeans slowly replaced the trade with Asian beads (Francis 2002: 170). The Chinese had been established bead producers and traders across the Philippine archipelago for centuries before the arrival of the Spanish. Once Manila became the main interchange for trade goods connecting Asia with the Euro-American trade routes, Chinese traders expanded and intensified their routes with the surrounding islands. Around AD 1570, Juan Gonzalez de Mendoza[4] reports that over 20 Chinese ships a year reached Manila (Gonzales 1853: 265). In 1588, the Englishman Francis Pretty already counted between 20 and 30 every year (Pretty 1905: 175). In his description of 1609, Antonio de Morga raised this number to 30 to 40 ships entering Manila in a year (Cummins 1971: 305). Trade on the Philippines flourished. Thus, de Morga also reports that some traders came from Manila, but others from as far afield as China, Japan, the Moluccas, Malaysia, Cambodia, Borneo, India, Persia, Turkey and even Portugal (Cummins 1971: 404–9). Still, Chinese entrepreneurs dominated trade in this region, which is why the Spanish attempted to drastically reduce the number of traders. Archaeological finds of shipwrecks near Palawan have brought to light an enormous number of Chinese beads. The *Royal Captain*, which was probably on its way from Manila to Borneo and has been dated to 1573–1620 on the basis of pottery, carried a cargo of red spiral beads and glass beads. Ethnographic works show that Chinese glass and Indian agate long dominated in the Philippines, while the first European beads were only obtained in greater numbers in the nineteenth century. The old trade beads, the old traders and the old routes persisted for a long time (Francis 2002: 170).

In contrast, in Indonesia the amount of European-produced beads, especially those from Germany and Italy, increased from 57.5% to 69% between the years 1909 and 1922. In the same interval, Indian beads decreased from 28.2% to 16.3%. Alongside items from Germany and Italy, Czech products were increasingly

[4] His name is variously written as Ivan Gonzales de Mendoca, Ivan Gonzales de Mendosa, and Juan Gonzales de Mendoza (Francis 2002: 248).

sought after, while on the Asian side beads from Japan entered the market. The decreasing quantities of Indonesian and Indian beads progressively made their manufacture less profitable, and with the beginning of the twentieth century they were gradually pushed out of the market (Francis 2002: 172).

For a long time, Chinese goods dominated Asian trade. It is only from AD 1863 that Chinese glass beads began to be replaced by European ones and that their trade was restricted by the colonial powers (Francis 2002: 174).

In India, the East India Company took over control of exchange in the early seventeenth century, including the trade in beads, which was documented in detail in the company's reports (Francis 2002: 175). In addition, beads were exported from India, but increasingly these were stone rather than glass beads. With the start of the twentieth century, Italy dominated the Indian bead trade, followed by Austria, Germany and England. The quantities and value of these beads were greater than those of indigenous ones, leading to the building of European glass factories in India which outcompeted traditional local producers. The return of the Indian glass beads only began during World War II and increased with Indian independence in 1947 (Francis 2002: 177).

In Asia, whether this be China, India, the Philippines or Indonesia, the production and trade networks built up over centuries were at first maintained, but eventually progressively replaced through European intervention. European beads were imported into the Philippines and Indonesia from early on, but played a subordinate role until the late nineteenth and the beginning of the twentieth century, when they were selected for economic and political reasons (Francis 2002: 180).

The multiple origins of beads

In sum, the origin of many identical-looking beads is difficult to determine. A good example are Indo-Pacific beads, which were first produced in India, but later also in Sri Lanka, southern Thailand or Malaysia. These beads were exported in large quantities from 200 BC into the seventeenth century AD and are found on archaeological sites in, amongst others, Thailand, Java, Sumatra, Malaysia, eastern and southern Africa, where they were probably introduced by Arab, Indian and Chinese traders.

Mosaic beads and Pelangi beads, which are also used as money in Palau, come from Indonesia. Their production probably began around AD 300 and they were exported until the end of the nineteenth century. Identical beads have been recovered from archaeological contexts in the Philippines, on Sumatra and on Borneo.

With its spiral beads, China imitated the sought-after Indo-Pacific beads and by AD 1200 the great demand for them made them the most traded items. They are found in the ninth and tenth centuries in Korea, in northern Sumatra and the Philippines. Archaeological finds allow us to suggest regional customs and preferences. Thus, in Indonesia primarily yellow beads and bracelets are found. These are so far absent from the Philippines, where instead beads and bracelets of an orange colour dominate. These patterns are not yet well explained. They could simply be the result of regional preferences, but could also depend on what traders in those regions offered or indeed reflect the low numbers of sites excavated so far.

Without further scientific analyses, it is impossible to determine the exact origin of many of the Palauan beads. What seems clear is that they could have arrived in Palau from several sources and at varying times, as detailed in the following section.

The route of the beads

One possibility for how beads reached Palau centres on the Philippines, an archipelago of more than 7000 islands located 450 miles west of Palau. From as early as 5000 BC, Filipinos traded with Indonesia, via Celebes and Timor. In their manoeuvrable dugout canoes, they upheld contacts across their island world and spread ideas, techniques and languages along their trade routes. While beads made from gold, shell and clay were produced on the islands, carnelian, agate, black and white patterned onyx and glass beads were imported from eastern India, and jade was brought from China. Burials dated to between 1000 BC and AD 500 contain numerous monochrome glass beads, including small Indo-Pacific beads, although there are hardly any hints of direct contacts with India. However, it is known that Filipinos entertained trade relations with China and Thailand (Dubin 1997: 239).

Maritime traders imported beads to the Philippines for several centuries, particularly Arab traders, who tightly controlled the Pacific exchange system between the eleventh and seventeenth centuries. However, the Chinese, who had already been trading in this region for several centuries, began to seriously compete with the Arabs from the tenth century and considerably expanded their activities from the thirteenth century onwards. In exchange for pearls from the Philippines, they brought gold, silver, jade, textiles, porcelain and glass beads. Sixteenth-century Spanish scholars report that beads were used as everyday currency in the Philippines (Dubin 1997: 239).

The earliest Indo-Pacific beads found during archaeological excavations in the Philippines are dated to 390–15 BC. Overall, 67% of bead finds in the Philippines are Indo-Pacific beads, which are thought to mostly originate from Funan and Srivijaya[5] (Francis 2002: 204). When production of Indo-Pacific beads in Srivijaya came to an end, probably due to a shift in power relations after the move of the capital at Jambi (1079–1082), Chinese beads reached the Philippines. Chinese pottery helps to date the arrival of beads to around 1127 (Francis 2002: 209).

Indo-Pacific beads were sought after across the archipelago and are, amongst others, found in graves on Luzon, on the Visayas and on the Batan islands. They were later replaced by Chinese beads, found on Palawan, Luzon, the Visayas and Mindanao. In addition, beads from eastern Java were also found in the graves (Villegas 1983: 34). According to Francis (2002: 209), it was probably Malaysian traders who brought the Indo-Pacific beads and Chinese traders who introduced the Chinese ones. But how did the beads reach Palau?

From early on, the inhabitants of Palau regularly sailed their outrigger canoes, up to 10m long and referred to as *keap*, to the Philippines to supply Chinese traders with *bêche-de-mer* sea cucumbers (Hernsheim 1883: 5; Kubary 2005: 143). In return, they most likely obtained their bead money. A further possibility is that bracelets and beads reached Palau as trade goods on early Chinese ships trading in the Pacific (Etpison 2014: 34).

However, Indo-Pacific beads are also found in Karawang (Java), and there, too, people entertained trade relations with China in the sixth and seventh centuries. Time and again, graves containing Chinese pottery and other goods alongside beads are found in various south-east Asian regions, for example in Plawangan in central Java. In Pekauman, eastern Java, different glass and stone beads and Chinese pottery of the Tang period (ninth century) were recovered. Further graves with Chinese goods at Palembang (Indonesia), in the Philippines, in Vietnam, Thailand and Malaysia, as well as written sources concerning seafaring, document that Chinese traders supplied these regions (Adhaytman and Arfin 1996: 27–30), which thus became a link between Indonesia, the Philippines and Palau.[6]

In contrast, Francis (2002: 190) believes that direct contact between Palau and eastern Java existed between 600 and 900 AD, as the beads were produced during that time. Although these beads were widely traded over a considerable period

[5] Srivijaya on Sumatra (a kingdom existing between the seventh and thirteenth centuries) entertained close relations to China and India and became a bead production centre (Adhaytman and Arfin 1996: 27–30).

[6] The relatively low number of beads in Palau rather speaks against a direct trade link with China.

of time, the overall amount circulating in Palau means that they must have been introduced there at a time when they were still being actively produced.

The question of how exactly bead money reached Palau can no longer be answered today. It is also unclear whether the beads and bracelets came to Palau by one single route or whether they were supplied over different lengths of time from different regions and via different trade partners. The fact remains that Indo-Pacific beads, bracelets, East Java beads and Chinese beads are found in the Philippines and Indonesia in graves dating between 500 BC and AD 1500 (Etpison 2014: 34; Fox 1970: 239–40). At this time, Palau was already in contact with Chinese traders in the Philippines who, in turn, exchanged goods with Indonesia.

In addition, in more recent years a new source of bead money has opened up: the acquisition of antique beads looted from archaeological sites. Since most excavations in the Philippines and in Indonesia have been carried out illegally, there is no detailed information on the sites and the context of the finds. Grave robbers generally open burials to access the sought-after gold and Chinese porcelain. Especially on Palawan and Luzon in the Philippines, the political problems of the last few years have prevented the proper archaeological recording of such graves. For the few sites excavated under research conditions, the focus has regrettably been on the study and recording of the gold and pottery, rather than the beads. Beads from funerary contexts can today be openly bought from antiques dealers in Manila and elsewhere.

The inflation of the *Udoud er Belau*

In his observations on Palauan money, the ethnographer Homer Barnett (1960: 37) writes that it 'can never be increased because its source is unknown'. However, since the 1960s, illegally excavated beads and bracelets are being offered for sale in antiques shops in the Philippines and Indonesia (Figure 4). Since the items found in graves look identical to Palauan bead money, Palauans began to believe that these islands were the origin of the beads. Thus, since the 1990s Palauans have increasingly been travelling to Manila, Bali and Jakarta to search the shops there for antique beads.

In 2010, Indonesia passed a law according to which objects older than 50 years can only be exported with permission of the minister for culture and tourism (The Jakarta Post, 02/10/2010). There is no such strict law concerning antiquities in the Philippines, and as the flight from Koror to Manila is only two hours long and leaves twice a week, the acquisition of Palauan money is now concentrated on the Philippines.

Figure 4. Display in an antiques shop in Manila, Philippines (© C. Dupont).

A rapid inflation of new beads in Palau is currently being prevented by two mechanisms. On the one hand, it is still relatively difficult to obtain a piece from the Philippines or Indonesia, as they are sold at very high prices. On the other hand, the number of graves excavated and recorded by professional archaeologists is increasing, and illegal grave robbery is consequently declining.

Over the last 20 years, the demand for beads has increased — and with that their price, which is now much higher than for the gold or porcelain objects found in the graves. To suit their Palauan customers, antiques dealers now frequently cut up the bracelets, perforate them and thread them onto black nylon string. Depending on size and quality, a segment of an orange bracelet can cost between 200 and 400 US dollars, a yellow segment between 300 and 800 dollars.

In the last 30 years, the so-called 'new/fake beads' from the Philippines and Indonesia have been imported into Palau in increasing numbers. Today, many women wear pieces of bead money around their necks which are much larger than the traditionally largest and most famous examples. Many of the smaller new beads are knowingly and unknowingly being used as gifts in the traditional exchange systems in Palau. In the last section, I will briefly trace some of the consequences of and local responses to this situation.

From inventarisation to registration

Over the many years of research and intensive study of Palauan bead money, the only attempt at producing an inventory of the beads in Palau remains the list produced by the ethnographer Robert Ritzenthaler in 1954. His results are based on his informant Targong from Ngarchelong. According to Ritzenthaler (1954: 14–15), at that point there were 2947 pieces of bead money in Palau, which could be divided into 282 different kinds. However, of these 282 kinds, only 209 were still in circulation in the 1950s; this means that following Ritzenthaler, only 2317 pieces were being actively exchanged. However, Ritzenthaler also admits that his list could contain errors and omissions, as it is based on intelligence gathered from just one local informant.

For the ethnographer, the Palauan monetary system was 'a frozen one. As all the money is not only of foreign manufacture, but also antique, no new money is coming in' (Ritzenthaler 1954: 15).

In the course of his work he admits having been told by other informants that new beads had been introduced by European traders; however, he claims to be unable to corroborate this fact (Ritzenthaler 1954: 15). In his writings, Ritzenthaler (1954: 15) is also of the opinion that the amount of money would decrease over time due to damage and losses:

> Although the money is handled and cared for with supreme solicitude, there are accounts of money being lost due to accidents, such as an outrigger capsizing, or a person, known to have buried their money, suddenly dying without revealing the hiding place. Some money was claimed to have been lost in the recent war due to bombings, or in the process of moving to evacuation centers. Cracked and broken beads are not acceptable, but must be written off as loss, unless the crack is so tiny that the piece can be passed off to the stupid or unobservant. Thus in recent years there has been a slow decrease in the number of pieces of Palau money, but there has been no resultant increase in the value of the remainder of the money, as might be expected. The logical explanation for this is that the increasing desirability of foreign money tended to lessen somewhat the demand for native money. The reduction in number of pieces, plus the impact of foreign money, has resulted in the decline in fluidity of native money from pre-contact to modern times (Ritzenthaler 1954: 15–16).

Unfortunately, Ritzenthaler's inventory of Palauan money contains numerous mistakes. There are instances in which categories, subcategories and names within the Palauan monetary system have been confused. In addition, Palauans do not exhibit their valuable possessions publicly, and it is unknown who owns how many pieces. Nevertheless, Ritzenthaler's list continues to be used in order to assign existing names to newly imported beads.

Today, no-one knows exactly how many beads exist in Palau. Since losses are rare and the rate of new imports high, it is likely that there are more beads now than at the time of Krämer's and Ritzenthaler's visits. This creates the problem of how to distinguish whether one is being offered a valuable antique or a newly imported item in exchange.

Counterfeit money is today referred to as *Udoud el kemanget a cosenged er ngii*, i.e. as money that must be looked at for a long time. Particularly members of lower-status clans or younger people, who do not have much experience or many comparative pieces at hand, cannot distinguish fakes or newly imported pieces from traditional bead money. In Palau, there are two opposing theories of how pieces newly imported from the Philippines or Indonesia can be distinguished from real Palauan money:

> When a person wishes to examine more closely the design on a polychrome bead for purpose of identification, he will rub the piece on his nose. Apparently the oil from the skin brings out the patterns more clearly (Ritzenthaler 1954: 35).

This phenomenon was already described by Kubary:

> The surface of the pieces, although rubbed smooth, is never completely polished and exhibits a certain roughness; this the Palauan connoisseur of money attempts to discover by rubbing the piece on his nose, as wetting it with the oily sweat makes the nature of the surface appear more clearly, as well as making the different ornaments stand out more distinctly, particularly on worn beads (Kubary 1885: 19).

Alongside this frequently repeated theory that rubbing beads on one's nose and the oil of the skin confer a special sheen on Palauan money, while fake beads remain grey and dull, a second theory states that real beads can cut through window glass and mirrors, while fake beads cannot. Yet since the newly imported beads and bracelet segments have the same source and are made from the same material as Palauan money, these two methods merely help to detect fakes made in other materials.

One possibility to distinguish Palauan money from new bracelet segments imported from the Philippines and Indonesia is by examining the drill holes in more detail. Since the material from which the bracelets are made is very hard, today diamond saws and drills are used to cut the pieces and to perforate them for suspension. These mechanically-created suspension holes are larger and show the spiral traces of the drill bits. Also, they are drilled straight through from one end to the other, while traditional pieces were drilled from both sides until the two perforations could be joined in the middle. Therefore, by introducing a small piece of cotton wool into the perforation and then removing it, one can see whether the hole is the same width all the way through – indicating a new piece – or is narrower in the middle, like the old ones. In addition, newer bracelet segments generally have the wrong proportions, they are too long and narrow, or too short and thick. Some beads, however, cannot be distinguished from the newly imported pieces, as material, form and colour are identical.

Alongside newly imported beads, there are now also cheap plastic and glass imitations, which have already entered circulation through exchange. Although the trained and experienced eye can easily tell them apart from Palauan money, the problem is that it would be impolite to turn down a piece offered in gift exchange. Even if it is an item that must be looked at for a long time, it is accepted with thanks or in silence. If it is a definite fake, it is pointed out politely that the item is too large and valuable and that one would prefer another piece. Should anyone declare publicly that the offered payment is in fact counterfeit money, then the matter generally ends in court and can even lead to the permanent break-up of relations within whole families and clans. In Palau, it is considered shameful to offer fake pieces in exchange.

Older Palauans insist that newly imported beads, even if made from the same material, are not the same and do not carry the same value as the original beads, which are connected to their own stories. In addition, many Palauans still believe that origin is a further important criterion of differentiation. Palauan money is valuable, because according to myth it comes from the gods. Each bead carries its own history which has united or divided people or has evened out debts between them. These beads bear the history of events between individuals and groups, and through reciting these histories during exchange they are recalled to the memory of those present. As a result, Palauan money could also be characterised as a symbolic object of cultural memory, or as an object of cultural self-assertion.

As Semper already described:

> One day — so myth tells us — one of these rupacks [*rubak*] went up to the sky, from where the kalids [*chalid*] looked down every night with their sparkling eyes, the stars. Of one of these sky dwellers, he stole one of the beautiful eyes, and once back in Palau they made their money from it. And it is this money which we here in Palau still use, and because it comes from the kalids [*chalid*], we think it so holy. That is also why you men from Angabard cannot imitate it, though you have tried often enough; we can still distinguish it easily from the real money of the kalids [*chalid*] (Semper 1873: 195).

Ever since it has become known that beads from Indonesia and the Philippines are circulating in exchange systems, mistrust has increased (Figure 5). Some Palauans are insecure, and named individuals are blamed for starting the import, others are accused of carrying and spending fake money. This insecurity has led to some definitely old pieces being redefined as new, imitated items.

Currently, the government is attempting to call for the registration of Palauan money. To achieve this, the individual items should be taken to the Bureau of Arts and Culture to be photographed and have their basic information and histories recorded, so that during exchanges they can be handed over with their certificates. However, the attempt to inventory only Palauan money seems almost impossible, as newly imported beads have now been in circulation for 30 years and have already gained value through the work they perform in exchanges.

In addition, there is no authority which could decide whether a given piece is original and admissible for registration or not. Therefore, all beads currently existing in the Palauan archipelago, whether newly imported or old, should be documented in order to prevent import of ever more items and the resulting

Figure 5. Proofing of Palauan money at a custom (© C. Dupont).

inflation. Yet this could lead to a shift in wealth which would have repercussions on prestige, status and power in this society. Traditionally, high-ranking clans own more and larger pieces of money, but by commercially acquiring beads from looted graves, families from lower-ranking clans now possess more and larger items than those traditionally known.

Since, as has already been mentioned, no-one likes to exhibit their money in public, this proposal for a new law has had a mixed reception. Among the people in favour of registration are the current President of Palau, Tommy Remgensau, and his wife. In contrast, traditional leaders such as Bilung Gloria Salii oppose the law. The issue of the registration of Palauan money was raised at the 21st Women's Conference, the Mechesil Belau Conference, on 21 November 2014, where the law was also opposed.

The influence of traditional leaders and especially of older women is still very noticeable in Palau. Although many politicians and even the President are in favour of registering bead money, this law and its implementation will not be successful as long as traditional leaders oppose it.

Summary

In sum, it can be stated that Palauan money consists of Indo-Pacific beads, East Java glass beads and Chinese spiral beads. Through their integration they were placed into a new social and symbolic context and acquired a new kind of value in traditional exchange systems on the Palauan islands. Now that it is possible to acquire new beads from antiques dealers in the Philippines, the threat of an inflation of indigenous money in Palau is looming. The so-called 'fake' or new beads are already being incorporated into exchange cycles, causing a shift in the relations of power, status and prestige on which the hierarchical social system in Palau is based. There is increasing conflict between political and traditional leaders, causing family feuds and blind accusations. The passing of a law regarding the registration of Palauan money is currently an important concern being discussed on the islands. It is hoped that this will stop the import of beads from the Philippines and prevent inflation.

Further work is currently being carried out to trace the multiple ways in which traditional power relations and status positions are bound up in the issue of categorizing money as original or new and to further explore the impact of introducing new items into established exchange systems.

Bibliography

Adhyatman, S. and Arifin, R. 1996. *Manik-Manik di Indonesia. Beads in Indonesia.* Jakarta, Ikrar Mandiriabadi.

Barnett, H. 1960. *Being a Palauan. Case studies in cultural anthropology.* New York/ Chicago, Holt, Rinehart and Winston.

Blair, E. H. and Robertson, J. A. 1973. *The Philippine islands 1493–1898. Volume 2.* Manila, Cachos Hermanos.

Cummins, J. 1971. *Sucesos de las Islas Filipinas by Antonio de Morga.* Cambridge, Cambridge University Press.

de Beauclair, I. 1963. Some ancient beads of Yap and Palau. *The Journal of the Polynesian Society* 72: 1–10.

Dubin, L. S. 1997. *Alle Perlen dieser Welt.* Köln, DuMont.

Etpison, M. 2014. *30 years Palau.* Koror/Palau, Neco Marine Corp.

Force, R. 1959. Palauan money: some preliminary comments on material and origins. *The Journal of the Polynesian Society* 68: 40–4.

Fox, R. 1970. *The Tabon caves: archaeological explorations and excavations on Palawan Island, Philippines.* Manila, National Museum (Monograph No. 1).

Francis Jr., P. 2002. *Asia's maritime bead trade. 300 B.C. to the present.* Honolulu, University of Hawai'I Press.

Gonzalez, J. 1853. *The history of the great and mighty kingdom of China and the situation thereof.* London: Hakluyt Society.

Hernsheim, F. 1883. *Südsee-Erinnerungen (1875–1880).* Berlin, Hofmann & Comp.

Keate, G. 2007. *Nachrichten von den Pelew-Inseln in der Westgegend des stillen Oceans. Aus dem Englischen übersetzt von Georg Forster*. München, Süddeutsche Zeitung Edition.

Krämer, A. 1926. *Palau. Ergebnisse der Südsee-Expedition 1908–1910. 3. Teilband. Abteilung V. Stoffliches. Abteilung VI. Geistige Kultur. II Ethnographie, B. Mikronesien. Band 3.* Hamburg, L. Friedrichsen & Co.

Krämer, A.1929a. *Palau. Ergebnisse der Südsee-Expedition 1908–1910. 4. Teilband. Abteilung VII. Geschichten und Gesänge. Abteilung VIII. Botanischer, Zoologischer und Palauwörter-Index. II Ethnographie, B. Mikronesien. Band 3.* Hamburg, L. Friedrichsen & Co.

Krämer, A. 1929b. *Palau. Ergebnisse der Südsee-Expedition 1908–1910. 5. Teilband. Abteilung IX: Zierkunst und Kulturvergleich. Abteilung X: Baiverzeichnis. II Ethnographie, B. Mikronesien. Band 3.* Hamburg, L. Friedrichsen & Co.

Kubary, J. S. 1889. *Ethnographische Beiträge zur Kenntnis des Karolinen Archipels.* Paderborn, Salzwasser Verlag GmbH.

Kubary, J. S. 2005. Die Palau-Inseln in der Südsee. In H. Kranz (ed.), *Das Museum Godeffroy 1861–1881. Naturkunde und Ethnographie der Südsee*: 115–49. Hamburg, Altonaer Museum.

Lautz, T. 1999. *Steinreich in der Südsee. Traditionelle Zahlungsmittel in Mikronesien. Dritter Sonderband der EUCOPRIMO (European Union to Search for, Collect, and Preserve Primitive and Curious Money).* Köln, Geldgeschichtliches Museum.

McCluer, J. 1790/92. *Journal of a voyage to the Pelew Islands in H.C. 'Snow Panther'.* Typescript of original British Museum manuscript, Palau Community Action Agency, Koror.

Müller-Wismar, W. 1917. Yap. In G. Thilenius (ed.), *Ergebnisse der Südsee-Expedition 1908–1910, II Ethnographie, B. Mikronesien, Band 2.* Hamburg.

Osborne, D. 1979. *The archaeology of Palau Islands: an intensive survey.* Honolulu, Bishop Museum Press.

Parmentier, R. 1987. *The sacred remains. Myth, history, and polity in Belau.* Chicago/Londong, University of Chicago Press.

Pigafetta, A. 1905. Of Fernandus Magalianes: the occasion of his voyage, and the particulars of the same, with the compassing of the world by the ship called San Victoria. In S. Purchas (ed.), *Hakluytus Posthumus or, Purchas his pilgrimes: Contayning a history of the world in sea voyages and lande travells by Englishmen and others. Volume 2*: 84–119. Glasgow, J. MacLehose & Sons.

Pretty, F. 1905. The third circum-navigation of the globe: or the admirable and prosperous voyage of Master Thomas Candish of Trimley in the countie of Suffolke Esquire, into the South Sea, and from thence round about the circumference on the whole earth, begun in the yeere of Our Lord 1568, and finished 1588. In S. Purchas (ed.), *Hakluytus Posthumus or, Purchas his pilgrimes: Contayning a history of the world in sea voyages and lande travells by Englishmen and others. Volume 2*: 149–87. Glasgow, J. MacLehose & Sons.

Ritzenthaler, R. E. 1954. *Native money of Palau.* Milwakee (WI), Milwaukee Public Museum (Publications in Anthropology 1).

Semper, K. 1873. *Die Palau-Inseln im Stillen Ocean.* Leipzig, Brockhaus.

Smith, M. and Good, M. E. 1982. *Early sixteenth century glass beads in the Spanish colonial trade*. Greenwood, Miss., Cottonlandia Museum.

The Jakarta Post, 10 February 2010. Antiquities on Sale. http://www.thejakartapost.com/news/2011/02/10/antiquities-sale.html [last accessed 11 March 2015].

Van Leur, J. C. 1955. *Indonesian trade and society: essays in Asian social and economic history. Selected studies on Indonesia by Dutch scholars. Volume 1*. The Hague, W. van Hoeve Ltd.

Vierke, U. 2007. *Die Spur der Glasperlen. Produktion, Handel und Aneignung von Glasperlen*. Saarbrücken, VDM Verlag.

Villegas, R. 1983. *Kayamanan: the Philippine jewelry tradition*. Manila, Central Bank of the Philippines.